# AN UNCERTAIN FRIENDSHIP

Theodore Roosevelt and Japan, 1906–1909

# An Uncertain Friendship

Theodore Roosevelt and Japan, 1906-1909

CHARLES E. NEU

HARVARD UNIVERSITY PRESS

Cambridge, Massachusetts

1967

*For Deborah*

# PREFACE

A little over a decade ago John Morton Blum noted in *The Republican Roosevelt* that Theodore Roosevelt, like G. A. Henty, "is more often remembered than reread." [1] Blum's work, along with the publication of *The Letters of Theodore Roosevelt*, did much to end this neglect and marked the beginning of a period in which historians have intensively studied Roosevelt and his times. As a result, we now have a deeper understanding of the man and his place in history. In the 1930's historians pictured Roosevelt as an impulsive and shallow statesman; now they are more appreciative of his skill and vision in both domestic and foreign affairs. Ironically, the pendulum of historical revision has swung so far in the direction of praise that there is a danger Roosevelt will become a figure almost larger than life, always wise and far-sighted, gravely balancing power and responsibility.

Nowhere is this danger greater than in the study of Roosevelt's foreign policy. Howard K. Beale, in his influential *Theodore Roosevelt and the Rise of America to World Power*, views Roosevelt as "primarily an international strategist with a peculiar *long range* conception of the United States as a world power," and Roosevelt's most recent biographer, William Henry Harbaugh, follows closely Beale's interpretation of Roosevelt's diplomacy. [2] Roosevelt would have been

[1] John Morton Blum, *The Republican Roosevelt* (Cambridge, Mass., 1954), p. 1.
[2] Howard K. Beale, *Theodore Roosevelt and the Rise of America to World Power* (Baltimore, 1956), p. 174.

pleased with a portrayal of his foreign policy that emphasized its disinterestedness and freedom from political expediency. Often, to be sure, Roosevelt did look far ahead and allow long-range goals and intellectual convictions to shape his policies toward other nations. Just as often, however, his foreign policy was based upon improvisation and a sensitive regard for domestic political realities. Roosevelt was without doubt a statesman of great stature, but he was also a Republican politician eager for continuing political success. This is only to suggest that with his numerous virtues Roosevelt combined most human ambitions and limitations, and that any study of his foreign policy ought to deal with him in his full complexity.

The revival of interest in Roosevelt as a person has not extended to his Far Eastern policy. Most of the work done on Roosevelt's relation to the Far East was completed in the 1930's. A. Whitney Griswold's *The Far Eastern Policy of the United States,* Tyler Dennett's *John Hay: From Poetry to Politics,* and *Theodore Roosevelt and the Russo-Japanese War,* and Thomas A. Bailey's *Theodore Roosevelt and the Japanese-American Crises,* are still valued — justifiably so — by historians, as are more recent works such as Edward H. Zabriskie's *American-Russian Rivalry in the Far East* and Howard K. Beale's *Theodore Roosevelt and the Rise of America to World Power.* Yet all of these books, while they remain immensely useful, have inevitably suffered from the passage of time. Viewpoints once unique now seem dated, and many new sources have become available since even the most recent of these books was written. A need remains, then, for taking another look at the whole of Roosevelt's Far Eastern policy. The present study, based upon a broad range of materials in American, British, Canadian, and Japanese archives, attempts to contribute to that need through a re-examination of Theodore Roosevelt's last great adventure in world politics, the Japanese-American crisis of 1906–1909.

I am indebted to many institutions and individuals for their generous support. My requests were invariably handled with courtesy and efficiency by the staffs of the Public Archives of Canada, the Public Record Office, the Bodleian Library, the Manuscript Division of the Library of Congress, the National Archives, the Division of Naval History, Department of the Navy, the Massachusetts Historical Society, and the Harvard University Library. Grants from Rice University, the Penrose Fund of the American Philosophical Society, and the Committee on American Far Eastern Policy Studies of Harvard University, were of great importance at various stages of my research. My thanks, too, to the editor of the *Pacific Historical Review* for permission to use portions of an article entitled "Theodore Roosevelt and American Involvement in the Far East, 1901–1909," which appeared in the November, 1966, issue, and to Mr. Mark Bonham Carter, Mrs. Richmond P. Hobson, and Mr. Henry Cabot Lodge, Jr., for permission to examine, respectively, the Asquith, Hobson, and Lodge papers. Quotations of Crown copyright material in the Public Record Office appear by permission of the Controller of H. M. Stationery Office.

Most important, however, were the people who helped along the way. Mr. Chong Kun Yoon of Washington, D.C., skillfully summarized Japanese documents. Frequent stays in Washington were made more pleasant by the hospitality of my brother, Arthur A. Neu, and of Miss Katherine E. Brand and Carol Piper. At the Manuscript Division, Miss Kate M. Steward often interrupted a busy schedule to offer every sort of assistance. A thorough reading of the manuscript by Professor Richard W. Leopold brought countless improvements in it. My greatest obligation, however, is to Professor Ernest R. May. He first suggested this study, and guided it through several stages with patient and imaginative criticism. Finally, my wife Deborah contributed, in more ways than she knows, to the completion of this book.

CHARLES E. NEU

Houston, Texas
April, 1967

# CONTENTS

The following abbreviations are used throughout the notes:

JA    Archives of the Japanese Ministry of Foreign Affairs (microfilm), Library of Congress.
NA    National Archives, Washington, D.C.
PRO   Public Record Office, London.

# CONTENTS

# I

# ROOSEVELT AND THE FAR EAST

The Spanish-American War swelled the nation's pride and strengthened its self-confidence. Spectacular victories and great territorial gains confirmed, for many Americans, the justice of the nation's cause and the splendor of its destiny. New possessions in the Far East heightened the aspirations of businessmen and missionaries, while the rise of the nation to world power brought fulfillment to the expansionist elite which, for over a decade, had urged the American people to exercise their great power responsibly in world affairs. The war and its consequences, however, had come more by accident than design. The nation had gone to war in 1898 because of an irrational public excitement over Cuba, not for the prestige and territorial acquisitions which the war ultimately brought. Understandably most Americans looked outward at the turn of the century without any firm concept of how the nation's power ought to be used beyond its own hemisphere. Expansionists sensed this lack of purpose among the people and wondered if the nation would preserve and enlarge its role in world events. Thus they mixed their anticipation of the future with a sense of somber responsibility. They shared Theodore Roosevelt's belief that "the twentieth century looms before us big with the fate of many nations"; they also shared his doubts over how well the

American people would play their part in these momentous events.[1]

Once war came, the foreign policy of William McKinley and John Hay pleased American expansionists, for under the leadership of these two men the United States made important departures in foreign affairs. The nation acquired colonies and defined its relationship to them, participated in the Hague Conference of 1899, proclaimed its interest in China, and laid the groundwork for hegemony in the Caribbean. The second Hay-Pauncefote Treaty, negotiated before Roosevelt took office and signed shortly after, cleared the way for an American-dominated isthmian canal and signified the growing Anglo-American rapprochement begun under McKinley. So much had McKinley and Hay accomplished that Tyler Dennett, writing in 1933, thought that "there was left to him [Roosevelt] little but to follow paths which McKinley, Root and chiefly Hay, had thought out and projected." [2]

Dennett underestimated the task Roosevelt faced. In all of the areas in which McKinley had set directions, much remained to be done. Roosevelt still had to secure a canal route, to define fully the nature of America's Caribbean hegemony, and to obtain European recognition of it, while encouraging Anglo-American understanding and solving vexing problems such as the Alaskan boundary dispute. At the same time, the scope of America's international involvement outside its own hemisphere was uncertain. On the very day of his death McKinley had declared that "isolation is no longer possible or desirable. . . . The period of exclusiveness is past." [3] But it fell to his successor to shape the rela-

[1] Theodore Roosevelt, *The Strenuous Life: Essays and Addresses* (New York, 1900), p. 20; Beale, *Theodore Roosevelt*, p. 173.

[2] Tyler Dennett, *John Hay: From Poetry to Politics* (New York, 1933), p. 349.

[3] Margaret Leech, *In the Days of McKinley* (New York, 1959), p. 587.

tionship of the United States to the balance of power in Europe and Asia and to lead the nation into a persistent participation in world affairs.

In actuality Roosevelt's opportunity was a limited one, for much depended upon domestic and foreign circumstances beyond the control of any one man. His policy toward Europe would have to be conditioned by the traditional American aloofness from the concerns of that continent. His policy toward the Far East could, on the contrary, capitalize upon the widespread belief in the importance of the nation's future there. But this belief might prove ephemeral, for it was not grounded in a well-defined concept of the nation's interests in the Orient. McKinley and Hay had pursued an ambiguous policy which aroused public opinion but charted no clear course for Roosevelt to follow.

Well before McKinley took office in March, 1897, American interest in the Far East had grown intense, particularly among businessmen, missionaries and intellectuals.[4] Some businessmen, such as cotton manufacturers and exporters, developed a direct economic stake in the China market, while others came to see China as a vast, untapped area in which to dispose of surplus industrial goods and in which to invest accumulated capital. The increasing number of American missionaries in China regarded that unformed nation as an exciting field for religious endeavor; and such prominent intellectuals as Brooks Adams and Alfred Thayer Mahan, fascinated by the future of China, viewed it as the focal point of the struggle among nations for world supremacy. For Adams the economic dominance of Asia was essential to maintain the momentum of American civilization;

[4] For the rise of American interest in the Far East see Tyler Dennett, *Americans in Eastern Asia* (New York, 1922); Walter LaFeber, *The New Empire: An Interpretation of American Expansion, 1860–1898* (Ithaca, 1963); Paul A. Varg, *Missionaries, Chinese and Diplomats* (Princeton, 1958).

for Mahan the fusion of Chinese and Western civilization was a crucial problem of the twentieth century.

All of these groups based their concern over China more upon future expectations than upon present realities. Thus by 1898, when the break-up of China seemed imminent, those Americans convinced of the vital importance of China felt a deep anxiety over the future. Yet the McKinley administration was sluggish in responding to this widespread dissatisfaction over the role of the United States in the Far East. Distracted by war with Spain and apparently convinced that the partition of China would not damage American markets, McKinley sensed no threat to the traditional goal of equal commercial opportunity for American citizens. By the summer of 1899, however, a mounting popular unrest made this passivity inadequate, and the administration moved toward both a more dramatic expression of its old policy and the inauguration of a new one.[5] The results were the Open Door Notes of September 6, 1899, and the Hay Circular of July 3, 1900. The first recognized spheres of influence and asked the powers to respect equality of commercial opportunity within them. Their substance was only a restatement of past policy, though their form was an important departure, for the United States had publicly and formally declared its policy and asked for the cooperation of the European powers. The Hay Circular went beyond the Open Door Notes in that it no longer accepted spheres of influence but instead sought the preservation of the "terri-

---

[5] For the origins of the Open Door Notes and Hay Circular see A. Whitney Griswold, *The Far Eastern Policy of the United States* (New York, 1938); Charles S. Campbell, Jr., *Special Business Interests and the Open Door Policy* (New Haven, 1951); Dennett, *John Hay*; Harvey Pressman, "Hay, Rockhill, and China's Integrity: A Reappraisal," *Papers on China*, 13 (December, 1959), 61–79, Center for East Asian Studies, Harvard University; and Paul A. Varg, *Open Door Diplomat, The Life of W. W. Rockhill* (Illinois Studies in the Social Sciences, vol. 33, no. 4. Urbana, Ill., 1952).

torial and administrative entity" of China. It marked a new
approach to the problem of China and had profound implications for the future of American policy there.

The full meaning of the Open Door Notes and the Hay
Circular was rooted in the motives and beliefs of four men.
Alfred E. Hippisley, a member of the Chinese Customs
Service, largely inspired the Open Door Notes in the hope
that an American declaration would preserve the Chinese
tariff and treaty ports and prevent a further deterioration
of the situation in China. Hippisley's influence was exercised
through William W. Rockhill, Hay's chief adviser on Far
Eastern affairs, who had, however, more far-reaching diplomatic objectives than his English friend. Rockhill believed
that the United States must actively participate in Asian
politics in order to preserve the integrity of China and thus
to maintain the balance of power in that region. The Hay
Circular rather than the Open Door Notes embodied his
views.

McKinley and Hay had more ephemeral purposes than
Hippisley and Rockhill. Both had only slight knowledge of
China and probably had no clear concept of American interests there. Both favored the Open Door Notes because they
sensed the need to appease alarmed businessmen and missionaries and thought the international situation favored a
successful démarche. Moreover, the notes seemed a fitting
expression of the nation's new position in the Orient. When
the Open Door Notes brought popular acclaim in the United
States and no overt rejection by the powers, Hay and Mc-
Kinley, alarmed by the possible consequences of the Boxer
rebellion, risked a second and bolder move in the summer
of 1900. In both cases, however, they were concerned with
the needs of the moment, not with the inauguration of a
long-term policy. When the entangling possibilities of any
defense of China's integrity became clear, McKinley and

Hay quickly retreated. McKinley, for example, was eager to remove American troops from the Boxer expedition, though such a withdrawal was certain to weaken American influence in whatever settlement the powers reached with China. And before the President's death Hay backed away from the broader purpose of preserving China's territorial and administrative entity to the more limited purpose of maintaining equality of commercial opportunity there. The extent of this retreat was not apparent to the American public, and it was only within the administration that a gap existed between America's pretensions and actual policy in China.

It was not at all clear how the new President would handle this disunified Far Eastern policy bequeathed by McKinley. Before 1901 Roosevelt had followed closely events in that region and had read avidly the writings of Adams and Mahan. He seemed to agree with most of what these two prophets wrote about America's stake in China, but he was also impressed with the potential power and geographical advantages of Russia and doubted whether, in the long run, its expansion into China could be halted.[6] He also realized, far more acutely than Adams or Mahan, the difficulties of leading the American people toward a commitment in China.[7] Prior to September, 1901, however, his convictions about American policy were tentative, not final, and too unformed to be an accurate guide for future actions. Only the experience of the presidency would bring the crystallization of scattered beliefs and the formation of a definite policy.

During the early years of his presidency Roosevelt provided little evidence that he intended to pursue a vigorous Far Eastern policy. He entered office convinced that public

[6] Beale, *Theodore Roosevelt*, pp. 175–179, 255–261.

[7] Roosevelt to Mahan, March 18, 1901, in Elting E. Morison (ed.), *The Letters of Theodore Roosevelt* (8 vols.; Cambridge, Mass., 1951–1954), III, 23. Hereafter cited as *Letters*.

opinion was "dull on the question of China" and personally
uncertain of what the "exact facts" were about the situation
there.[8] Instead of attempting to alter such public apathy,
Roosevelt left Far Eastern affairs until 1904 largely in the
hands of John Hay, who, as the President knew, believed
America's hands were tied in the Far East.[9] Hay accepted
Russia's exceptional position in Manchuria, though he hoped
to secure a commercial open door there, and when confronted with Russian encroachments in Manchuria in 1902
and 1903 he issued a series of diplomatic protests of varying
strength. But in these exchanges Hay was always conscious
of the restraints on American policy.[10] He warned Roosevelt
that it was "out of the question that we should adopt any
scheme of concerted action with England and Japan" and
continually reminded the President of the limitations im-
posed on American diplomacy by public indifference to Far
Eastern affairs.[11] Hay adhered to this policy despite two
overtures from Great Britain in 1903 seeking American cooperation against Russian expansion.[12]

Roosevelt accepted Hay's advice, though in 1903 he
seemed to chafe under the frustrations of American policy
and spoke of "going to 'extremes' with Russia." For a time
in the summer of that year Roosevelt seemed to feel the
American people were becoming aroused and might support
a more vigorous defense of American interests in China and
Manchuria.[13] Before this conviction hardened, however,

[8] *Ibid.*

[9] Dennett, *John Hay,* pp. 403–404.

[10] Edward H. Zabriskie, *American-Russian Rivalry in the Far East* (Philadelphia, 1946), pp. 65–100; and Raymond A. Esthus, *Theodore Roosevelt
and Japan* (Seattle, 1966), pp. 7–13.

[11] Hay to Roosevelt, April 25, April 28, and July 22, 1903, quoted in
Dennett, *John Hay,* pp. 400, 404–405.

[12] G. W. Monger, *The End of Isolation: British Foreign Policy, 1900–
1907* (London, 1963), pp. 124–125, 131.

[13] Roosevelt to Hay, July 18, July 29, 1903, *Letters,* III, 520, 532; and
Roosevelt to Brooks Adams, July 18, 1903, quoted in Beale, *Theodore
Roosevelt,* pp. 179–180.

Japan stepped forward to challenge Russian advances in Manchuria and Korea.

The President was understandably delighted to have Japan protecting American interests in the Far East. As his concern over Russian expansion had increased and as his awareness of the administration's helplessness had grown, he had turned more and more to Japan as a balance against Russian power on the mainland of Asia. Roosevelt had long believed that Japan was the nation "most menaced" by Russian expansion and that Japan, not the United States or some European power, would ultimately have to "contest with Russia the control of the destiny of Asia." [14] In protecting its own vital self-interests Japan was also protecting interests less vital to the welfare of the United States. In short, Japan was, as Roosevelt put it, "playing our game" in the Far East.[15] There was, of course, the danger that Japan would grow too strong, particularly as one Japanese victory followed another in the Russo-Japanese War, and eventually Roosevelt risked his own personal prestige to end the war and maintain a balanced antagonism in the Far East.[16] He sought to achieve by indirection what the American people would not allow more direct diplomacy to secure. In doing so, he surely realized that the balance between Japan and Russia offered at best uncertain protection for American interests. He could only hope that Japan would exercise its new preponderance of power in the Far East with restraint and wisdom, and therefore not expose the very limited effort which the United States could make in that region.[17]

Roosevelt's mediation of the Russo-Japanese War has ob-

[14] Roosevelt to Cecil Spring Rice, March 16, 1901, *Letters,* III, 15; Roosevelt to Hermann Speck von Sternburg, July 12, 1901, *Letters,* III, 117.
[15] Roosevelt to Theodore Roosevelt, Jr., February 10, 1904, *Letters,* IV, 724.
[16] Beale, *Theodore Roosevelt,* pp. 312–314.
[17] Roosevelt to Spring Rice, June 13, 1904, *Letters,* IV, 829–832.

scured the fact that from 1901 through 1905 he was pursuing a cautious and unadventurous Far Eastern policy which was a natural reflection of his absorption in domestic affairs. Throughout these years he faced the arduous task of fixing his leadership upon his party and nation and achieving election in his own right in 1904. With considerable anxiety Roosevelt pursued these goals; what energy he gave to foreign affairs had to be focused on problems which the American people, as he put it, felt "keenly about." China was not such a problem, but the Alaskan boundary controversy, the isthmian canal and American hegemony in the Caribbean were.[18] By late 1904 these foreign policy issues were solved, America's world prestige was firmly established, and Roosevelt was triumphantly elected. But no sooner were Roosevelt's political yearnings consummated than the progressive impulse began to reach beyond the state onto the national level. Sensing the change in the air, Roosevelt was determined to guide the reform movement, and after re-election in 1904 he became the advocate of a wide range of social and economic measures, including expanded federal control over the nation's railroads. By May, 1906, he had secured the passage of the Hepburn Act, perhaps his most impressive legislative achievement and, as George E. Mowry has pointed out, a "landmark in the evolution of federal control of private industry." [19] Lesser measures were also enacted, making a good beginning, but much remained to be done. Though foreign affairs could intrude unexpectedly, the challenges of the future seemed to lie in the domestic rather than in the foreign arena.

This was all the more true because of the changing mood of the American public. By the beginning of Roosevelt's

[18] Roosevelt to Mahan, March 18, 1901, *Letters*, III, 23.
[19] George E. Mowry, *The Era of Theodore Roosevelt, 1900–1912* (New York, 1958), pp. 197–211.

second term the nation was becoming less jingoistic, and enthusiasm over America's imperial adventure waned as the many burdens of empire both in the Far East and the Caribbean became more apparent.[20] There was a noticeable turning inward of the people toward domestic concerns, which Roosevelt sensed and often berated. Sometimes he fought against public apathy over foreign problems, as in the case of naval expansion, but more often, as in the case of Caribbean intervention, he became more cautious. Generally Roosevelt was inclined to join the people in their growing concentration upon the reformation of American society.

Thus before November, 1904, Roosevelt was preoccupied with solidifying his domestic political base; after that date, while he undertook a limited initiative in the Far East, his energies were increasingly absorbed in the tide of domestic reform, and when the prolonged Japanese-American crisis of 1906–1909 brought an opportunity to unite the American people behind a more forceful Far Eastern policy, Roosevelt refused to grasp it. The crisis seemed a distraction, not an opportunity, and it was with a heavy heart that Roosevelt, after October, 1906, grappled with the exasperating problem of California's discrimination against Japanese residents. As the crisis spread far beyond Roosevelt's original expectations it vexed and puzzled him and finally required all his skill and persuasiveness before a solution was achieved. Since the approach of the American government depended as much on the temperaments and beliefs of the President and his Secretary of State as on the circumstances themselves, we must look briefly at the two men who dominated American Far Eastern policy from 1906 to 1909.

Theodore Roosevelt was a man of astonishing intellectual and physical vigor, a great natural leader who displayed,

[20] Richard W. Leopold, *Elihu Root and the Conservative Tradition* (Boston, 1954), p. 50.

during his presidency, an almost instinctive feel for the major currents of his era.[21] He was, however, a complex and contradictory figure. His boyishness and spontaneity drew some men to him, while his vindictiveness and ruthlessness alarmed others. A voracious reader who eagerly exchanged ideas with learned men, he placed less value on words than on action. In fact, his words were a misleading guide to his motives, for he used them more to influence other men than to express his own inner thoughts. In conversation Roosevelt seemed impetuous and surprisingly frank, yet he was, during his presidency, generally cautious and shrewd in action. Publicly and privately Roosevelt constantly emphasized public duty, patriotism, and character, though he was essentially a professional Republican politician often forced to compromise his own creed of behavior. Only through compromise could Roosevelt become the most popular political leader of the first decade of this century. Despite this popularity, he had a deep and constant anxiety over his own standing with the people. Combined with it was a craving for political power unrestrained by the fact that his fierce, compulsive energy could spin dangerously out of control. Ironically, as John Morton Blum observes, Roosevelt performed most effectively and responsibly when his freedom of action was sharply circumscribed by many competing forces.[22]

In foreign affairs Roosevelt understood the interdependence of the world and the fragile nature of the balance of power which prevented conflict among "civilized" nations. He wanted the United States to use its great power to help

[21] The most penetrating sketch is John Morton Blum's *The Republican Roosevelt* (Cambridge, Mass., 1954); but see also Henry Pringle, *Theodore Roosevelt: A Biography* (New York, 1931), superficial but full of insights; William Henry Harbaugh, *Power and Responsibility: The Life and Times of Theodore Roosevelt* (New York, 1961), largely a summary of recent scholarship; and Beale, *Theodore Roosevelt,* a major reinterpretation.

[22] Blum, *The Republican Roosevelt,* p. 123.

maintain world order, for such a course would strengthen the fiber of the American people, give the nation its rightful place in world affairs, and encourage the spread of Western civilization. Roosevelt thought, despite evidence of British decline, that "the twentieth century will still be the century of the men who speak English," and this conviction influenced many of his policies.[23] But his concept of civilization, a mixture of industrial development, governmental stability, and military might, did not prevent his full acceptance of a non-Western nation such as Japan.[24] With all of these beliefs Roosevelt coupled an understanding of the relationship of power and diplomacy and of public opinion and foreign policy. He saw the need for naval strength if the nation's weight was to be felt in the councils of the great powers; he saw, too, the need for public acceptance of his major foreign objectives. Roosevelt cared deeply about national honor and world order, but more than either he cared about continuing political success at home. And this fact often shaped and limited his foreign policy.

Roosevelt exercised a strong, if somewhat uneven, leadership over American foreign policy. In areas he considered of secondary importance, he allowed subordinates considerable autonomy. Thus from 1901 to 1904 John Hay retained his control of Far Eastern policy, and after 1905 Elihu Root dominated relations with Latin America. In the first case Roosevelt wished the United States to play only a defensive role in the Far East; in the second, Root's good neighbor policy seemed the best answer to the growing hostility in Latin America and to growing apathy at home. Yet in events of major importance, such as the mediation of the Russo-Japanese War or the Japanese-American crisis of 1906–1909,

---

[23] Roosevelt to Spring Rice, March 16, 1901, *Letters,* III, 16.
[24] See Beale, *Theodore Roosevelt,* pp. 22–38, for an interesting discussion of Roosevelt's imperialism.

Roosevelt watched closely day-to-day developments and also determined major goals. Then he held in his own supple hands all the strands of American policy.

For the historian Roosevelt poses many problems of interpretation. His egotism, sense of history, and volubility led to a huge correspondence which, in its every fullness and plausibility, tends to impose Roosevelt's own pattern upon events. Moreover, Roosevelt often ennobled and distorted his motives and failed to suggest their actual complexity. There is, then, the constant danger of overemphasizing Roosevelt's role in events and his interpretation of them. In foreign affairs, for example, he sometimes spoke in terms of long-range strategic and policy goals when he was, in truth, more influenced by domestic political considerations or by a shifting combination of long and short-term goals, of far-sighted statesmanship and political opportunism.

Roosevelt's chief adviser in foreign affairs after John Hay's death in July, 1905, contrasted sharply to the President himself. Outside a small circle of intimates and working associates, Elihu Root seemed a distant, cold man, with a precise, analytical mind and a tight control upon his enormous energies.[25] Calm, unpretentious, and self-possessed, he had a passion for order, stability, and administrative efficiency. His desire was to make the government work through a balancing of power and responsibility. In two successive cabinets Root was the strongest figure next to the President. To Roosevelt he was a close friend, a wise and selfless counselor who possessed restraint, patience, and humor, along with

[25] Philip C. Jessup's *Elihu Root* (2 vols.; New York, 1938), is a detailed, friendly study, while Richard W. Leopold's *Elihu Root and the Conservative Tradition* is a briefer and more critical assessment. Two discussions of Root as secretary of state, by James B. Scott in *The American Secretaries of State and Their Diplomacy*, ed. Samuel Flagg Bemis (10 vols.; New York, 1927–29), IX, 193–282, and by Charles W. Toth in *An Uncertain Tradition: American Secretaries of State in the Twentieth Century*, ed. Norman Graebner (New York, 1961), pp. 40–58, are of little value.

little political ambition and a passive attitude toward his place in history. Their very differences seemed to draw the two men together.

Thus if Roosevelt, in retrospect, seems larger than life, Root's influence appears too small. His most recent biographer, Richard W. Leopold, remarks that "Root's record on paper can never fully convey his strength, character, and insight." [26] Because of his self-effacement and his reluctance to elaborate his beliefs, Root's role in policy-making is often difficult to trace, though we know that Roosevelt always listened to him on domestic as well as foreign problems. Root understandably lacked Roosevelt's broad knowledge and vision in foreign affairs, though he shared the President's belief that the United States must play an important role in the world. At the same time, however, he thought that "to keep the country out of trouble . . . in the right way, is the main object of diplomacy." [27]

After 1905 Root largely directed the administration's Latin American policy, and he had much to do with furthering international arbitration and easing Canadian-American relations. It was in Far Eastern policy that Root's part was smallest. "Of all the important matters which Root handled in the Department of State," Philip C. Jessup observes, "those involving the Far East were least distinctively his own." [28] Before Root actively assumed his new duties, Roosevelt had taken over Far Eastern policy and set the future course of the administration in that region. Root accepted Roosevelt's broad goals of disengagement in the Far East and friendship with Japan, and during the Japanese-American crisis of 1906–1909 the two men completely agreed on major policies.[29]

[26] Leopold, *Elihu Root,* p. 194.
[27] Jessup, *Elihu Root,* II, 4.
[28] *Ibid.,* II, 3.
[29] A different view is in Raymond A. Esthus' "The Changing Concept of the Open Door, 1899–1910," *Mississippi Valley Historical Review,* 46 (December, 1959), 435–454.

Root's role in this crisis was more to implement policy than to create it, and in this way he figured prominently in the various negotiations with Japan during Roosevelt's last three years in office.

There was one other man who ought to have been an important presidential adviser on Far Eastern affairs. William Howard Taft had been Governor General of the Philippines, had visited Japan three times, and was in a position as Secretary of War from 1904 to 1908 constantly to influence the President.[30] In contrast to Roosevelt or Root, Taft had a first-hand impression of Japan and its statesmen. Perhaps because of this, throughout the Japanese-American crisis Taft was surprisingly calm and consistently less concerned than Roosevelt or Root over future relations with Japan.[31] Within his own immediate sphere of responsibility, Taft presided phlegmatically over the bitter inter-service debate on the defense of the Philippines. Significantly, it was the President, not the Secretary of War, who ordered strengthened defenses for those islands and an investigation into the strategic planning deficiencies of the army and navy.

In the autumn of 1907 Taft made another important journey to Japan to converse with leaders of the Japanese government. At that time he was impressed by the domestic difficulties of the ministry of Prince Kimmochi Saionji and urged Washington to accept an administrative solution to the problem of Japanese immigration. His reports brought an important shift in the administration's attitude toward that problem. Even in this mission, however, Taft largely reported what Saionji and Foreign Minister Tadasu Hayashi told him,

[30] The only biography of Taft is Henry F. Pringle's *The Life and Times of William Howard Taft* (2 vols.; New York, 1939), which is weak on Taft's tenure as secretary of war and on his attitude toward foreign affairs. On Taft's relations with Japan, see also Ralph E. Minger, "Taft's Missions to Japan: A Study in Personal Diplomacy," *Pacific Historical Review*, 30 (August, 1961), 279–294.

[31] For Taft's views on Japan see Pringle, *Taft*, I, 296–304, II, 712.

and acted more as a diplomatic messenger than as a creator of policy. Though a genial companion and an able administrator, the Secretary of War had a noticeable absence of ideas about American Far Eastern policy, and he tended to reflect the views of strong, opinionated men around him — particularly those of Theodore Roosevelt. So well did Taft assimilate Roosevelt's position that the Japanese government thought he would be in every way a safer president than Theodore Roosevelt.

Root and Taft were the only government officials upon whom the President drew consistently for advice and assistance in his dealings with Japan. Neither ambassadors nor subordinate officials in the State Department had much impact upon the President's policy. The American ambassador in China, William W. Rockhill, was a good friend and longtime counselor on Far Eastern affairs who undoubtedly approved of Roosevelt's policy toward Japan. But Rockhill's only important contribution during the crisis of 1906–1909 was to encourage American acquiescence to Japan's sphere in southern Manchuria.[32] The American ambassadors in Japan from 1906 to 1909 lacked a close personal relationship with the President. The first, Luke Wright, was a Tennessee Democrat who left his party in 1896 to support McKinley. Wright became a member of the Philippine Commission in 1900, Governor General in 1904, and in early 1906 reluctantly agreed to become the nation's first ambassador to Japan. He served until May, 1907, when he was replaced by Thomas J. O'Brien, a Michigan Republican and former minister to Denmark. While both men were conscientious diplomats and sympathetic to Japan, they knew little about Japanese politics and exercised no influence on Roosevelt or Root except as informants. Needless to say, the President took neither man into his confidence and used either Taft or John Callan

<hr />

[32] Varg, *Open Door Diplomat*, pp. 83–90.

O'Laughlin, Washington correspondent of the *Chicago Tribune,* for sensitive missions to Japan.

Within the State Department, Francis M. Huntington Wilson supervised some smaller aspects of the Japanese-American immigration dispute. This arrogant, fastidious Yale graduate had by the age of thirty-one risen from second secretary of the Tokyo legation to third assistant secretary of state. Unfortunately he had left Japan in May, 1906, with an intense antagonism toward that nation's culture and people. Though able and knowledgeable, he was also ungenerous in his interpretations of Japan's motives and a consistent advocate of a tougher, more active Far Eastern policy until his resignation in 1913.[33] Years later Root remembered him as a "person of the most dangerous character for diplomatic service" but in 1907 Root described him as a "good and genuine man" with the advantage of a close friendship with Henry W. Denison, an American adviser to the Japanese Foreign Office.[34] Both Roosevelt and Root valued Huntington Wilson's ability, though seldom his policies, and he left no imprint upon the broad course of Roosevelt's Far Eastern policy because of his anti-Japanese views.

The President, the Secretary of State, and the Secretary of War all shared several common assumptions throughout the crisis with Japan which began in October, 1906. These were an admiration for Japan's achievements as a nation coupled with a desire for friendship in the future. Roosevelt had largely altered his views toward Japan since the 1890's. Then he was hostile because of Japan's opposition to American acquisition of Hawaii, though his hostility was mixed with respect for Japan's rapid development as a modern nation. After 1900, however, the ominous growth of Russian

[33] Francis M. Huntington Wilson, *Memoirs of an Ex-Diplomat* (Boston, 1945), pp. 72, 165, 174.
[34] Jessup, *Elihu Root,* I, 457; Root to Roosevelt, July 21, 1907, Roosevelt Papers.

imperialism in China caused Roosevelt increasingly to regard Japan as the nation best fitted to contain that imperialism, stabilize the Far East, and lead China into the circle of "great civilized powers." Like Alfred Thayer Mahan, he believed that Japan was a good, if incomplete, example of the fusion of Western and Oriental civilizations.[35]

Roosevelt was, however, uneasy over the extent of Japan's triumph in the Russo-Japanese War and the violent riots in Tokyo protesting the terms of the Treaty of Portsmouth. He could not understand how Japan's statesmen had failed to moderate the expectations of their people and worried that Japan "might get the 'big head' and enter into a general career of insolence and aggression." Victorious Japan, unlike other powers with interests in the Orient, would have "but one care, one interest, one burden." [36] Yet most of Roosevelt's experience with Japan throughout the peace negotiations and after made this prospect seem unlikely. And he attempted to make it more remote by approving the renewal of the Anglo-Japanese Alliance in 1905 and endorsing the friendly exchange of views between Secretary of War Taft and Prime Minister Taro Katsura in July of that year.[37]

In his last years in office Roosevelt shaped his Far Eastern policy around the belief that Japan would exercise its power with responsibility and restraint. His pro-Japanese views were, if anything, held more strongly by Secretary of State Root, who described Japan as a "liberal and progressive constitutional Empire," and thought that nation would become the England of the Orient.[38] Both Roosevelt and Root were to have these beliefs severely tested in the years stretching

[35] Beale, *Theodore Roosevelt*, pp. 264–270.

[36] Roosevelt to Spring Rice, June 13, 1904, *Letters*, IV, 830; Roosevelt to Spring Rice, March 19, 1904, *Letters*, IV, 760.

[37] An excellent analysis of Taft's conversation with Katsura is in Raymond A. Esthus', "The Taft–Katsura Agreement — Reality or Myth?" *Journal of Modern History*, 32 (March, 1959), 46–51.

[38] Jessup, *Elihu Root*, II, 7; Leopold, *Elihu Root*, p. 60.

from 1906 to 1909, when their faith in Japan at times wavered and they were filled with doubts over the future of Japanese-American relations. Yet their conviction that these two nations could work together in friendship was never shattered. Without this conviction, they could not have guided the United States so successfully through the crisis of the ensuing years.

# II

## CALIFORNIA AND JAPAN

The Russo-Japanese War marked the end of an era of good feeling in Japanese-American relations. In the decades prior to that conflict most of the American people had watched with sympathy Japan's emergence as a modern nation, while their government had pursued a benevolent policy toward Japan which reflected this popular feeling. Despite tensions over Hawaii in the 1890's, the nation looked upon Japan almost as a protégé, with similar interests in the Far East; and when Japan's opposition to Russian expansion brought war in 1904, American approval of Japan's cause and apparent war aims was overwhelming. Most editorial writers agreed with Theodore Roosevelt that Japan was "playing our game" in the Far East and that its victory over Russia and predominance in Southern Manchuria would benefit American commerce there. They expected Japan to expand its trade but not to pursue a monopolistic policy offensive to Great Britain and the United States.[1]

[1] Payson J. Treat, *Japan and the United States, 1853-1921* (Stanford, 1928), p. 187; Winston B. Thorson, "American Public Opinion and the Portsmouth Peace Conference," *American Historical Review*, 53 (April, 1948), 439-464; two recent accounts of Japanese-American relations are William L. Neumann's *America Encounters Japan: From Perry to MacArthur* (Baltimore, 1963), and Raymond A. Esthus' *Theodore Roosevelt and Japan*.

But the year 1905 was an important turning point in relations between the United States and Japan. Japan's victory over Russia made it the dominant power in Asia, with hegemony over Korea, extensive rights in Manchuria, and unknown ambitions in China proper. Japan achieved its new position at a time when many Americans, impressed by the reforms of the Manchu dynasty, believed China was finally transforming itself into a modern and civilized state.[2] Now a potential conflict appeared between Japanese and American interests in the Far East, and after 1905 there was less exultation of Japan's progress and more skepticism over Japan's future aims in the Orient. This subtle shift in American attitudes, paralleled by a less friendly Japanese view of the United States, was the beginning of a long, uneven decline in Japanese-American relations.[3]

In the months following the Portsmouth Conference, Japan's rapid consolidation of its new position in southern Manchuria and Korea quickened fears of a "Japanese peril." Favoritism in railway rates, combined with restrictions on the entry of foreign merchants into Manchuria, created suspicion among some Americans, as did the slow pace of negotiations with China for the opening of Manchurian customs houses. The impact of this discrimination was intensified by a trade depression in Manchuria and led to investigations and protests by British and American merchants.[4] In March, 1906, the State Department responded by complaining to Japan over trade conditions in Manchuria. Though Washington showed little inclination to begin a serious dispute, Amer-

[2] Jessie Ashworth Miller, "China in American Policy and Opinion, 1906–1909" (unpublished Ph.D. dissertation, Clark University, 1940), pp. 6–27.
[3] Eleanor Tupper and George E. McReynolds, *Japan in American Public Opinion* (New York, 1937), p. 17.
[4] Charles Vevier, *The United States and China, 1906–1913: A Study of Finance and Diplomacy* (New Brunswick, 1955), pp. 35–43.

ican diplomats continued to watch the Manchurian situation closely.[5]

These fears of Japanese commercial aggressiveness did not diminish as business conditions in the Far East slowly improved, for they were stimulated more by a vague foreboding over America's future in the Pacific than by present commercial realities. On the Pacific Coast, more oriented toward Asia and still geographically isolated from the rest of the nation, the Japanese threat loomed far larger in men's minds and was intensified by a growing uneasiness over Japanese immigration.[6] This immigration became noticeable in the 1890's but it brought no significant protest from Californians until 1900, when over 12,000 Japanese entered the United States. That year a mass meeting in San Francisco urged the extension of Chinese exclusion laws to include the Japanese, and less than a year later Governor Henry T. Gage called the attention of the California legislature to the Japanese problem.[7] Aroused by these protests, the Japanese government prohibited the issuance of passports to coolies for the continental United States, but the restriction proved ineffective, largely because of the continued emigration of laborers to the Hawaiian Islands. Nonetheless, prior to the outbreak of the Russo-Japanese War the anti-Japanese agitation on the Pacific Coast was only in its infancy.[8]

By 1905 Japanese immigration was still numerically small (less than 15,000 in 1904), but was beginning to alarm many Californians who feared a great influx of Japanese laborers after the end of the war. They realized that Japanese im-

[5] *Foreign Relations, 1906,* I, 170–177, 210–213.
[6] J. Ingram Bryan, "Japan's Capacity for the Supremacy of the Far East," *Harper's Weekly,* 50 (August 18, 1906), 1166.
[7] H. A. Millis, *The Japanese Problem in the United States* (New York, 1915), pp. 11–13.
[8] Raymond L. Buell, "The Development of the Anti-Japanese Agitation in the United States," *Political Science Quarterly,* 37 (December, 1922), 609.

migrants were more aggressive and ambitious than the Chinese had been and had behind them a powerful and sensitive government fresh from its victory over Russia. Before 1905 anti-Japanese agitation had been an offshoot of the drive for Chinese exclusion; after that year it achieved a separate and permanent importance in California society.[9] Four ominous developments in the early months of 1905 reflected this new trend. The California legislature passed a resolution asking for restrictive laws against the "immoral, intemperate, quarrelsome men bound to labor for a pittance"; the *San Francisco Chronicle,* the most influential paper on the Pacific Coast, began a rabid anti-Japanese campaign; and on May 5 the San Francisco Board of Education resolved to segregate Japanese children in the primary grades of the city's school system. Two days later the Japanese-Korean Exclusion League was founded. It promptly endorsed the board's resolution and urged the extension of the Chinese exclusion laws to the Japanese and Koreans.[10]

The President's reaction to these events was ambiguous. He knew better than most of his countrymen the resentment with which the Japanese would regard agitation against them in the United States. "You cannot feel as badly as I do," Roosevelt wrote the journalist George Kennan in May, 1905, "over such action as that by the idiots of the California Legislature." Yet he sympathized with the Californians' objections to the Japanese and realized that their "very frugality, abstemiousness and clannishness make them formidable to our laboring class." In Hawaii the Japanese remained an

[9] For the background and nature of anti-Japanese agitation in California see Roger Daniels, *The Politics of Prejudice: The Anti-Japanese Movement in California and the Struggle for Japanese Exclusion* (Berkeley, 1962); and Fred H. Matthews, "White Community and 'Yellow Peril,'" *Mississippi Valley Historical Review,* 50 (March, 1964), 612–633.

[10] Ruth H. Thomson, "Events Leading to the Order to Segregate Japanese Pupils in the San Francisco Schools" (unpublished Ph.D. dissertation, Stanford University, 1931), pp. 47–50, 112–118.

"alien mass" and already presented a serious problem. If the California legislature had passed a courteous resolution calling for the restriction of Japanese immigration, the President would have approved, but he was "keenly mortified" by the insulting terms of the actual resolution.[11] Roosevelt's agreement with the basic purpose of the Californians was not surprising, for he had long favored restrictions on the masses of immigrants flocking to American shores. He shared the prejudices of organized labor and of many other Americans against these impoverished newcomers.[12] In the spring of 1904 the President signed a Chinese exclusion act, and a year later he forwarded to the State Department a plan for stopping the passage of Japanese laborers from Hawaii to the mainland of the United States. But the State Department, deprived of leadership for several months after John Hay's death, took no action, though from time to time it received reports on the mounting influx of Japanese laborers.[13]

Apparently the President was irritated rather than alarmed by the anti-Japanese agitation in California. "The feeling on the Pacific slope," he said, ". . . is as foolish as if conceived by the mind of a Hottentot." Asking Ambassador Lloyd Griscom to let the Japanese government know that the American government and people had no sympathy with the anti-Japanese fever among certain "small sections" of the people along the Pacific slope, he vowed that during his presidency "the Japanese will be treated just exactly like the English, Germans, French or other civilized peoples; that is, each man, good or bad, will be treated on his merits." [14] At a farewell dinner in September, 1905, for Kentaro Kaneko, a special

[11] Roosevelt to George Kennan, May 6, 1905, *Letters*, IV, 1168–70.
[12] Blum, *The Republican Roosevelt*, p. 113.
[13] A. L. C. Atkinson to Roosevelt, June 12, 1905, and William Loeb to Acting Secretary of State Loomis, June 15, 1905, NA, RG 59:2542/1.
[14] Roosevelt to Henry Cabot Lodge, June 5, 1905, and to Lloyd Griscom, July 15, 1905, *Letters*, IV, 1205–1206, 1274–1275.

Japanese envoy to the United States during the Russo-Japanese War, he expressed some concern over the future of Japanese-American relations because of the agitation against the Japanese on the Pacific Coast; but if he entertained any real doubts of his ability to control the situation, he gave no sign of them.[15] When a delegation of Californians called upon him in December to discuss the introduction of a Japanese exclusion bill, Roosevelt used strong language in condemning it and threatened to veto a bill that passed unanimously.[16] And as if to provide a final answer to the Californians, in his annual message he urged nondiscriminatory immigration restriction which would not single out men on account of their nationality or creed.[17] This, however, did not deter the introduction of Japanese exclusion legislation in early 1906 by Representatives Everis Hayes and Duncan McKinley, Republicans of California. As events would soon demonstrate, the Californians were as determined as the President.

In 1905 and 1906 the anti-Japanese agitation in California was not as widespread or powerful as the movement against Chinese immigration had been. It was still a localized, class affair centered in San Francisco, where organized labor was strong and controlled the municipal government. In that city the possibility of an outbreak became increasingly real as 1906 progressed. The great earthquake of April, 1906, destroyed large parts of San Francisco and created an atmosphere in which violence thrived. Hostility toward Japanese residents was intensified by their spread into previously white areas of the city and by the rapid increase in Japanese restaurants which served workingmen. Many incidents oc-

[15] Kamikawa Hikomatsu (ed.), *Japan-American Diplomatic Relations in the Meiji-Taisho Era,* trans. by Kimura Michiko (Tokyo, 1958), pp. 265–266.

[16] *San Francisco Chronicle,* December 7, 1905, as quoted in Thomson, "Events," 50, 120.

[17] *The Works of Theodore Roosevelt* (20 vols., National Edition; New York, 1926), XXV, 319–320. Hereafter cited as *Works.*

curred, including attacks on prominent Japanese and the boycotting of Japanese restaurants by organized labor.[18] By August, Tokyo newspapers reported the extreme feeling against Japanese in San Francisco.[19] The climax to these developments came on October 11, 1906, when, carrying out its earlier threat, the Board of Education ordered the segregation of Japanese children in the primary schools.

Despite the passage of many years, the origins of the school order remain obscure. It may have been associated with the political fortunes of the Union Labor party administration, led by Mayor Eugene Schmitz and by the party's boss, Abraham Ruef. It was a curious coincidence that a labor government should be dominated by these two men, for both were more interested in advancing their own political fortunes than labor's cause. First elected in 1901, Schmitz was re-elected in 1903 and again in November, 1905. His final victory had for the first time given the party complete control of the municipal government and was followed by an orgy of corruption remarkable even for that era of city government. Nevertheless, by the summer of 1906 Schmitz's successful handling of the city's rehabilitation effort raised the prestige of his administration to new heights and greatly stimulated both his own political ambitions and those of the "Curly Boss."

Schmitz hoped to become governor of California, while Ruef schemed to replace Senator George C. Perkins in 1909. Ruef expected to secure a return on the many favors he had done for the state's regular Republican organization over the years. Just as the time was approaching when he might do so, the position of the Schmitz administration began slipping as quickly as it had risen. In the autumn of 1906 a serious crime wave, beyond the control of the police, aroused many

[18] Daniels, *Politics of Prejudice*, pp. 32–34.
[19] *Japan Weekly Mail*, August 11 and 25, 1906.

citizens. Moreover, certain Union Labor supervisors, by their exhibition of sudden wealth, helped substantiate the widespread rumors of corruption. Two prominent San Franciscans, Fremont Older and Rudolph Spreckels, had long been convinced of this fact and on October 20, with their backing, the San Francisco graft prosecution was formally inaugurated.[20]

The school order may have had its origins in the hopes of Ruef and Schmitz to strengthen their public support before the forthcoming graft trials; perhaps they even expected to divert public attention from their own misdeeds. The careers of both men held ample precedent for such a maneuver. During the mayoralty election of 1903 Ruef had attempted to use anti-Chinese sentiment against Franklin K. Lane, the Democratic nominee. And Schmitz had endorsed the anti-Japanese movement in May, 1905, several days after the Board of Education resolved to segregate Japanese pupils. The Mayor, however, seemed in no hurry to initiate anti-Japanese measures, for the Board of Education was not given the funds to carry out its resolution and the issue lapsed until the autumn of 1906. By that time the former Chinese school was no longer fully occupied and could be used for Japanese students without additional expenditures. Moreover, in August the Japanese-Korean Exclusion League asked that the board's resolution be implemented. Perhaps prodded by the demands of their union supporters and eager to improve their own political fortunes, Schmitz and Ruef ordered the Board of Education to act.[21]

Yet in the autumn of 1906 neither Schmitz nor Ruef seemed anxious over his political position. Ruef knew that

[20] Walton Bean, *Boss Ruef's San Francisco: The Story of the Union Labor Party, Big Business, and the Graft Prosecution* (Berkeley, 1952), pp. 31–35, 64–66, 81–83, 145, 156–163.
[21] Bean, *Boss Ruef's San Francisco*, p. 38, and Thomson, "Events," 145–146, 156–160.

a graft prosecution was being organized from early 1906, but showed no concern until after the public announcement of its organization was made, while Schmitz actually left for Europe on October 1.[22] The board may only have been taking advantage of the favorable circumstances created by vacancies in the old Chinese school to strike a long-contemplated blow at the Japanese, without closely considering the immediate political needs of the Schmitz administration. For several years influential parents had complained about the presence of Japanese children in the public schools, and local officials, in justifying school segregation, emphasized the age of the Japanese pupils in the primary schools and claimed that grown orientals with low moral standards ought not to sit beside young girls.[23] Neither of these reasons was convincing, for the problem of overaged Japanese students could have been solved by simple administrative regulations, while the testimony of local educators, along with several careful investigations, showed that Japanese pupils in the San Francisco public schools were exemplary students.[24] But the Board of Education, influenced by the climate of intolerance in San Francisco, may simply have been attempting to carry out the wishes of the majority of its constituents.

What began as a local, routine decision soon became, to the surprise of Schmitz and his associates, a national and international issue. The Japanese Consul General in San Francisco, Kisaburo Uyeno, already had called the attention of municipal officials to the restaurant boycott and to the assaults on Japanese. The day after the board resolved to

[22] Thomson, "Events," 156–157.
[23] George Kennan, "San Francisco Notes," December 3, 1906, Kennan Papers; Julius Kahn, "The Japanese Question From a Californian's Standpoint," *The Independent*, 62 (January 3, 1907), 26–33.
[24] George Kennan, "The Japanese in the San Francisco Schools," *Outlook*, 86 (June 1, 1907), 246–252; and Victor H. Metcalf, *Report on the Situation Affecting the Japanese in the City of San Francisco, California*, November 26, 1906, Senate Doc. 147, 59th Cong. 2d Sess.

segregate Japanese pupils, Uyeno protested that such action would deprive many Japanese children of all school privileges and would create resentment in Japan.[25] Though the board agreed to establish schools for smaller Japanese children nearer their homes, it refused to alter its order in any other way, leaving both Uyeno and the Japanese Association of America dissatisfied.[26] In a statement widely circulated in Japan, the latter claimed that "the Japanese people in San Francisco . . . are being subjected to such insult as no other nation except the Chinese has been subjected to since the founding of the United States." "If Japan remains humiliated," the association warned, "her prestige will be lost forever." [27]

Dispatches to American newspapers from Tokyo reported a "storm of popular indignation" over the discrimination against Japanese school children. Though these descriptions of the popular reaction were no doubt overdrawn, there was cause enough for alarm in Washington in late October. Kentaro Kaneko, now back in Japan and serving as a financial adviser to the Japanese government, telegraphed Roosevelt, his old Harvard classmate, that Japan "painfully regrets" the school segregation.[28] The *Japan Weekly Mail* confirmed his impression by pointing out the "excitement and indignation" and the "profound sorrow and disappointment" created among the Japanese people, while Ambassador Luke Wright thought a "marked feeling of irritation against the United States" had developed in the public mind. Wright claimed

[25] "Notes from the Japanese Embassy, October 25, 1906," NA, RG 59:1797/5–6.
[26] Arthur G. Butzbach, "The Segregation of Orientals in the San Francisco Schools" (unpublished Master's thesis, Stanford University, 1928), pp. 31–32.
[27] Japanese Association of America, "The Expulsion of the Japanese School Children," San Francisco, October 20, 1906, NA, RG 59:1797/64.
[28] *Literary Digest,* 33 (November 3, 1906), 621–622; Kentaro Kaneko to Roosevelt, October 26, 1906, Roosevelt Papers.

that more incidents could cause a "total change of sentiment which might result in a boycott or some other form of retaliation." [29]

Part of the reaction of the Japanese press was due to the cumulative effect of the anti-Japanese agitation on the Pacific Coast, combined with irritation over American suspicion of Japan's Manchurian policy and resentment over incidents such as the killing of Japanese seal-poachers in the Pribilof Islands in July, 1906. Part was also a product of sensational journalism and of Japanese domestic politics. One prominent representative of the yellow press, the *Yorozu Choho,* said that Americans "have almost gone mad with the agitation for excluding Japanese." The *Hochi Shimbun,* an organ of the *Kenseihonto* (Orthodox Constitutional Government Party), reflected the desire of the party and its leader, Count Shigenobu Okuma, to bring about the downfall of the ministry of Prince Kimmochi Saionji. The *Hochi* complained that the "Japanese authorities concerned who sit idly by and look at the affair like disinterested parties are incapable in the highest degree." "If the United States," it threatened, "does not put an end to the anti-Japanese agitation, this country must take some decisive measures for retaliation." [30] Government and independent organs — such as the semi-official *Japan Times,* the *Kokumin Shimbun,* speaking for former Prime Minister Taro Katsura, and the influential, independent *Jiji Shimpo* and *Asahi Shimbun* — were not yet seriously aroused. [31]

The weakness of the Saionji ministry and the mood of the

[29] *Japan Weekly Mail,* October 27, 1906; Wright to Root, October 22, 1906, NA, RG 59:1797/41.

[30] *Yorozu Choho,* October 19, 1906, *Hochi Shimbun,* October 20, 1906, NA, RG 59:1797/44–45.

[31] *Japan Times,* October 23, 1906, *Kokumin Shimbun,* October 20, 1906, *Jiji Shimpo,* October 20, 1906, *Asahi Shimbun,* October 17, 1906, NA, RG 59:1797/43–58.

Japanese people justified the concern of Wright and the *Weekly Mail*. Spurred by the reported severity of the initial Japanese reaction, Roosevelt and Root had been quick to make a conciliatory gesture. On October 23 the Secretary of State informed the Japanese that the school order was the result of local labor agitation which should be ignored by the rulers and people of Japan. The United States wanted Japanese residents treated as if they were from the most friendly European nation, and the President had ordered the Department of Justice to make a full investigation.[32] But Tokyo had not waited for the official explanation from Washington. On the day of Root's message, Foreign Minister Tadasu Hayashi instructed Ambassador Shuzo Aoki "to call the serious attention of the Secretary of State" to conditions in San Francisco. Japan had hoped, Aoki was to inform Root, that the American government would quickly remedy the situation, but instead it was "daily growing worse." The Japanese-American treaty of 1894, which had guaranteed Japanese residents both full personal protection and most-favored-nation treatment, was clearly violated by the school segregation order. In closing, Aoki was to say that "the hostile demonstration in San Francisco has produced among all classes of people in Japan a feeling of profound disappointment and sorrow. Happily that feeling up to this time is unmixed with any suggestion of retaliation because it is firmly believed that the evil will be speedily removed."[33]

The reasons for this threatening protest and Saionji's subsequent course, which prevented a rapid settlement of Japanese-American difficulties, deserve some explanation. Saionji, scion of a court family, was a prominent government bureaucrat (but not a *genro*); the most powerful *genro*, Aritomo

---

[32] Root to Wright, October 23, 1906, NA, RG 59:1797/4.
[33] Hayashi to Aoki, October 23, 1906, Telegram Series, JA.

Yamagata, regarded him with suspicion because of his affilia-
tion with a popular party. When Hirobumi Ito left active
politics in 1903 Saionji replaced him as the leader of the most
numerous party in the lower house, the *Seiyukai*. Ito originally hoped to form a party which would cooperate with
the government, but Yamagata and the military officers and
conservative bureaucrats whom he led opposed sharing
power with political parties of any sort. Saionji's noble rank
and government service, not his role as a party leader, explain his appointment as premier. The cabinet of Yamagata's
protégé, Taro Katsura, resigned in late 1905 because of the
dissatisfaction in Japan over the terms of the Treaty of Portsmouth. Katsura suggested that Saionji form a ministry to replace his own, and Yamagata reluctantly agreed after Saionji
had pledged a continuance of Katsura's policies. Katsura and
many Japanese newspapers viewed Saionji's tenure as a temporary one which would allow postwar readjustments to occur and thus permit Katsura's return to power. Understandably, from the time of its formation in January, 1906, the
Saionji Ministry could not steer an independent course in
either foreign or domestic affairs and leaned heavily on the
advice of the *genro*.[34]

In part the *genro* chose Saionji because they felt he could
best control the difficult postwar situation in Japan. The violent dissatisfaction of the public and political parties over
the settlement of the Russo-Japanese War was unprecedented and led to riots and martial law in Tokyo. The compromise peace offended members of the *Seiyukai* and *Ken-*

[34] For the Japanese political background see Jackson H. Bailey, "Prince
Saionji: A Study in Modern Japanese Political Leadership" (unpublished
Ph.D. dissertation, Harvard University, 1959), pp. 143, 145, 149, 152;
Roger F. Hackett, "Yamagata Aritomo: A Political Biography" (unpublished
Ph.D. dissertation, Harvard University, 1955), pp. 292, 302, 322, 365–366;
Lawrence A. Olson, Jr., "Hara Kei, A Political Biography" (unpublished
Ph.D. dissertation, Harvard University, 1954), p. 180.

*seihonto,* who during the war developed exaggerated notions of what Japan's postwar position on the Asiatic mainland should be.[35] Saionji succeeded in muffling much of the discontent within the *Seiyukai,* but Okuma led the *Kenseihonto* in outspoken attacks upon the government. The members of the ruling group were sensitive to the criticisms of Okuma, for he had a wide popular following based upon years of opposition to the rule of the Satsuma-Choshu oligarchy and upon his advocacy of political parties and responsible parliamentary government. He had encouraged the trend toward broader popular participation in government while most of the *genro* had attempted to suppress it directly or indirectly through their manipulation of the parties. Only a year after the Tokyo riots, Okuma was again exciting the general restiveness among the people by attacking the government's policy on the potentially explosive issue of discrimination against Japanese residents in the United States.[36] Wright reported that Foreign Minister Hayashi was "nervous and fear[s] an anti-American agitation among the people with disagreeable consequences, as I do." [37]

Both fear and opportunism moved Japanese leaders to make a strong plea for a rapid adjustment of the San Francisco school order. Saionji himself had a reputation as a moderate and internationalist in foreign affairs, while his foreign minister, Hayashi, was one of the chief architects of the Anglo-Japanese Alliance. The cabinet had no desire for trouble with the United States during a period of postwar readjustment when it was organizing new spheres of influ-

[35] Robert A. Scalapino, *Democracy and the Party Movement in Prewar Japan: The Failure of the First Attempt* (Berkeley, 1953), pp. 187–188.

[36] Joyce C. Lebra, "Japan's First Modern Popular Statesman: A Study of the Political Career of Okuma Shigenobu" (unpublished Ph.D. dissertation, Radcliffe College, 1958), pp. 216, 260–263.

[37] Wright to Root, telegram, October 21, 1906, NA, RG 59:1797/1.

ence on the Asiatic mainland, nationalizing Japanese railroads, and facing military and naval demands for expanded
programs. But the cabinet, like the Japanese people, was
highly conscious of Japan's new position in world affairs and
sensitive to insults to the nation's honor. It was, at the same
time, poorly informed about conditions in the United States
and probably assumed that the Roosevelt administration
could control the anti-Japanese agitation in California far
more effectively than in fact it could. Thus Saionji, eager to
strengthen his position with the *genro* and uneasy over
Japanese public opinion, may have behaved more chauvinis-
tically than his own sense of policy would have dictated.
And he felt he could afford to do so because the American
government was in a position to satisfy promptly the demands of Japan. In the early months of the Japanese-
American crisis Saionji, like Roosevelt, largely viewed his
nation's diplomacy in terms of domestic needs.

What the American government saw, however, was merely
the vigor with which Japan's leaders spoke. Although Ambassador Aoki delivered his government's note in a softened
paraphrase, its words still stung. Root was conciliatory,
emphasized the local nature of the anti-Japanese agitation
and the warm friendship which the American people in
general had for Japan. He gave assurances that, though the
Department of State was still collecting information, the
President was determined to do everything in his power to
correct injustice and abuses.[38] But his cordiality masked the
deep concern over the nature of the Japanese protest. Aoki's
manner and language, reported the *New York Times,* were
regarded as "very unusual" and produced a "decided sensation" at the State Department. There the impression was

[38] "Note from the Japanese Embassy," October 25, 1906, NA, RG
59:1797/16, and Aoki to Hayashi, October 25 and 31, 1906, Telegram Series,
JA.

that Japan would go to considerable lengths to defend its interpretation of the treaty of 1894.[39]

The mood of the administration by late October, 1906, was tense. The cabinet, meeting on October 26, felt that the situation was grave and would require delicate treatment to avoid an open rupture. It decided that Victor Metcalf, Secretary of Commerce and Labor and a former congressman from California, should go on a mission to San Francisco to gather badly needed information on the anti-Japanese disturbances there and to demonstrate to Japan the good will and activity of the federal government.[40] A day later Metcalf received a memorandum composed by Root at the President's request which indicated the anxiety in Washington and the importance attached to his mission. Reflecting many of Roosevelt's views, the Secretary of State described the Japanese as a "proud, sensitive, warlike" people who were so "ready for war" that they could take the Philippine Islands, the Hawaiian Islands, and "probably the Pacific Coast" from the unprepared United States. "The subject," wrote Root, "is not one of some far distant, possible evil, but is an immediate and present danger to be considered and averted now, today." Even without war, Japan, because of its commanding position in China and Manchuria, could harm American trade in the Orient. Moreover, in any controversy which might arise the attitude of the United States would be unjustifiable, both to Japan and to the world, for the things done in San Francisco were not only violations of the 1894 treaty with Japan but "intrinsically unfair and indefensible." San Francisco's action was an "exhibition of . . . provincial and uninstructed narrowness and prejudice"; the United States must not be forced into an unjust quarrel "by the action of a few ignorant . . . men who wish to

[39] *New York Times,* October 26 and 28, 1906.
[40] *Washington Star,* October 26, 1906, Roosevelt Scrapbooks.

monopolize the labor market of San Francisco." Rather than reach this humiliating crisis, Root argued that the entire power of the federal government should be used.[41]

The President, as he confessed to his son Kermit, was "being horribly bothered about the Japanese business" and was scornful of the "infernal fools in California" who threatened to lead the nation "into a war in which it was wrong." He was concerned over the control of mobs and demagogues on the Pacific Coast and thought it possible that he might "have to use the army in connection with boycotting or the suppression of mob violence." [42] No doubt with this in mind, he instructed Metcalf to warn the San Francisco authorities that any failure to protect the Japanese would lead to the use of all the force of the United States, "both civil and military." [43] These incidents could, as Roosevelt so sharply realized, "bring war with Japan" and he sought to lessen the impact of past and perhaps future events by reassuring the Japanese government of his good intentions. Through Kentaro Kaneko, Roosevelt explained to Hayashi his difficulties and determination in dealing with San Francisco. He also let Ambassador Aoki and the *Osaka Mainichi's* Washington correspondent look over a draft of the Japanese portion of his annual message, which praised Japan and censured California. And finally, the *New York Tribune* carried an officially inspired statement of the legal and

[41] Root, "Confidential Memorandum for Secretary Metcalf Regarding the Exclusion of Japanese Children from the Public Schools and the Boycotting of Japanese Restaurants in San Francisco," October 27, 1906, NA, RG 59:1797/13.

[42] Roosevelt to Kermit Roosevelt, October 27, 1906, and to Eugene Hale, October 27, 1906, *Letters*, V, 474–476.

[43] *Message from President Roosevelt to Congress, transmitting the final report of Secretary Metcalf on the situation affecting the Japanese in the City of San Francisco, California*, Senate Doc. 147, 59th Cong., 2d Sess.; before leaving for Panama Roosevelt authorized Root to use the armed forces to protect the Japanese. Roosevelt to Root, October 29, 1906, *Letters*, V, 484.

constitutional aspects of the administration's controversy with San Francisco. If Japan understood Roosevelt's predicament, perhaps it would await a solution with more patience.[44]

The President's assurances, Root's conciliatory telegrams, and the dispatch of Metcalf to the Pacific Coast, all encouraged moderation in Japan. In late October Count Okuma voiced his faith in the ability of the United States to render justice to Japan. But at the same time he warned that "we are controlling ourselves simply for the reason that America has been the most friendly nation to us during the last fifty years. . . . I hope before long the friendly relations of the two countries will be settled as before; if not, I must say to the Japanese as a nation that we can not bear injustice from any nation whatever." [45] Okuma summed up the feeling of most of the Japanese press, which was circumspect but convinced that something must be done to right the offense against Japanese school children. Wright reported that influential Japanese newspapers were showing a more "quiet tone of confidence" and that the public was prepared to await the ordinary legal and diplomatic delays. "Yet underneath [it] all," he said, "is a current of feeling which shows how nearly the implied racial discrimination has touched home." This feeling was being suppressed because of the unique friendship between the two nations and would soon pass unless other incidents occurred.[46]

During November the Japanese press remained calm. The *Jiji Shimpo* and *Asahi Shimbun* spoke of Roosevelt's "powerful personality" and of their confidence in the American

[44] Wire from the *Osaka Mainichi*'s Washington correspondent, October 27, 1906, NA, RG 59:1797/58; Aoki to Hayashi, October 31, 1906, Telegram Series, JA; *New York Tribune*, as quoted in Aoki to Hayashi, October 27, 1906, Telegram Series, JA.

[45] *Japan Weekly Mail*, November 3, 1906.

[46] Wright to Root, October 31 and November 9, 1906, NA, RG 59:1797/55 and 63.

government.[47] This forbearance was encouraged by Foreign Minister Hayashi, who told delegates from the *Seiyukai* and *Kenseihonto* that the views of the United States coincided with those of Japan and that an amicable settlement would be reached. Both political parties resolved to be patient since the American government was seeking a rapid solution.[48] Hayashi was also patient, as Aoki advised, and awaited further developments and Roosevelt's annual message. Nevertheless, the government retained its firm position that the treaty of 1894 gave Japanese children most-favored-nation rights in education, which the federal government was bound to enforce.[49]

Most of the American press from the very start of the school crisis sympathized with the indignation felt by the Japanese government and people. American papers generally deplored the anti-Japanese agitation and emphasized its local character. The *Washington Evening Star* remarked that American "interests in the Far East . . . are too heavy and important to be placed in jeopardy by a wanton insult of the dominant power." [50] Ambassador Aoki thought that "not a single paper east of the Rocky Mountains" approved of the action of the San Francisco authorities. Aoki's judgment, however, overlooked the considerable doubts among editorial writers over the legal power of the federal government to end discrimination against Japanese students. Even the pro-Roosevelt *Outlook* argued that the federal government could not by treaty confer educational rights within states upon foreign citizens.[51]

[47] *Jiji Shimpo*, November 18, 1906, *Asahi Shimbun*, November 14, 1906, NA, RG 59:1797/80 and 82.

[48] Wright to Root, November 24, 1906, NA, RG 59:1797/77.

[49] Aoki to Hayashi, November 10, and Hayashi to Aoki, November 13, 1906, Telegram Series, JA.

[50] *Literary Digest*, 33 (November 3, 1906), 621–622.

[51] Aoki to Hayashi, October 28, 1906, Telegram Series, JA; *Outlook*, 84 (December 29, 1906), 1049–1051.

While the press and people of both nations awaited developments in Washington, the Roosevelt administration pondered several possible solutions to the school crisis. One was legal and would be based on court action to uphold Japanese treaty rights; the other was diplomatic and would involve negotiations with Japan for the restriction of immigration. The legal approach offered considerable hope if, as the administration assumed from the start, the school order was a violation of the treaty of 1894 with Japan. On his arrival in San Francisco, Metcalf told Consul General Uyeno that the United States guaranteed the Japanese all public school privileges that were accorded the most-favored-nation and that as long as San Francisco segregated just Japanese pupils it was violating the treaty. He offered the cooperation of United States District Attorney Robert Devlin if the Japanese wished to make a test case in the California courts.[52] However, Metcalf and Devlin soon discovered that the treaty contained no general most-favored-nation clause — that instead it contained two separate ones providing for most-favored-nation treatment in navigation and commerce and in residence and travel. Metcalf doubted that the term "residence" included education. Though the California statute under which the Board of Education acted was perhaps vulnerable to attack, its weaknesses were at best technical deficiencies which the legislature could remedy. Metcalf recommended that if any test case was to be tried successfully, the treaty with Japan should be amended to include a more general most-favored-nation clause.[53]

This news produced a divided reaction within the administration. Root and Second Assistant Secretary of State Alvey A. Adee were skeptical of Metcalf's legal reasoning. Root thought, as the Japanese argued, that education was

[52] Uyeno to Hayashi, November 1, 1906, Telegram Series, JA.
[53] Metcalf to Roosevelt, November 2, 1906, NA, RG 59:1797/37.

included in the clause guaranteeing equal rights of residence, particularly considering the purpose with which the treaty was negotiated.[54] But James Brown Scott, the department's solicitor, cogently pointed out a new problem. Assuming that education was covered in the term "residence," Scott predicted the California Supreme Court would rule the treaty provision not to be violated so long as San Francisco provided separate Japanese schools of equal quality. In short, equal schools were not identical ones, and the courts surely would not endow Japanese with greater rights than the American Negro.[55] Though Metcalf brought out in his final report the additional fact that Japanese children were really denied any education because of the distance of the new oriental school from their homes, he made clear that it would be a formidable task to sustain in the courts (1) that the term "residence" included education, and (2) that separate schools were not equal ones.

The President's uncertainty with the legal problems involved indicates that he never placed much faith in reaching a solution to the San Francisco school crisis through the courts. On November 8, the day on which he left for the Panama Canal (and after he had received Metcalf's initial report), Roosevelt assured Aoki that he entirely concurred with the Japanese interpretation of the treaty. Upon returning home November 27 and consulting with Metcalf, Roosevelt wrote him that "if our treaty contains no 'most favored nation' clause then I am inclined to feel as strongly as you do that we had better take no action to upset the action of the Board of Education." However, on December 5 Roosevelt thought the suit in the California courts should be

[54] Memorandum of Adee to Bacon, November 3, 1906, NA, RG 59:1797/20; Root to Attorney General William H. Moody, November 13, 1906, NA, RG 59:1797/53–54.
[55] Scott, "The Discrimination Against Japanese Subjects in California," November 27, 1906, NA, RG 59:1797/61.

pressed "as rapidly as possible." [56] It is unlikely that Roosevelt was convinced of the efficacy of legal action by Root, for the latter had probably been persuaded by Scott's memorandum that, as he put it later, there was an even chance the courts would decide the present arrangement of separate but equal schools did not violate the treaty.[57]

Roosevelt felt the question of whether the treaty did or did not permit school segregation was not the main point at issue, for even if the state could segregate Japanese pupils, the exercise of such technical rights put the United States morally in the wrong and justified Japan's strong resentment. And if segregation was illegal, the enforcement of a court ruling against the hostile Californians might be politically costly. In urging legal action, the President was probably coercing the San Francisco authorities as part of a larger plan to bring them to a settlement.[58] For while Metcalf was exploring the San Francisco imbroglio, Roosevelt was evolving a more plausible approach based upon the exclusion of Japanese laborers.

Soon after the eruption of the school crisis, the President recalled later, he had been informed by men speaking for the labor organizations of San Francisco that "the real objection was to the incoming of Japanese laborers. . . . They asserted unequivocally that the trouble was not with the attendance of the Japanese at the schools; that this was merely a symptom of the irritation. They exprest their entire willingness to support any arrangement which would secure the exclusion of all Japanese laborers. They stated that if this object could be achieved they would . . . be glad to

[56] Aoki to Hayashi, November 10, 1906, Telegram Series, JA; Roosevelt to Metcalf, November 27, 1906, to Root, December 5, 1906, *Letters*, V, 510, 521.

[57] Root to Wright, February 5, 1907, NA, RG 59:1797/156.

[58] Roosevelt to Gillett, March 14, 1907, *Letters*, V, 618; in December legal preparations were completed and on January 17, 1907, two actions were initiated, one in California, the other in federal, courts.

have the school question arranged." Secretary Metcalf, senators and representatives from California, and other prominent Californians all agreed "that there was a most intense feeling as to the absolute necessity of excluding all Japanese laborers . . . and thus preventing the upgrowth on the Pacific Slope of a situation which might lead to race conflict, and which would surely lead to the lowering of the status of our own wageworkers." [59] The primary representative of the San Francisco labor organizations to whom Roosevelt referred was Samuel Gompers, president of the American Federation of Labor, who had long opposed oriental immigration to the United States. Gompers was in contact with Mayor Schmitz, Olaf Tveitmoe (president of the Japanese-Korean Exclusion League), and other labor leaders on the Pacific Coast, and passed on their views to the President.[60]

Information provided by the President's own advisers indicated that Japan might agree to an exclusion arrangement. Commissioner General of Immigration and Naturalization Frank P. Sargent believed that the trouble was due to the movement of Japanese laborers from Hawaii to the Pacific Coast. He did not think it would be too difficult to get the Japanese government to agree to further restrictions, since it was already refusing passports to laborers for the mainland of the United States. Both Third Assistant Secretary of State Huntington Wilson, recently returned from Japan, and Ambassador Wright also thought that Japan could be convinced to check quietly the influx of laborers.[61] Aoki agreed with the President that the immigration of all Japanese working-

[59] Roosevelt to Gillett, March 11, 1907, *Letters,* V, 611–612.
[60] Samuel Gompers, *Seventy Years of Life and Labor* (2 vols.; New York, 1925), II, 162, 165–166.
[61] Sargent to Charles Denby, October 31, 1906, NA, RG 59:1797/49; memorandum by Huntington Wilson, October 22, 1906, NA, RG 59:1797/2; Wright to Root, October 21, 1906, NA, RG 59:1797/1.

men should be stopped.[62] In the early part of November Roosevelt concluded that the San Francisco school order would be repealed if the immigration of Japanese laborers to the Pacific Coast could be halted, and he began to lay the groundwork for such a compromise.

For a number of reasons the President was sensitive to the demands of organized labor and to sentiment on the Pacific Coast. Aside from his prejudices against the masses of oriental and European immigrants, he was concerned with the political position of the Republican party in the autumn of 1906. In the congressional elections of that year Roosevelt supported all Republicans for re-election, but saw the party's House majority sharply reduced. The American Federation of Labor carried out the policy shift announced in the spring of 1906 and actively campaigned against several Republican standpatters who opposed "Labor's Bill of Grievances." In several congressional districts Roosevelt sent in an impressive array of Republican orators to counter the activity of the A. F. of L. The Republicans won in those particular districts but Roosevelt was worried about the general election reversal and the hostility of labor, which he feared might unite against his party.[63]

Not only in the nation, but also in California, the position of the Republican party seemed to be weakening. California's government for many years had been in the grip of the Southern Pacific Railroad and its associated economic interests, and the state had given both McKinley and Roosevelt large presidential majorities while sending a heavily Republican delegation to Congress. In 1906 California had no Democrats in Congress, and its Republicans — Senators George C. Perkins and Frank P. Flint, and most of the

[62] Roosevelt to Metcalf, November 27, 1906, *Letters*, V, 510.
[63] Rowland H. Harvey, *Samuel Gompers: Champion of the Toiling Masses* (Stanford, 1935), pp. 176–183; Mowry, *Era of Theodore Roosevelt*, pp. 208–209.

congressional delegation — were conservative machine men. But the Republican hold on the state was becoming uncertain due to a number of changes in California politics and society. Since the turn of the century the Democratic party had been increasing in strength and had nearly won two gubernatorial elections. Moreover, the Southern Pacific's economic position was no longer so dominant as it once had been, for other business groups and organized labor were demanding recogition and power. Within the Republican party a reform group was emerging opposed to the regular organization and favoring many social and humanitarian reforms advocated by Roosevelt. These reformers, appearing strongly first in Los Angeles and San Francisco in 1906, soon found that city corruption could be met only on the state level and so in May, 1907, were to form the Lincoln-Roosevelt League.[64] In the long run this movement, if successful, might improve the political prospects of the party; but in the short run it would bring dissension and weakness. Even many conservative Republicans were dissatisfied with the ruthlessness and corruption of the Southern Pacific's rule, and in the gubernatorial election of 1906 the Republican nominee, James N. Gillett, won by only 8,000 votes over the progressive, anti-Southern Pacific, Democratic candidate, Theodore Bell.[65]

The President's concern over organized labor and the fortunes of his party in California had once before led him to show unusual deference for anti-oriental feeling on the Pacific Coast. In the spring of 1904 Roosevelt had compromised his own convictions and recommended to Congress a Chinese exclusion law, regardless of the outcome of pending treaty negotiations.[66] He pursued a Chinese immigration

---

[64] George E. Mowry, *The California Progressives* (Berkeley, 1951), *passim*.

[65] *Los Angeles Times*, October 13, 17, 22, and November 2, 1906.

[66] Harbaugh, *Power and Responsibility*, pp. 296–297.

policy which balanced demands for vigorous exclusion against appeals for the fair treatment of Chinese immigrants.[67] But the *New York Journal of Commerce and Commercial Bulletin* remained convinced that Roosevelt had surrendered to anti-oriental sentiment on the Pacific Coast.[68] And the Chinese people, offended at the brutal treatment given emigrants to the United States, instituted a damaging boycott against American goods. The experience with China probably reinforced Roosevelt's belief that Japanese laborers would have to be excluded in a manner acceptable to Japan.

By the autumn of 1906 Roosevelt still had time to secure a settlement satisfactory to both California and Japan, for the anti-Japanese agitation lacked a broad base. But as Roosevelt probably realized, it might become a potent force affecting state politics. Prominent Californians such as David Starr Jordan, president of Stanford University, and Chester Rowell, editor of the *Fresno Morning Republican* and a founder of the Lincoln-Roosevelt League, believed that the feeling against Japanese immigration was widespread. Many Californians who felt indifferent to the economic threat feared racial complications which would further damage the homogeneity of their society.[69] These fears had not yet formed into a compelling demand for exclusion legislation or discriminatory measures against Japanese residents, though as Japanese spread into rural areas and as the Progressive impulse gathered momentum, the Japanese problem would, despite the efforts of Roosevelt, become a major issue in California politics.[70]

[67] Beale, *Theodore Roosevelt*, pp. 212–249.

[68] *New York Journal of Commerce and Commercial Bulletin,* October 11, 1907, Roosevelt Scrapbooks.

[69] Chester H. Rowell, " 'Orientophobia,' A Western Editor's Views on the White Frontier," *Collier's,* 42 (January 30, 1909), 29; Chester H. Rowell, "The Japanese in California," *World's Work,* 26 (June, 1913), 195–201; David Starr Jordan, "Japan in California," *Boston Evening Transcript,* December 30, 1906, Roosevelt Scrapbooks.

[70] Daniels, *Politics of Prejudice,* pp. 45–52.

With the feelings of both California and Japan in mind, Roosevelt prepared that portion of his annual message dealing with the San Francisco school crisis. His purpose in delivering it, he wrote at the time, was twofold. On the one hand, he wanted to let California and the rest of the people know that no "political considerations would interfere for a moment with my using the armed forces of the country to protect the Japanese if they were molested in their person and property." Roosevelt apparently felt a warning was necessary, though Metcalf in his final report discounted the violence against the Japanese and told of the assurances given by San Francisco officials that Japanese residents would be protected. Second, by praising Japan the President sought to "smooth over . . . [the Japanese] feelings so that the Government will quietly stop all immigration of coolies to our country." These feelings, Roosevelt reasoned, had been wounded by the anti-Japanese agitation, and the great difficulty in getting Japan to take his view on immigration matters would be the irritation felt by the government and, more important, by the Japanese people. Such a message, aside from helping to achieve his diplomatic aims, would reflect Roosevelt's profound admiration of the Japanese and his strong personal reaction to the ugly provincialism that threatened to involve the great nations in a prolonged quarrel.[71]

While preparing verbally to lash California, Roosevelt strove behind the scenes to lessen the impact of his message. Amid rumors of an intended attack, he assured California representatives and senators that he had a plan on foot which would solve their difficulties and warned them to drop all hopes for exclusion legislation. Many Californians left the President's office with the feeling that he was on

---

[71] Roosevelt to J. St. Loe Strachey, December 21, 1906, and to Metcalf, November 27, 1906, *Letters*, V, 532–533, 510–511.

their side. With a few of the state's political leaders, Roosevelt went further and told of his plan to praise Japan in order to secure the exclusion of laborers. And one prominent member of the Senate Foreign Relations Committee, presumably Henry Cabot Lodge, announced that the President would scold California for the benefit of Japan without making any real move against the state.[72]

On December 4 the President delivered his anxiously awaited message. Describing Japan as a nation that "won in a single generation the right to stand abreast of the foremost and most enlightened peoples of Europe and America," Roosevelt deprecated the hostility toward Japanese residents and predicted that "it may be fraught with the gravest consequences to the Nation." Prejudices against people of a nation equal to our own, he said, were "unworthy"; "shutting them out from the common schools" was a "wicked absurdity"; and the failure to treat the Japanese well was a "confession of inferiority in our civilization." The President went on to say that if the United States hoped for a growing role in the Pacific it would have to treat other nations as it expected to be treated. He warned that the federal government, where it had the power, would "deal summarily" with citizens who acted badly, and in other cases asked that the states take action. And he recommended not only naturalization for the Japanese, but also an amendment of United States statutes to give the President power "to protect aliens in rights secured to them under solemn treaties which are the law of the land." Nevertheless, the federal government was not altogether helpless, and in the Japanese matter the President vowed that "everything that is in my power will be done, and all of the forces, both military and civil, of the United States which I may lawfully employ, will be so employed." "There should," he concluded, "be no

[72] *New York Times,* December 1–8, 1906.

particle of doubt as to the power of the National Government completely to perform its own obligations to other nations." [73]

The President's message had an immediate impact in Japan, where the press unanimously lauded his friendly gesture. In the United States, many eastern papers approved of Roosevelt's strong language, but many other papers, without regard to party lines, maintained that the whole subject was one for the courts.[74] The *New York Times* thought that the message was "for export" and argued that the President could not enforce treaty rights through executive action before the issue was adjudicated in the courts. Few editorial writers asked, as did "Ignotus" in the *North American Review*, if the nation could "retain its lofty seat [as a world power] after it has admitted that it cannot compel the School Board of one of its cities to obey its law?" [75]

However, Roosevelt had badly misjudged the effect his extreme language would have on Congress and on the people of California. Democrats in both the Senate and the House were alarmed by the President's invasion of states' rights, and Senator Isidor Rayner of Maryland introduced a resolution denying the federal government's right to enter into treaties relating to the public school systems of states. Even Senator Henry Cabot Lodge thought that Roosevelt "put it a little too strongly when he referred to the army and navy." The *New York Times* reported the President's remarks excited "fierce indignation" and "unbounded wrath" among the surprised California delegation.[76] All along the Pacific Coast,

[73] *Works*, XV, 385–388.

[74] Wright to Root, December 11, 1906, NA, RG 59:1797/92; *Literary Digest*, 33 (December 15, 1906), 890–891.

[75] *New York Times*, December 6, 1906; "Ignotus," "Is the United States a World Power?" *North American Review*, 183 (December 7, 1906), 1107–1119.

[76] Lodge to William Sturgis Bigelow, December 6, 1906, Lodge Papers; *New York Times*, December 5 and 6, 1906.

particularly in San Francisco, the President's scolding seemed to harden and excite anti-Japanese sentiment. The *Sacramento Union* predicted that "not even the big stick is big enough to compel the people of California to do a thing which they have a fixt determination not to do," while the *San Francisco Chronicle* spoke of Roosevelt's "impotent rage." The Japanese-Korean Exclusion League went so far as to denounce any diplomatic settlement of the immigration question and continued to demand exclusion legislation from Congress. A poll by the *Literary Digest* early in January, 1907, found most leading Pacific Coast papers hostile both to President Roosevelt and to Japan.[77]

The President quickly sensed the need for conciliation. The day after his message, he outlined to various members of Congress his idea of an arrangement with Japan for the reciprocal exclusion of laborers.[78] On December 18, in a message forwarding Metcalf's report to Congress, he agreed to the segregation of Japanese young men from white children and hoped that it would not be necessary to test the school order in the courts.[79] In effect, the President and the Secretary of State had reached a more complex view of the whole crisis. Initially Roosevelt and Root thought the anti-Japanese agitation in California was confined to scattered labor agitators and could be disregarded, and they assumed the United States could draw heavily upon its traditional friendship with Japan. By late December both men had come to see more of the depth and explosive potential of the anti-Japanese feeling and recognized the necessity of compromising with it. But they did not yet see the extraordinary difficulties which would arise in their

[77] *Literary Digest,* 33 (December 15, 1906), 890–891, and *ibid.,* 34 (January 12, 1907), 43–44.

[78] *New York Times,* December 6–8, 1906.

[79] Message from Roosevelt to Congress, December 18, 1908, Senate Doc. 147, 59th Cong., 2d Sess.

dealings with the Japanese government, nor sense the extent to which traditional assumptions about Japanese-American friendship had been eroded by popular suspicion in both nations. In short, by late 1906 no particularly large obstacles seemed to block an early settlement, and Roosevelt and Root anticipated that the crisis with Japan would pass almost as quickly as it had begun.

# III

# THE WIDENING CRISIS

Soon after the San Francisco school order had precipitated a crisis in Japanese-American relations, Theodore Roosevelt began to search for a solution which would satisfy both Japan and California. Without a quick resolution of the crisis, the anti-Japanese agitation on the Pacific Coast would intensify, damaging the position of the Republican party, weakening the friendship of the two nations, and ultimately imperiling the basis of Roosevelt's Far Eastern policy. Yet it was by no means certain that the friendship of Japan could be preserved if the demands of California were entirely met. Roosevelt had already sought to retain Japan's good will by using conciliatory language in diplomatic communications and by praising in his annual message that nation's accomplishments. To Californians he had given prolific assurances that he would protect their state's vital interests. Having laid the groundwork for compromise, Roosevelt by early 1907 faced the necessity of devising a diplomatic strategy to achieve his goals. Californians had repeatedly told him that Japanese immigration rather than school segregation was the real issue in their state, and therefore it seemed obvious to seek a repeal of the school order in return for a cessation of most Japanese immigration. Success would depend upon a delicate sense of timing, considerable persuasiveness, and the nature of the proposal made to Japan.

For some time various members of the Roosevelt administration had thought about the problem of Japanese immigration, and by the turn of the new year they saw clearly how it focused on the passage of laborers from Hawaii to the mainland. Commissioner General of Immigration Frank P. Sargent, who had just returned from Hawaii, described the arrangements between Japanese immigration agents, Hawaiian hotel-keepers, and large employers of Asiatic labor on the mainland (such as the Northern Pacific and the Great Northern Railways), through which Honolulu was being used as a "transhipping station" for Japanese laborers. Despite attempts of the Japanese Consul General to discourage this traffic, Sargent predicted the movement of Japanese laborers to the mainland would continue unless the American government found a way to stop it.[1]

Several proposals since the summer of 1905 had been aimed at this troublesome phenomenon. The most recent had come in late November, 1906, when Third Assistant Secretary of State Huntington Wilson suggested legislation forbidding the movement of all alien laborers from Hawaii to the mainland. The Japanese would agree to such legislation, Huntington Wilson claimed, "so long as they are not asked to do anything injurious to their 'face' (the thing dearest to the Oriental)." Soon after Huntington Wilson's proposal, Foreign Minister Hayashi himself explained to Ambassador Wright that, since Japanese passports were issued with the phrase "to Hawaii only," the United States could prevent Japanese from leaving Hawaii by amending its immigration laws to authorize the enforcement of such passport restrictions.[2]

[1] Sargent to Roosevelt, January 2, 1907, NA, RG 59:2542/17 and 18.
[2] Huntington Wilson to Bacon, November 20, 1906, NA, RG 59:2542/7; Wright to Root, December 26, 1906, NA, RG 59:2542/19.

The President ignored this suggestion and instead sought a different solution. From early in the school crisis he had been hoping for an understanding with Japan for the reciprocal exclusion of laborers. He actually preferred a "general immigration restriction bill, by which we could keep out all people who have difficulty in assimilating with our own," but he feared that such a bill could not be obtained. Instead, Roosevelt could only assume that Japan "of her own accord and of her own initiative will propose a reciprocal arrangement by which American laborers will be kept out of the Japanese possessions and Japanese laborers out of American possessions." Unless this was accomplished, the steady growth of the number of Japanese laborers on the Pacific Coast would sooner or later cause an "explosion of feeling." [3] David Starr Jordan encouraged Roosevelt's view and reported he had received many assurances from Japanese friends "that Japan has but two interests in this matter, to do what the United States wishes and at the same time to save her face." [4]

By January, 1907, if not before, the President, with the concurrence of the Secretary of State, hoped for a treaty containing that understanding.[5] Many factors had encouraged Roosevelt to bargain for a mutual exclusion treaty instead of seeking the minimum goal of an informal arrangement by which Japan would consent to legislation barring the movement of laborers from Hawaii to the mainland. A formal treaty would have many advantages when the time came to negotiate with the Californians, for it would offer them a more substantial victory than a mere informal agreement and would be less dependent on the good will of Japan. Despite his recognition of Japan's emergence as a great,

[3] Roosevelt to Strachey, December 21, 1906, *Letters,* V, 532–533; Roosevelt to David Starr Jordan, January 9, 1907, Roosevelt Papers.
[4] Jordan to Roosevelt, January 3, 1907, Roosevelt Papers.
[5] Roosevelt to Sir Edward Grey, December 18, 1906, *Letters,* V, 528–529.

civilized power, Roosevelt assumed he could force his wishes upon the Japanese government and arrange a solution which would quickly satisfy his own domestic needs. Apparently Roosevelt was not yet deeply impressed with the restiveness of Japanese public opinion or the difficulties of the Saionji ministry, for the only concession he was ready to offer Japan was the continued immigration of laborers to Hawaii. Thinking in terms of a short-term crisis, Roosevelt thought that words alone would sufficiently appease Japan's pride.

No subordinates within or without the State Department had proposed such a one-sided solution. The burden of the advice of such men as Commissioner General Sargent and Ambassador Wright was that Japan would agree to an informal restriction of immigration, but not to a public treaty of mutual exclusion. In early January a thoughtful memorandum by Huntington Wilson emphasized the difficulties of achieving such a treaty at this time. The most pressing problem, Huntington Wilson perceived, was finding a suitable quid pro quo for Japan. In return for the exclusion of laborers, the United States could offer to relinquish its extraterritorial privileges in Korea upon notice of Japan's willingness to open to Americans suitable courts of justice, but this arrangement would be "lacking in mutuality." A second possible quid pro quo was the naturalization of Japanese, which would be a "sop" to Japan without being of much importance to the United States. Neither of these proposals offered much hope, Huntington Wilson argued, in the present circumstances. Aoki was not "influential in Japan because of his German marriage and his strong German affiliations and because he is regarded in Japan as 'High Collar' (excessively pro-European)." Wright, on the other hand, was not "capable of forming the necessary close relations with the Japanese in power and above all with Mr. [Henry W.] Denison, the powerful American advisor of the Tokio Foreign Office." Denison, who would be in the United States in March or April, was "perhaps the one man who could find the way out." [6]

Implicit in Huntington Wilson's memorandum was the warning that Japan would not relish trading a treaty of mutual exclusion for the withdrawal of the school segregation order. Roosevelt and Root, however, ignored the advice of the department's single Far Eastern expert and proceeded with their plan. On January 8 or 9, 1907, Root sent a long letter to Aoki on the reciprocal restriction of immigration. Root began by rejecting Aoki's suggestion that the United States should stop the movement of laborers from Hawaii to the Pacific Coast by enforcing the "to Hawaii only" restriction in their passports. This would, in Root's opinion, require legislation by Congress, and he hesitated to ask for it "lest it should be misinterpreted by the people of Japan." He agreed, however, that some measure was necessary to prevent the growing anti-Japanese feeling among Pacific Coast laborers. That was the "real question" in California, for the attempt to exclude Japanese from the public schools, the restaurant boycotts and street assaults were "but symptoms of this underlying opposition to a successful labor competition." Japan and the United States could strike at the cause of this feeling if Japan would suggest a treaty providing that "neither Government should admit to its territories citizens of the other country except upon passports issued by the Government of that other country and that neither Government should issue such passports to laborers." Hawaii would be excepted if the treaty included a provision allowing the United States to enforce the limitations of Japanese passports issued to Hawaii only, for such a provision would have

[6] Huntington Wilson to Root, January 3, 1907, NA, RG 59:2542/83.

the force of law and would make legislation by the Congress unnecessary.[7]

Root's indirectness stemmed from his theory that the best way to prevent a hostile reaction among the Japanese was to persuade Japan itself to propose the exclusion of laborers. Apparently this approach had some effect on Aoki, who was impressed by the "friendly spirit" with which Root offered the proposition.[8] The Japanese government, however, had no intention of accepting such a one-sided treaty, and Hayashi attempted to clarify the Japanese position in several conversations with Ambassador Wright in mid-January. Hayashi explained that Japan did not wish its laborers to enter any country where they were not wanted; nor did Japan wish to restrict American laborers coming within its territory. The Saionji ministry would not consider the proposed reciprocal exclusion treaty, for it was too one-sided and would bring severe criticism in Japan. He was aware, Hayashi told Wright, of the difficulties growing out of the immigration of Japanese laborers and he would lay the question before the cabinet to find a solution "after the school question is satisfactorily settled." Wright was left with the impression that with the repeal of the school order Japan would readily agree to the restriction of laborers.[9]

A few days after his conversations with Hayashi, Wright discussed with Henry W. Denison the desirability of a formal convention. Denison, who since 1880 had been legal adviser to the Japanese Foreign Office, reminded the American ambassador of the domestic problem of the Japanese government and suggested Japan might agree to a treaty if naturalization was conceded. Wright was intrigued with the idea

[7] Root to Wright, January 14, 1907, NA, RG 59:2542/18b.

[8] Root to Oliver Wendell Holmes, March 6, 1907, NA, RG 59:2542/55a; Aoki to Hayashi, January 9, 1907, Telegram Series, JA.

[9] Wright to Root, January 11, 23, 1907, NA, RG 59:1797/106 and 127; and Hayashi to Aoki, January 19, 1907, Telegram Series, JA.

of naturalization, but concluded that unless the San Francisco school order was repealed any settlement would be difficult. Instead of telegraphing this important information, Wright sent it by mail and it arrived too late to have any direct bearing on the course adopted in Washington.[10]

As early as late December, 1906, the Japanese government had made clear its desire to settle the immigration controversy quietly and informally. When the United States brushed aside these overtures and instead sought a formal agreement, Japan reversed Washington's order of priority by insisting that a settlement of the school crisis must precede any adjustment of the immigration question. Though from many points of view this was an expedient course for Japan to take, it was precisely what Ambassador Aoki had been recommending since the middle of December. At that time Aoki advised that Japan should be slow in responding to American proposals for immigration restriction "as the immigration question will have to be used for a lever for settling the difficulties in San Francisco." By early January, 1907, Aoki's optimism had waxed and he thought that concessions on immigration should hinge on securing both the withdrawal of the school order and the naturalization of Japanese. Despite Root's doubts that a naturalization bill could pass Congress, Aoki regarded naturalization as a question awaiting adjustment between himself, Roosevelt, and Root and therefore urged that the negotiations be centered in Washington.[11] Hayashi did not follow this last suggestion; nor did he immediately demand naturalization as a quid pro quo. But the general strategy pursued by Japan was in accord with Aoki's views.

Impatient over the failure of the Japanese government to

---

[10] Wright to Root, January 22, 1907, NA, RG 59:2542/41.
[11] Aoki to Hayashi, December 15, 1906, January 9, 14, 1907, Telegram Series, JA.

answer his proposal to Aoki, Root in late January asked Wright to prod Hayashi. In an interview on January 28, Hayashi reported that he had conferred with the members of the cabinet, all of whom agreed that when the San Francisco school order was withdrawn some arrangement with the United States might be found to prevent the immigration of laborers to the Pacific Coast. But the cabinet wanted more time to consider this. Moreover, any arrangement would have to exempt immigration to Hawaii and protect the amour propre of the Japanese people. Japan would not object to legislation by the United States preventing immigration of laborers from Hawaii to the mainland if a means could be found to reduce the existing tension. Hayashi, who still apparently had some hope in a judicial settlement, suggested it might be better to wait for the outcome of the pending suits. But Wright was uncertain of the results and thought that even favorable ones might increase the tension on the Pacific Coast. Japan's firm reply revealed the inadequacy of Root's original proposal.[12] If any agreement was to be reached, Washington would have to demand less and offer more.

Both Hayashi and Saionji attempted to quiet dissatisfaction in Japan over the slowness with which the school controversy was being settled. In late January Saionji reassured the Diet of the government's confidence that a suitable solution would be found, while Hayashi told the Diet's budget committee that the San Francisco affair had not been made a subject of diplomatic discussion because the sympathies of the United States were with Japan. Japan would utilize diplomacy only in the unlikely event that the lawsuits turned out unfavorably. On January 29 Hayashi reaffirmed the government's position, though he now added that Japan did

[12] Root to Wright, January 28, 1907, and Wright to Root, February 1, 1907, NA, RG 59:2542/18b and 1797/153.

"not intend to wait forever." [13] The Saionji ministry's caution in handling public opinion and its reluctance to accept a formal settlement were justified by the press reaction to leaks emanating from Washington in early February reporting that negotiations were in progress for a treaty of reciprocal exclusion. Despite a denial from Hayashi, the rumor excited considerable apprehension in the Japanese press.[14] Leading independent and opposition newspapers denounced such a solution as one-sided and unacceptable to Japan. The *Hochi Shimbun* accused the government of a "self-humiliating attitude" and "sluggish diplomacy"; it preferred an armed clash to "yielding to outrage." Rejecting any reciprocal labor exclusion, the *Asahi Shimbun* spoke of the "deep significance" of the San Francisco affair. And the moderate, English-language *Japan Weekly Mail* predicted that Japan would be "profoundly offended" if the government yielded on the labor question to settle the difficulties in San Francisco.[15]

Before Japan's rejection of a treaty of reciprocal exclusion reached Washington, Roosevelt decided to include the California congressional delegation in the final phase of the negotiations to end the school crisis. Whatever plan Japan ultimately accepted, the cooperation of the Californians was crucial if it was to be traded for rescinding the school order. Roosevelt was eager to convert the California delegation to his point of view and to enlist its aid in bringing the San Francisco Board of Education to Washington and in discouraging any anti-Japanese legislation by the California legislature. A resolution of the California Senate on January 29 protesting the federal government's interference with the

[13] *Japan Weekly Mail,* January 26, 1907; *Official Gazette,* January 29, 1907, NA, RG 59:1797/159.

[14] *Japan Weekly Mail,* February 9, 1907.

[15] *Hochi Shimbun,* February 2–4, 1907, *Asahi Shimbun,* February 6, 1907, NA, RG 59:1797/160–163; *Japan Weekly Mail,* February 9, 1907.

rights of the state in the school controversy lent reality to Roosevelt's fear of discriminatory legislation. Many other anti-Japanese measures awaited discussion.[16] Finally, the time available to conclude the negotiations was at a premium since the short session of Congress would end in March and congressional approval would be needed for any settlement, whether in the form of a treaty or of legislation.

On January 30, 1907, Roosevelt, Root, and Metcalf conferred with the California delegation. The President pledged the Californians to secrecy, but the promise was not taken very seriously by several members of the delegation. Two days later the *Washington Post* learned the President had told the Californians this:

> We must act immediately in removing all causes of friction between the United States and Japan. The San Francisco school question must be disposed of, if possible, without waiting for the decision of the courts. Foreign Minister Hayashi declares that if the courts decide unfavorably, the anti-Japanese movement in California will be considered to represent the opinion of the whole United States, and that this would require diplomatic adjustment. This can have only one meaning, and you can understand it. The situation is more serious than you imagine.
>
> That mayor of yours, the bassoon player, whose tune is hot air, may think war with Japan would not amount to much, but we are dealing with a nation of proud and brave people. You do not know their resources. . . . We must do all we can to remove any possible cause of war. If trouble comes, it must not be our fault.[17]

Roosevelt insisted the Californians must aid him in removing the irritation between the two nations and explained that he hoped to arrange a treaty of mutual exclusion with Japan.

[16] Thomson, "Events," 55–56.

[17] *Washington Post*, February 1, 1907, in Esme Howard to Grey, February 4, 1907, PRO, FO 371/269, and *Washington Post*, February 7, 1907, Roosevelt Scrapbooks.

Before this could be done, the San Francisco authorities must end the segregation of Japanese school children. The Secretary of State seconded Roosevelt's appeal, in more temperate language, and added that the proposed treaty should concede most-favored-nation treatment in the schools to Japanese children in the United States.[18]

The Californians were surprised at the seriousness of the situation and impressed by the President's exposition. They agreed to the terms of the proposed Japanese-American treaty of mutual exclusion and gave up their demand for immediate exclusion legislation. Moreover, they consented to send telegrams (1) to their influential friends, asking them to restrain anti-Japanese feeling among the people of California; (2) to Governor Gillett, urging him to induce the California legislature to defer action on all matters affecting Japanese-American relations until they communicated with him further; and (3) to the San Francisco Board of Education and the superintendent of schools, inviting them to come to Washington to confer with the President. With the California delegation backing the administration's program, the chances for a swift settlement with Japan seemed bright. The next day leading California legislators granted the delegation's request, and within a few days Mayor Schmitz joined his Board of Education on a trip to Washington.[19]

The President, however, secured the cooperation of the Californians at a cost, for some of the conferees left convinced war was imminent and soon revealed their fears to newspaper reporters. The press was flooded with rumors of war, which played upon the suspicion of Japan that had risen since the end of the Russo-Japanese War.[20] As early as December, 1906, the *Nation* complained that Japan had

[18] *Ibid.*
[19] *New York Times*, January 31, February 1–2, 1907.
[20] *New York Times*, February 5, 1907.

suddenly replaced Germany as the United States' next enemy. A few weeks later Finley Peter Dunne's Mr. Dooley reflected the changing attitude toward Japan when he explained to his friend Hennessy that "th' friendship ceminted two years ago with blood an' beers is busted . . . befure very long thim little brown hands acrost th' sea will hand us a crack in th' eye." [21]

In early February, 1907, the war rumors achieved a much wider currency. Richmond Pearson Hobson, a handsome and popular Spanish-American War hero soon to enter Congress, claimed he had seen an ultimatum sent by the Japanese government and predicted Japan "is spoiling for a war with this nation. . . . She is only waiting until she can negotiate loans in Europe." [22] Some members of Congress, conscious of American commercial and military weakness in the Pacific, imagined a powerful Japan seeking predominance there. Senator George C. Perkins of California predicted a struggle for supremacy in the Pacific between the United States and Japan which would "converge to a point of inevitable conflict of interests," and Representative William E. Humphrey of Washington felt that without energetic action the United States would "be driven from the Pacific Ocean within five years." [23] The administration was alarmed by sentiment in Congress and had William Howard Taft ask many prominent legislators to stop inflammatory addresses by their colleagues. The brief flurry of war rumors, deprecated by most of the nation's press, soon disappeared. Many Americans, however, remained uneasy over relations with Japan and the future of American interests in the Pacific. [24]

[21] *Nation*, 83 (December 6, 1906), 476–477; *New York Times*, January 6, 1907.

[22] *New York Times*, February 2, 1907.

[23] *Los Angeles Times*, February 2, 1907; *Congressional Record*, 59th Cong., 2d Sess., pp. 4151–4156.

[24] *Los Angeles Times*, February 2, 1907; *Literary Digest*, 34 (February 9, 1907), 193–194.

Roosevelt's conference with the California congressional delegation not only led to rumors of war but also to a new proposal by the Secretary of State to the Japanese government. On January 31 Root suggested a treaty of reciprocal exclusion, including a guarantee of most-favored-nation treatment for Japanese school children. The Secretary of State feared, Aoki reported, that the courts might rule against the contention of the federal government in the test cases and therefore urged the conclusion of a treaty in time to submit it to the Senate for approval during the present session. This would settle the school controversy by treaty provision instead of running the risk of an "impossible situation" arising out of an adverse court decision. Root was encouraged by Aoki's response to his suggestion, but he was also deeply concerned about deteriorating conditions on the Pacific Coast and convinced of the need for prompt action if the increasing tension there was not to culminate in an exclusion act. Moreover, he saw no chance of settling "the school question independently and in advance of the immigration question." [25]

The response from Tokyo to this modified proposition did nothing to relieve Root's anxiety. Wright telegraphed that Hayashi was disturbed by reports coming from Washington and picked up by the opposition press in Japan that a settlement would be reached on the basis of the mutual exclusion of laborers. He rejected school privileges as a quid pro quo, for the Japanese people believed they had most-favored-nation school rights under the existing treaty. At this juncture, however, Hayashi finally came forth with a formal offer of his own. If the school order was first repealed, he said, Japan would enter into a treaty of reciprocal exclusion provided those Japanese not within the excluded class entering the United States would be entitled to naturalization. Root im-

[25] Aoki to Hayashi, February 1, 1907, Telegram Series, JA; Root to Wright, February 1, 1907, NA, RG 59:2542/22.

mediately and emphatically rejected Hayashi's counterproposal. "It is wholly useless," he said, "to discuss the subject of naturalization at the present time," for no statute embodying it could pass Congress "in the present hot-headed condition of some members." [26]

With Japan's rejection of the terms proposed by the United States, the outlook seemed bleak. Roosevelt and Root, ignoring much evidence to the contrary, had been confident Japan would accept a treaty of reciprocal exclusion. When Japan's initial reaction was unfavorable, they had offered to include a most-favored-nation clause which would ensure an end to school segregation through the courts if bargaining with San Francisco officials failed. But the Saionji ministry still found the proposed treaty unacceptable, and it seemed that the two nations had reached a deadlock. Root thought it doubtful that the courts would rule that segregation violated Japan's treaty rights. And he informed Wright that unless some treaty arrangement was made to prevent the influx of Japanese laborers, Congress would pass exclusion legislation.[27] Moreover, both he and Roosevelt would soon face San Francisco officials without any treaty near completion. It is curious that neither the Secretary of State nor the President immediately picked up the idea, suggested earlier by both Hayashi and Huntington Wilson, of ending the passage of Japanese laborers from Hawaii to the mainland by legislation. Apparently a treaty of reciprocal exclusion had become an *idée fixe*, and only at the last moment did they grasp this alternative as the basis of a temporary settlement.

Explanations from Tokyo of the Japanese position did little to end the diplomatic impasse. Wright thought the Saionji cabinet was anxious to meet the wishes of the United States but feared an outcry against a one-sided treaty. Therefore

[26] Wright to Root, February 4, 1907, and Root to Wright, February 5, 1907, NA, RG 59:1797/155–156.

[27] Root to Wright, February 5, 1907, NA, RG 59:1797/156.

it sought naturalization as a "sop" to public opinion, not as something intrinsically important. Hayashi confirmed Wright's speculations in an interview on February 9. With considerable candor, the Foreign Minister admitted that probably under the present treaty Japan had no right to object to the school ordinance. But the Japanese people, he explained, believed they had such a right, and to accede to Root's proposition would effect the exclusion of Japanese laborers without any corresponding concession. For the cabinet it was largely a matter of preserving Japan's amour propre, and Hayashi again asked for a private agreement to repeal the school order in return for the exclusion of Japanese laborers.[28] With Japan holding firm and with the San Franciscans now in Washington, the administration would have to move quickly if even a temporary settlement was to be reached.

Mayor Schmitz had been eager to accompany the superintendent of schools and the San Francisco Board of Education to Washington. Under indictment for extortion and with his trial imminent, he sought to regain as much prestige as possible by casting himself in the role of the disinterested statesman, willing to sacrifice local for national interests by repealing the school order in return for a Japanese exclusion treaty. As Schmitz realized, the people of the Pacific Coast regarded Japanese exclusion as far more important than school segregation.[29] His supporters, reported the *San Francisco Chronicle,* were "delighted with the prospect of the indicted Mayor returning from the national capital covered with glory and acclaimed the savior of the country from a war with Japan." [30]

[28] Wright to Root, February 6, 9, 1907, NA, RG 59:1797/157 and 170.
[29] For discussions of Schmitz's motives, see Franklin Hichborn, *"The System" as Uncovered by the San Francisco Graft Prosecution* (San Francisco, 1915); Thomson, "Events," 152–153; and Buell, "Development of Anti-Japanese Agitation," 637.
[30] *San Francisco Chronicle,* February 4, 1907.

As the San Franciscans journeyed East, numerous letters and telegrams to the President from California businessmen indicated a growing willingness there to readmit the Japanese children if laborers were excluded.[31] The President must have been pleased by this tendency to see things his own way, for he was deeply impressed with the feeling against the Japanese on the Pacific Coast springing from labor competition and racial antipathy, "the extent of which," he wrote George Kennan, "fairly astounds me." Roosevelt was convinced the Pacific Coast would "without a moment's hesitation" accept war rather than unrestricted Japanese immigration, and he regarded the school crisis and its complications as "one of the most difficult situations with which I have had to deal." [32] At times the insults to Japan by the Californians, which made the conclusion of an immigration agreement with Japan more difficult, loosened the President's self-restraint. "The San Franciscans," he wrote his son Kermit, "are howling and whooping and embarrassing me in every way, and their manners are simply inexcusable." [33] But however strong the President's private feelings, his public ones were conciliatory and persuasive. Without the good will of these same San Franciscans, no agreement with Japan could be reached.

Mayor Schmitz and his retinue of local officials reached Washington on February 8, 1907, proclaiming their open-mindedness and readiness to make concessions. The next day the first of several conferences with the President and the Secretary of State began. Years later Roosevelt recalled telling the San Franciscans that he "was in entire sympathy with the people of California as to the subject of immigration of the Japanese in mass," but that he "wished to accomplish

[31] *New York Herald*, February 4, 1907, Roosevelt Scrapbooks.
[32] Roosevelt to Kennan, February 9, and to Andrew D. White, February 4, 1907, Roosevelt Papers.
[33] Roosevelt to Kermit Roosevelt, February 4, 1907, Roosevelt Papers.

the object they had in view in the way that would be most courteous and most agreeable to the feelings of the Japanese." It was an "intolerable outrage," Roosevelt stormed, "to use offensive and insulting language" about the Japanese.[34] Roosevelt and Root impressed upon the San Franciscans that their problem was not a local one but one that involved the whole country, with peace or war hanging in the balance. Richmond P. Hobson was later told that the President said "war was imminent," but one doubts that he had to go this far to convince Schmitz and his associates of the wisdom of compromise. Roosevelt's main argument was that they would be serving their own self-interest by rescinding the school order in return for the exclusion of laborers. It was a valid point without any hyperbole. Root restrained the President during his moments of vehemence by clicking his pencil on a big mahogany table.[35]

When pressed by the San Franciscans about the scope and nature of the proposed treaty with Japan, the President was noticeably vague and kept insisting on the necessity of meeting Japan halfway before a treaty could be concluded.[36] Roosevelt was actually without a precise plan, for by February 9 little chance remained of getting a treaty of exclusion on acceptable terms. Yet the new solution to which the administration had turned — legislation to prohibit Japanese laborers moving from Hawaii to the Pacific Coast — was in an uncertain stage of development. It probably was not until February 9 or 10 that Roosevelt and Root, at the suggestion of Lodge, seized upon the idea of attaching such an amendment to the immigration bill currently deadlocked in a conference committee.[37] Writing to Lodge on February 11, Root

[34] Roosevelt, *An Autobiography,* pp. 379–380.
[35] Jessup, *Elihu Root,* II, 13; Hobson to Grizelda Hobson, October 28, 1908, Hobson Papers.
[36] *Washington Post,* February 10, 1907, Roosevelt Scrapbooks.
[37] John A. Garraty, *Henry Cabot Lodge: A Biography* (New York, 1953), p. 407.

included a copy of the clause he had drawn up as an amendment to the bill. It gave the President the power to refuse foreign citizens entry into the continental United States from another country, insular possessions, or the Canal Zone, if the passports issued for these destinations were being used by holders to enable them to come to the mainland "to the detriment of labor conditions therein." As Root explained the amendment to Lodge, "from the Japanese point of view all that the President will be doing under such a provision will be to enforce the limitations that Japan herself puts into her passports, while, from our point of view, the provision will enable the President to keep Japanese laborers out unless Japan undertakes to force them upon us directly, which she is apparently far from wishing to do." Japan, Root speculated, might be willing under present conditions of excitement to do "*sub silencio* what she cannot make a treaty binding herself to do, viz: really stop the direct emigration of laborers to this country." The amendment would allow the United States to "run matters along without injury until quieter conditions prevail, so that a permanent arrangement can be made." [38]

On February 12 Root suggested this plan to immigration bill conferees, who were receptive. Speaker Joseph G. Cannon, however, would not agree to break the deadlock in the conference committee unless the House version of the immigration bill, which lacked a literacy test, was accepted. Both Roosevelt and Lodge then sacrificed their support of the literacy test and the major legislative roadblock was cleared.[39] The San Franciscans also accepted the amendment and quickly came to a final, written agreement with the President, which provided for the segregation of Japanese

[38] Root to Lodge, February 11, 1907, NA, RG 59:2542/37.

[39] *Boston Evening Transcript*, February 12, 1907; Blair Bolles, *Tyrant From Illinois: Uncle Joe Cannon's Experiment with Personal Power* (New York, 1951), pp. 68–77.

students only when their advanced age or inadequacy in English made this necessary. As soon as Congress passed the amended immigration act, the school segregation order would be revoked. Roosevelt thought the San Franciscans had been "most reasonable." [40]

No trouble seemed likely to arise in Congress, despite Senator Lodge's fear of delay so late in the session. Lodge urged Roosevelt "to say 'hurry' " to any senators he encountered, but the President showed no signs of concern.[41] He was, however, careful to spread the impression that the solution was agreeable to Japan and that he would now seek an exclusion treaty. This last point was of particular importance to Californians in the House, who were at first inclined to oppose the amendment but finally supported it as a temporary expedient. On February 16 the Senate passed the amended immigration act over the opposition of southern Democrats, and two days later the House followed suit. In each house the measure was approved by an almost straight party-line vote.[42]

Henry Cabot Lodge was pleased with the amended immigration act. "It was," he wrote, "rather a good stroke." The school order, which had placed the United States in the wrong, would now be repealed and the position of the United States would become "correct." "The good management of the President and Mr. Root," he thought, "has opened a door by which we can obtain a final settlement of this vexed question." [43]

The Gentlemen's Agreement was not embodied in any one

[40] *New York Times,* February 16, 1907; Roosevelt to Gillett, March 9, 1907, *Letters,* V, 609.

[41] Lodge to Henry L. Higginson, February 18, 1907, Lodge Papers; Lodge to Roosevelt, February 13, 1907, Roosevelt Papers.

[42] *Los Angeles Times,* February 14, 1907; *Congressional Record,* 59th Cong., 2d Sess., pp. 3099–3232.

[43] Lodge to Henry White, February 23, 1907, and to Higginson, February 18, 1907, Lodge Papers.

diplomatic note; nor had it yet reached its final form. At the completion of the first stage of the negotiations in February, 1907, it consisted of two interrelated parts. The first was an American prohibition of the passage of laborers from Hawaii to the mainland; the second was a verbal assurance from Hayashi that Japan would continue the order already in force under which no passports were granted to skilled or unskilled laborers for the mainland of the United States, with the exception of farmers having an interest or share in their produce or crops. Japan would also continue to insert in all passports issued to laborers the destination of the holder.[44] Each nation viewed the permanence of the Gentlemen's Agreement differently. The United States regarded it as a temporary expedient, a prelude to a formal treaty. In contrast, Japan thought additional measures were unnecessary and would only consider a treaty if immigration did not sufficiently decrease or if the United States offered extremely attractive terms. Each position reflected the respective domestic imperatives of the Roosevelt administration and the Saionji ministry. Only after much travail would a permanent compromise be achieved.

Even before the amended immigration act became law, Roosevelt was eager to begin negotiations for an immigration treaty with Japan. He did not want the Japanese "to shy off" because of the Gentlemen's Agreement, for with the school order soon to be removed the United States now had the "right basis" for a settlement.[45] Following the President's wishes, Root suggested to the Japanese government on February 19 that negotiations for a treaty should begin.[46]

Hayashi knew of the President's intention to follow the Gentlemen's Agreement with some sort of "conventional ad-

[44] Wright to Root, February 23, 1907, NA, RG 59:1797/190.
[45] Roosevelt to Root, February 15, 1907, and to Strachey, February 22, 1907, *Letters*, V, 589, 597–598.
[46] Root to Wright, February 19, 1907, NA, RG 59:1797/173.

justment." [47] Nevertheless, he impressed Wright as pleased with the solution, as did Prime Minister Saionji, who said that the cabinet appreciated the efforts of Roosevelt and Root.[48] But Foreign Minister Hayashi turned down Root's suggestion of renewed treaty negotiations. This refusal no longer resulted entirely from a reluctance to enter into any kind of formal commitment, for the government had by this time determined on several concessions (a customs union with Korea, naturalization, and possibly tariff advantages) which would make it feasible from a domestic standpoint. However, both Hayashi and Aoki believed that the most valuable possible quid pro quo — naturalization — was temporarily out of the question because of popular feeling in the United States. Therefore they preferred to wait for a quieter period when Japan might obtain more. Japan should be, Aoki suggested, "in no hurry to close the question . . . between Japan and the United States," while operating its passport system in "good faith." [49]

With Japan refusing to negotiate, the United States could do little. In his written agreement with Schmitz, Roosevelt had been careful to promise to seek a mutual exclusion treaty with Japan and exclusion legislation only if the amendment to the immigration law proved ineffective. Thus he was able to drop treaty negotiations and observe the workings of the Gentlemen's Agreement. The President still was pleased with the results of his own labors and with the attitude of the Japanese government, for if a permanent solution had not been achieved, at least the basis for one had been laid. Both California and Japan were partially satisfied and time had been gained to devise a more effective arrangement if one

[47] Aoki to Hayashi, February 18, 1907, Telegram Series, JA.
[48] Wright to Root, February 21, March 19, 1907, NA, RG 59:1797/189 and 2542/73.
[49] Aoki to Hayashi, February 18, 1907, Hayashi to Aoki, February 23, 1907, and Aoki to Hayashi, February 23, 1907, Telegram Series, JA.

was needed. The President may be forgiven for boasting "that I doubt if any President could have done more to secure peace than I have done." [50]

The Japanese press generally accepted the Gentlemen's Agreement without enthusiasm. Many newspapers felt that more had been surrendered than gained and that naturalization would have made the solution an equitable one. The *Chuwo Shimbun*, for example, was "uneasy" but realized that Japan must wait with "patient resignation." The *Japan Times*, conciliatory throughout the Japanese-American difficulties, acquiesced in the settlement but thought that "the restrictions cannot but touch keenly our sense of sacrifice, if not of pride. . . . The loss of an advantage once enjoyed legitimately cannot but be felt sharply." [51] In an interview with the *Mainichi Dempo*, Foreign Minister Hayashi encouraged acceptance of the Gentlemen's Agreement by pointing out that the United States had a treaty right to exclude Japanese laborers but refused to exercise it. He called upon Japan to appreciate the forbearance of the American government and to be grateful to President Roosevelt. Later, when questioned in parliament, Hayashi argued that Japan had to take what it could get and not jeopardize all by claiming too much. [52]

Despite Hayashi's efforts, criticisms of the government's emigration policy continued to be voiced. Opposition and some independent newspapers, the emigration companies, and Japanese residents on the Pacific Coast and in Hawaii were dissatisfied with the Gentlemen's Agreement. The most extreme complaint came from the *Hochi Shimbun*, which urged the Japanese people "to rise in indignation." Hayashi's

[50] Roosevelt to Andrew Carnegie, February 17, 1907, *Letters*, V, 592.

[51] *Literary Digest*, 34 (April 6, 1907), 531; *Chuwo Shimbun*, February 19, 1907, *Japan Times*, February 20, 1907, NA, RG 59:1797/175 and 179.

[52] *Mainichi Dempo*, February 20, 1907, NA, RG 59:1797/178; *Japan Weekly Mail*, March 16, 1907.

diplomacy, the *Hochi* claimed, had all along been "incompetent," and now the nation ought to drive him from office and rely "upon the strength of righteousness" to deal with the United States.[53] The *Mainichi Dempo* thought the Gentlemen's Agreement was the price of Japan's "indifference and *laissez faire* foreign policy" and urged Japanese diplomats to cease being too humble and conciliatory. Perhaps the most cogent criticism came from Count Okuma, recently retired as leader of the *Kenseihonto*. Japanese statesmen, he said, seemed to have left things entirely in American hands, and when a disadvantageous settlement resulted Japan could only acquiesce.[54]

The most concrete evidence of opposition came from persons associated with the emigration companies, who organized the *Taibei Doshikwai* to oppose any restriction on Japanese laborers entering the United States. Though this pressure group lacked support from any important newspapers or politicians, its creation indicated that some elements of Japanese society were disturbed by the recent course of events. And a warning that this minority sentiment might become dominant came in early March from the *Japan Weekly Mail*. The *Weekly Mail*, commenting upon the anti-Japanese measures being debated in the California legislature, "greatly feared" that if the agitation against Japanese continued "something in the form of retaliation will be attempted on this side." "Japanese patience," the *Weekly Mail* predicted, "is not inexhaustible." [55]

The administration's ingenious compromise met with more enthusiastic approval in the United States, where most of

---

[53] *Japan Weekly Mail*, February 23, 1907; *Hochi Shimbun*, March 12, 1907, NA, RG 59:2542/76.

[54] *Mainichi Dempo*, February 19, 1907, NA, RG 59:1797/176; *Japan Weekly Mail*, March 30, 1907.

[55] Wright to Root, March 3, 1907, NA, RG 59:1797/188; *Japan Weekly Mail*, March 9, 1907.

the press believed the Gentlemen's Agreement would make all sides happy until a new treaty was negotiated. Some eastern editors were angry at the disingenuousness of California's outcry against the Japanese school children; others were disappointed that the school question was not settled in the courts. And the *Nation* was puzzled by Roosevelt's retreat from his "lofty" message to a position of favoring the exclusion of Japanese laborers.[56] On the Pacific Coast, even those papers strongly for Japanese exclusion welcomed the new arrangement. The *San Francisco Chronicle* thought that "as a result of the school trouble, the cause of exclusion has been put forward to a point which its most ardent advocates could not have dreamed reaching in so short a time." The *Chronicle,* however, along with the Japanese-Korean Exclusion League, regarded the agreement as only a modus vivendi, and both were determined to press for Japanese exclusion legislation.[57] The Reverend Herbert Johnson, a longtime friend of the Japanese in California, predicted many Californians would continue to demand Japanese exclusion because they trusted neither Roosevelt nor Japan. And the hapless Mayor Schmitz, instead of being greeted in triumph, found that his mission was widely regarded as a failure.[58] Roosevelt's plan may have temporarily stilled the strife on the Pacific Coast, but unless it worked with great effectiveness and speed anti-Japanese agitation would soon reappear.

As March began the President thought he had the "Japanese business in good shape."[59] Within a few days he expected the San Francisco Board of Education to readmit the Japanese pupils. Then he would issue an executive order

---

[56] *Literary Digest,* 34 (February 23, 1907), 275–276; *Nation,* 84 (February 21, 1907), 168.

[57] *Literary Digest,* 34 (March 2, 1907), 320; *San Francisco Chronicle,* February 20, 1907.

[58] Herbert B. Johnson, *Discrimination Against the Japanese in California* (Berkeley, 1907), p. 85; Thomson, "Events," 154.

[59] Roosevelt to Gillett, March 4, 1907, Roosevelt Papers.

halting the flow of Japanese laborers to the mainland. However, sudden developments in the California legislature threatened to deprive the administration of the fruits of victory after they seemed secure. On February 28 the Assembly passed the Drew Bill, prohibiting aliens from holding property for more than five years without becoming naturalized. The Senate on March 7 defeated a bill which might have forced the San Francisco Board of Education to segregate Japanese school children but two days later passed a resolution opposing the naturalization and immigration of Japanese.[60] By March 10 Roosevelt was again excited, fearful that he already had waited too long before taking "open action" and certain that "if we let things drift we may get in a very bad situation." That evening Root submitted to Roosevelt a telegram for Schmitz. "I don't like to have you telegraph him," Root wrote the President, "but he ought to be stirred up for he practically guaranteed the legislature." Angrily the secretary asked: "Did you ever see such idiots?"[61]

The President's telegram warned both the Mayor and the Governor that anti-Japanese agitation in the legislature would probably make the Gentlemen's Agreement inoperative, and he asked Gillett to secure the suspension of further action until the receipt of a letter.[62] The next day the response of Schmitz and Gillett indicated that Roosevelt still controlled the situation. Denying any intention of repudiating the agreement and arguing that he was working to achieve it, Schmitz ended grandiloquently by saying: "Command me further." Gillett forwarded Roosevelt's telegram to the Assembly with a supporting message and the Assembly

[60] *Journal of the California Assembly,* 37th Sess. (1907), 1204, *Journal of the California Senate,* 37th Sess. (1907), 1567, 1651–1652, Thomson, "Events," 55–56.

[61] Roosevelt to Root, March 10, 1907, *Letters,* V, 610; Root to Roosevelt, March 10, 1907, Roosevelt Papers.

[62] Roosevelt to Gillett, March 10, 1907, in *Journal of the California Assembly,* 37th Sess. (1907), 1787.

complied by voting to take no further action on Japanese measures during the remainder of the session. "The Big Stick," the *New York Times* correspondent remarked, "has broken its record for swift and determined action." [63]

However, Gillett also telegraphed the President asking if he objected to a pending measure to submit the question of the exclusion of Japanese laborers to the voters of California.[64] Roosevelt, who already had written Gillett two long expositions on his policy, now sent a telegraphic summary. In these communications the President repeated his warning that insulting or discriminatory action against Japan might make the Japanese government unwilling to carry out its part of the agreement. Only California would suffer if Japan did break the Gentlemen's Agreement, for the United States, in Roosevelt's judgment, would never "consent to the exclusion of Japanese laborers save on substantially the terms upon which we have now secured their exclusion." The Californians should not be deluded into action against their own best interests by "unwise and sinister agitators." Roosevelt objected to any vote by California, for the question of Japanese exclusion could be handled only by the federal government. The latter had "the affair in hand" and could "in all human probability secure the results that California desires." [65] These powerful messages from the President sealed the capitulation of the California legislature and cleared the way for the consummation of the Gentlemen's Agreement. On March 13, 1907, the Board of Education readmitted the Japanese children. The next day Roosevelt issued his executive order and allowed the test cases to be dropped. Schmitz, the President remarked, "has acted like a trump." [66]

[63] Schmitz to Root, March 11, 1907, NA, RG 59:2542/55; *New York Times,* March 12, 1907.

[64] Gillett to Roosevelt, March 11, 1907, in *Journal of the California Assembly,* 37th Sess. (1907), 1855–1856.

[65] Roosevelt to Gillett, March 9, 11, 12, 1907, *Letters,* V, 608–615.

[66] Roosevelt to Root, March 12, 1907, Roosevelt Papers.

The final implementation of the Gentlemen's Agreement brought a resurgence of pro-Japanese feeling in the United States during the spring of 1907. Speaking before the American Society of International Law, Elihu Root described the way in which modern wars were made by people rather than by governments, and voiced his belief that the people of America and Japan had refused to break their friendship over the recent immigration dispute.[67] The effect of Root's address was reinforced by the warm reception given General Tamesada Kuroki, a senior army officer who accompanied a Japanese naval squadron on its visit to the Jamestown Exposition. Kuroki's arrival in New York City brought the formation of a local Japanese Society. Inspired by the occasion, the *Outlook* predicted future historians would note "as the most significant fact of the twentieth century the coming together of the East and the West."[68]

After months of complex negotiations, American relations with Japan seemed once more destined for a quiet and peaceful period. Though Roosevelt thought that "we shall now be able to accomplish by direct negotiations with Japan just what we desire," he seemed ready to observe the working of the Gentlemen's Agreement before again beginning treaty negotiations. "As the matter stands now," Root explained, "we are in a position to go on and negotiate a treaty when the excitement has died out a little more, if a treaty is found to be necessary."[69]

Both the President and Secretary of State thought the Gentlemen's Agreement would probably work effectively. They accepted the assurances of the Japanese government and did

[67] Root, "The Real Question Under the Japanese Treaty and the San Francisco School Board Resolution," *American Journal of International Law*, 1 (January and April, 1907), 273–286.

[68] *Literary Digest*, 34 (May 25, 1907), 822; *Outlook*, 86 (June 1, 1907), 230–232.

[69] Roosevelt to Gillett, March 14, 1907, *Letters*, V, 618; Root to Holmes, March 6, 1907, NA, RG 59:2542/55a.

not yet understand how complex the task of stopping the immigration of Japanese laborers would be. Nor did they foresee how even a trickle of immigrants would feed the growing anti-Japanese movement in California. In retrospect, of course, the Gentlemen's Agreement of February, 1907, only began the task of keeping Japanese laborers out of the United States. But to Roosevelt and Root it seemed, in the spring of 1907, to have largely ended it.

Several officials in Washington, acquainted with the intricacies of Japanese immigration, were well aware of the weaknesses of the Gentlemen's Agreement and pressed their views upon the President and the Secretary of State. They pointed out that no provision had been made (1) to halt the illegal entry of Japanese laborers from Mexico; (2) to guard against the abuse of transit rights granted to Japanese; or (3) to restrict the entry of farmers (who could hardly be distinguished from laborers).[70] These warnings made some impression on Root, for on April 17 he sought to open discussions with Hayashi over tighter limitations on farmers. At the same time Root suggested to Hayashi that treaty negotiations be resumed since the order of the school board had been repealed and the excitement in both nations had subsided.[71] Nearly a month later, when Wright interviewed the Japanese Foreign Minister, Hayashi assured him of the care with which passports were being issued to farmers and announced that his government had no intention of changing its system of granting such passports. While he agreed that the excitement seemed to have passed, he was reluctant to begin treaty negotiations and feared that to reopen the matter now would be like applying a match to powder. Wright thought the Saionji cabinet, in its present insecure position, could not

---

[70] Memorandum by Commissioner General Sargent, February 21, 1907, and memorandum by Huntington Wilson, March 19, 1907, NA, RG 59:2542/54 and 63.

[71] Root to Wright, April 17, 1907, NA, RG 59:2542/76a.

conclude a treaty of reciprocal exclusion without bringing about its own downfall.[72]

Developments in San Francisco prevented the administration from pursuing these negotiations. On May 20 and 21, in the midst of a bloody street-railway strike, mobs attacked and damaged Japanese restaurants and a Japanese bath house. The situation in San Francisco seemed to be deteriorating with the collapse of the Union Labor party machine. The confession of bribery by Abe Ruef in early May doomed the Schmitz administration, and on June 13 the Mayor was convicted of extortion and his office was declared vacant. Prior to the selection of a reform mayor on July 16, however, the city was in the hands of several acting mayors who lacked real power. While San Francisco languished without effective leadership, the police force remained under the control of Chief Joseph F. Dinan, an unsavory holdover from the former regime.[73]

Root had hardly learned of the new troubles in San Francisco when, on May 25, Ambassador Aoki called the attention of both the President and Secretary of State to conditions in San Francisco.[74] Neither needed any prodding, for they realized that the new incident once again put the United States in the wrong and that the tightening of the Gentlemen's Agreement would be delayed until it was settled. Root immediately had District Attorney Devlin and Governor Gillett begin investigations and asked Gillett to enforce the treaty rights of the Japanese through the use of special police protection. Despite Gillett's willingness to cooperate, no consensus could be reached on the causes of these attacks. The Acting Japanese Consul in San Francisco, Kazuo Matsubara, claimed they were premeditated and motivated by racial

[72] Wright to Root, May 15, 1907, and memorandum from Hayashi, undated, NA, RG 59:2542/97 and 118.
[73] Bean, *Boss Ruef's San Francisco*, pp. 211, 227–230.
[74] The episode can be followed in NA, RG 59:1797/204–232.

prejudices, while the reports received through Gillett and Devlin interpreted the violence as a by-product of the conflict between union and non-union workers. Chief Dinan assured investigators the Japanese would be protected, and Root on June 5 conveyed to Aoki the official regrets of the American government over the incident. The Japanese could secure their claims through the courts, with the assistance of the United States District Attorney. By acting swiftly Root had prevented the incident from becoming a formal diplomatic one, but he had no control over the ensuing war scare which it precipitated.

The first news of the incidents in San Francisco brought little response from the Japanese press, where the belief prevailed that the situation would be speedily corrected.[75] By early June, however, the conciliatory attitude of Japanese newspapers began to change. The extreme wing of the *Kenseihonto,* in search of an issue to use against the Saionji ministry, decided to capitalize on the San Francisco disturbances. On June 5 a *Kenseihonto* delegation called on Hayashi and complained of the government's policy toward China and toward the anti-Japanese agitation in the United States. The party organ, the *Hochi Shimbun,* along with other sensational papers, violently denounced the "San Francisco outrages." The *Hochi* argued that the nation could "no longer place any confidence either in the assurances of the American Government or in the diplomatic ability of our own authorities," and urged the Japanese people to take diplomacy into their own hands.[76] Soon the council of the *Kenseihonto* passed a resolution saying that the anti-Japanese acts were not of a temporary nature and that the federal government must be held responsible for its failure to prevent them.

[75] Wright to Root, May 28, 1907, NA, RG 59:1797/423.
[76] *Japan Weekly Mail,* June 8, 15, 1907; *Hochi Shimbun,* June 13, 1907, NA, RG 59:1797/238.

No doubt the *New York Times* exaggerated in reporting that "popular indignation has reached a degree never before witnessed in the history of Japan's relations with the United States," but the agitation begun for domestic political purposes did show a tendency to spread to more moderate sections of the press.[77] Wright wrote that leading newspapers expressed surprise or annoyance over the recent outbreaks in San Francisco, while those of the second or lower ranks went to extremes.[78] The *Nichi Nichi Shimbun* predicted, "even traditional friendship will not escape a rupture, should incidents like those that have occurred in San Francisco be repeated," and asked for the prompt enforcement of treaty rights. And the *Japan Times*, though dismissing the possibility of any break in the unparalleled friendship of the two nations, denounced "the indignity and oppression suffered by our compatriots in America." [79]

Japanese on the Pacific Coast may have joined the efforts of the *Kenseihonto* to capitalize on the apparent dissatisfaction of the Japanese people with the settlement of the school and immigration questions. The *New York Times* reported "authoritatively" that they were unhappy with the policy of both Aoki and Hayashi and had formed a league with members of the *Kenseihonto* in Japan to overthrow the Saionji ministry. Whatever the truth of this report, and the collateral one that Aoki would be recalled, a delegate sent by the Pacific Coast Japanese to represent their interests did arrive in Japan in late May.[80]

Rumors of war, spread by the sensational press in America and Japan, filled the air throughout June, 1907. The *Literary*

[77] *Literary Digest*, 34 (June 22, 1907), 977–979; *New York Times*, June 7, 1907.
[78] Wright to Root, June 12, 1907, NA, RG 59:1797/247.
[79] *Nichi Nichi Shimbun*, June 6, 1907, quoted in *New York Times*, June 7, 1907; *Japan Times*, June 13, 14, 1907, NA, RG 59:1797/272 and 274.
[80] *New York Times*, June 10, 11, 1907; Aoki to Hayashi, June 13, 1907, Telegram Series, JA.

*Digest* complained that despite Kuroki's visit "the sinister and bewildering rumors continue to circulate," and Mr. Dooley, in a lighter vein, described Theodore Roosevelt under a bed trying to learn to say "Spare me" in Japanese. Respectable American papers insisted there was no possibility of war and denounced the political opposition in Japan as well as American jingoes and the "hoodlums" in San Francisco. But, while alleging the crisis to be artificial, they acknowledged that friction could become real if reckless talk continued.[81] Perhaps some editorial writers saw, as did the *Nation,* an imitation of the process used by the yellow journals from 1895 to 1898 and feared the war scare would spread from the press to the people. For though a belief in immediate war did not seem common, one sensitive observer, the French journalist André Tardieu, found the opinion of an inevitable struggle between the United States and Japan widely held in America.[82] Ambassador Aoki felt that "the vague impression of a strife between Japan and the United States looming at a distance gains ground more and more in the mind of the public," and Alfred Thayer Mahan expressed the feelings of many Americans when he spoke of the "menacing appearance" of the Japanese question for the future.[83]

Speculation upon the future of Japanese-American relations was widespread in the European press, particularly in Great Britain, Germany, and France.[84] British papers regarded Japanese-American difficulties with great concern and generally deplored the talk of war. But it was widely realized

---

[81] *Literary Digest,* 34 (June 22, 1907), 977–979; *Outlook,* 86 (June 22, 1907), 345–346.

[82] *Nation,* 85 (July 11, 1907), 26; André Tardieu, *Notes sur les États-Unis* (Paris, 1908), p. 280.

[83] Aoki to Hayashi, June 13, 1907, Telegram Series, JA; Mahan to Leopold James Maxse, May 30, 1907, Mahan Papers.

[84] *Literary Digest,* 33 (November 24, 1906), 751; 33 (December 29, 1906), 969; 34 (January 26, 1907), 125–126.

that if war came, no British government could side with Japan and survive.[85] Germany, on the contrary, was a fertile source of war rumors. So intense did these become in June that the American naval attaché in Berlin, Commander W. L. Howard, spent a "number of anxious days and nights" running down alarming reports. Howard became convinced that Japan was actually preparing for war with the United States.[86] French journals did not view a conflict as imminent, but many agreed with the *Paris Figaro* that the United States and Japan would "sooner or later have to settle their accounts in the Pacific." The European press had not focused so intensively on American foreign relations since the turn of the century.[87]

In the Philippines the air was also heavy with rumors of war, both within and without the American military establishment. The commanding general of the Philippines Division, Leonard Wood, who had long been suspicious of Japan's intentions in the Far East, heard of alleged negotiations between former Filipino insurgents and the Japanese government. Some Filipinos seemed to believe Japan was about to drive out the United States and establish a Philippine republic. W. Cameron Forbes, a Boston banker whom Roosevelt had appointed to the Philippine Commission, discussed the possibility of war with Filipino political leaders and was assured that most would favor the United States. Even Emilio Aguinaldo thought many of the people, perhaps a majority, would defend the existing government against a Japanese attack.[88]

[85] *North American Review,* 184 (January 18, 1907), 204–205; *English Review of Reviews,* 35 (January 1907), 3.

[86] Commander W. L. Howard to Captain R. P. Rodgers, July 1, 1907, NA, RG 38:ONI General Correspondence, Case No. 8444.

[87] *Literary Digest,* 35 (July 27, 1907), 114–115.

[88] Hermann Hagedorn, *Leonard Wood: A Biography* (2 vols.; New York and London, 1931), II, 80; Journal of W. Cameron Forbes, II, March 19, July 9, August 18, November 20, and December 6, 1907, Forbes Papers.

Officially the administration took no notice of the disturbing rumors.[89] Its only comment was through an inspired article in the *Washington Post,* which reported that high officials regarded the agitation in Japan as nothing more than the working of Japanese politics and that the only danger was from the constant sensationalism of newspapers in both nations.[90] In private, however, both the President and the Secretary of State were worried over the implications of the new outbreak. On June 7 Root informed Roosevelt that the San Francisco affair was "getting on all right as an ordinary diplomatic affair about which there is no occasion to get excited. All the trouble is being made by the leprous vampires who are eager to involve their country in war in order to sell a few more newspapers." [91]

The President himself was "concerned about the Japanese-California situation and . . . [saw] no prospect of its growing better." [92] Ambassador James Bryce was surprised by the anxiety Roosevelt revealed in an interview on June 7 and reported how he dwelled on the difficulties of making the San Francisco police properly protect Japanese residents. Though he had arranged to have troops in the area, he was hesitant to use them now that the need for them seemed real. A few days later Roosevelt explained to Henry White, the American ambassador to France, how the use of troops would have to be completely warranted or it would do harm, for "in a democracy like ours a public servant must continu-

[89] On May 28, 1907, Foreign Minister Stephen Pichon instructed Ambassador Jules Jusserand to offer the good offices of France in arranging conversations between the United States and Japan leading to an agreement on Far Eastern affairs. Roosevelt politely declined the offer and was embarrassed by its leakage to the American press. Jusserand to Pinchon, June 14, 1907, *Documents Diplomatiques Francais,* 2d Series, XI (Paris, 1950), 45–48, and *Washington Post,* June 8, 1907, as quoted in Aoki to Hayashi, June 5, 1907, Telegram Series, JA.

[90] *Washington Post,* June 12, 1907, Roosevelt Scrapbooks.

[91] Root to Roosevelt, June 7, 1907, Roosevelt Papers.

[92] Roosevelt to Henry White, June 15, 1907, Roosevelt Papers.

ally keep in mind . . . how far he can arouse and guide public sentiment so that it will justify him." Roosevelt's reluctance to offend California by the employment of force was increased by his belief that "the utterances of the extremists in Japan have begun to make an unpleasant feeling in this country." [93]

On the surface the Saionji ministry remained as calm as the Roosevelt administration and gave no signs of succumbing to the new wave of protests. Foreign Minister Hayashi estimated to Wright that 70 percent of the feeling displayed by newspapers and politicians was for political effect, and Count Okuma confirmed this impression by privately admitting his public statements were entirely political.[94] The rapid investigation initiated by the United States government, in addition to its expression of regrets over the San Francisco violence, aided Hayashi in deferring any diplomatic steps and in expressing hope for a judicial settlement of the Japanese claims. The government's position was further strengthened by the widespread approval of a Franco-Japanese Agreement on Far Eastern affairs signed June 10. Three days later the government moved to quiet the press by warning Tokyo newspapers to cease publishing inflammatory material on the American question.[95]

By mid-June the offensive of the *Kenseihonto* against the ministry seemed to be flagging. It had failed to gain the complete cooperation of the Daido Club (Count Katsura's party), and had met with strong opposition from the *Seiyukai*, which continued to support the Saionji cabinet. Hayashi soon announced that Aoki would remain at Washington, and the Foreign Office succeeded in softening a

[93] Bryce to Grey, June 8, 1907, PRO, FO 371/269; Roosevelt to Henry White, June 15, 1907, Roosevelt Papers.

[94] Wright to Root, June 12, 1907, NA, RG 59:1797/247.

[95] *Japan Times*, June 19, 1907, NA, RG 59:6351/23; *New York Times*, June 14, 1907.

resolution of the Japanese Chambers of Commerce intended for chambers in the United States.[96] As first adopted it suggested Japan might resort to a boycott if incidents continued; as finally sent the resolution merely expressed fear that a continuation of incidents would retard commerce. By late June leading Japanese newspapers were beginning to counsel moderation, while the opposition seemed to be abandoning the idea of making the recent injuries to Japanese businesses a subject of diplomatic protest.[97]

The decision on June 27 of the San Francisco Board of Police Commissioners to refuse licenses to six Japanese employment bureaus did not interrupt the trend toward moderation in Japan, despite the lament of the *Japan Times* that the new act "throws the favorable turn of affairs to the winds." [98] Nor did the announcement of the cruise of the United States battle fleet to the Pacific excite the Japanese press. The *Kenseihonto* continued its agitation, and *Tokyo Puck* published a virulent anti-American issue, but the failure of a joint meeting of organizations interested in the "American affair" on July 22 indicated the isolated character of these efforts. Neither important businessmen nor representatives of the Daido Club attended, and Okuma delivered a relatively quiet speech.[99] By late July, satisfaction over the friendly American reception of Admiral Gombei Yamamoto, a former naval minister and elder statesman, helped to close the discussion of events in San Francisco.[100] Once more the Saionji cabinet had weathered sharp attacks on its policy toward the United States. But its maneuverability in future

[96] *Japan Weekly Mail*, June 22, 29, 1907; *New York Times*, June 22, 1907.
[97] Wright to Root, July 10, 1907, NA, RG 59:1797/298; Wright to Root, June 27, 1907, NA, RG 59:1797/270.
[98] *New York Times*, July 4, 1907; *Japan Times*, July 3, 1907, NA, RG 59:1797/301.
[99] *Tokyo Puck*, 3, No. 17, NA, RG 59:1797/290; *Kokumin Shimbun*, July 23, 1907, NA, RG 59:1797/318.
[100] Wright to Root, July 26, 1907, NA, RG 59:1797/314.

immigration negotiations had been further narrowed by the willingness of domestic foes to exploit foreign complications and by the residue of bitter feeling left in Japan over the treatment of Japanese citizens in California.

By late June the peak of the war scare had also passed in the United States. Richmond Hobson, who throughout these years traveled widely preaching hatred of Japan and the need for a United States navy second to none, predicted war would come at any moment.[101] Some other politicians were also attempting to exploit popular fears of Japan, but most political leaders did not do so. William Jennings Bryan, Representative Joseph Cannon of Illinois, and Representative John Hull of Iowa, chairman of the House Committee on Military Affairs, regarded war as unlikely, though Hull believed a large element in Japan outside of the ruling classes would welcome it. These men sensed more accurately than Hobson the mood of the nation, for only occasional stirrings could be detected among the people.[102] The Venice, California, Chamber of Commerce offered to form a volunteer torpedo service called the "Rough Riders of the Sea," and former soldiers from all parts of the country offered their services in case of war.[103] The War Department received complaints of Japanese spies mapping military installations, and some officers indicated their own nervousness by seizing innocent Japanese near them. The Commander of the Department of the East, General Frederick Grant, complained

[101] New York Times, July 8, 1907. Governor George R. Carter of Hawaii added to the scare by telling a reporter that "Japan would fight the United States at the drop of the hat should the occasion arise, and you can take it from me that Uncle Sam would know it was more than a slight tickling at the ribs before he got through with the trouble" (New York Times, June 30, 1907).

[102] New York Times, July 10, 12, 16, 1907.

[103] Venice Chamber of Commerce to Board of Coast Defense, Washington, D.C., June 18, 1907, No. 403, General Board Papers; Philip Hayward, Hanging Rock, Ohio, to Taft, July 9, 1907, NA, RG 94:1262672.

of the poor condition of the army, while some journalists wrote of the country's lack of enough trained artillerymen for the existing coast defense batteries.[104] But these warnings only slightly affected the American people. Theodore Roosevelt's generation had already experienced war and was turning with increasing absorption to the task of domestic reform.

The rumors of conflict between the United States and Japan continued at a lower pitch throughout the summer and were, to a varying degree, a constant presence for years to come.[105] Though their popular impact was never great, they did leave a legacy of suspicion and fear in each nation, which, as we shall see, subtly affected the policy of each government.

[104] *New York Times*, July 12, 21, 1907; *Literary Digest*, 34 (February 2, 1907), 159.

[105] George Kennan, "The Russo-Japanese Treaty," *Outlook*, 114 (September 20, 1916), 149–152.

# IV

## "THE NEED OF PREPAREDNESS"

Primarily through the efforts of Theodore Roosevelt, the Japanese-American crisis of 1906–1909 was fused with American naval policy. Roosevelt drew upon his wide knowledge of naval affairs and his understanding of the relationship between power and diplomacy to insist upon a close coordination of diplomacy and naval strategy throughout the years of crisis with Japan. He did so because he realized the two nations could conceivably stumble into war, not because war seemed likely either in the immediate or more distant future. However remote the chance of conflict might be, Roosevelt believed he had a duty to prepare the American people for it.

Long before coming to the presidency Roosevelt had acquired an intense interest in naval affairs. The tales of his uncles about their experiences in the Confederate navy awakened this interest in his youth, and it developed further in the 1890's, when Roosevelt grasped the relationship between world power and naval strength and served for a time as assistant secretary of the navy. By the turn of the century his views had matured, and during his presidential years they changed little. He believed the United States needed warships equal in numbers with "the greatness of our people" if its voice was to be heard in world affairs. National prestige and the effectiveness of America's diplomacy were closely intertwined with naval power. And if the nation's vital interests were challenged, the navy could then adequately defend them.[1]

Before 1901 Roosevelt had been a zealous advocate of naval expansion; after 1901 he employed presidential power to further these beliefs. His first annual message contained a vigorous call for more warships, and from 1901 to 1905 he drove the Congress hard in this direction. In four years Roosevelt secured ten battleships, four armored cruisers, and seventeen other vessels of different classes, along with an increase in naval appropriations from 85 to 118 million dollars per year. He also strove to reform the American naval establishment, for though the navy, unlike the army, had performed with tolerable efficiency during the Spanish-American War, it was still in a critical and confusing period of transition. Roosevelt failed to achieve a sweeping administrative reorganization, promotion by selection rather than seniority, and a system of fortified overseas naval stations. He did, however, partially remedy the navy's acute personnel shortage, create a permanent fighting fleet composed of capital ships, and support reformers within the navy in their efforts to improve naval gunnery and battleship design.[2] By 1905 the fighting effectiveness of the fleet had been greatly improved, though many serious deficiencies remained. While aware of these defects, Roosevelt seemed to feel that nothing more could be accomplished either in naval reform or fleet expansion. In early 1905 he predicted that "for some years now we can afford to rest and merely replace the ships that are worn out or become obsolete, while we bring up the personnel." In December he informed the Congress that for

[1] Beale, *Theodore Roosevelt*, pp. 3–4, 38–39.
[2] Harold and Margaret Sprout, *The Rise of American Naval Power, 1776–1918* (Princeton, 1939), pp. 259–262, 270–279.

the immediate future the navy would not have to be increased. A single battleship each year, to replace worn-out units, would do.[3]

Many motives influenced the President to call a halt to naval expansion. The United States was already the world's third naval power, due to become the second in 1907 with the completion of pending construction. Roosevelt had reached his mark, for there was no need to challenge Britain's naval primacy.[4] Moreover, the growing navy encountered increasing domestic opposition, as peace advocates and those who refused to recognize the involvement of the United States beyond its own hemisphere questioned the purpose of such a large, offensive navy. While lamenting the failure of the people to learn "the need of preparedness, and of shaping things so that decision and action can alike be instantaneous," Roosevelt was sensitive to this opposition and distracted by his own growing absorption in domestic reform.[5] In short, by late 1905 the political costs of naval expansion seemed greater than the benefits it might bring. Pleased with his own spectacular accomplishments in strengthening the navy, Roosevelt felt the nation could afford to rest.

If Roosevelt thought further naval expansion would be too difficult, he must have been even more impressed with the futility of pressing for further naval reforms. The public was apathetic over what appeared to be rather technical deficiencies in the navy's personnel and material, while powerful vested interests in the Congress and Navy Department opposed any change in the navy's antiquated bureau system. Congress preferred dealing with largely autonomous bureaus rather than with a highly centralized naval general staff; it

[3] Roosevelt to Wood, March 9, 1905, *Letters*, IV, 1136; *Works*, XV, 308–309.
[4] Roosevelt to Wood, March 9, 1905, *Letters*, IV, 1136.
[5] Roosevelt to Root, February 16, 1904, *Letters*, IV, 731.

also feared that a general staff system would threaten civilian control of the navy. The most powerful congressional stand-patter in naval affairs was Senator Eugene Hale of Maine, the long-time chairman of the Naval Affairs Committee and a member of the Senate's Republican oligarchy. Until the turn of the century Hale had been a champion of naval expansion, but in the years following the Spanish-American War his enthusiasm had waned and he had come to oppose most changes in naval administration, in the naval promotion system, and in battleship design.[6] Hale's resistance to change was reinforced by the various bureau chiefs who, while theoretically under the control of the Secretary of the Navy, in practice had great power, since the secretary generally lacked extensive knowledge of naval affairs and served only a short time in office. The secretary could turn for guidance to the General Board, created in 1900 as a concession to those who wanted a more centralized naval administration, but it was only an advisory body with no executive function or extensive staff. It advised the secretary on naval strategy, war plans, and building programs, and achieved consider-able influence under the chairmanship of Admiral of the Navy George Dewey. It did little, however, to repair major defects in the structure of the Navy Department.

Under this system many burdens, if they were to be borne at all, fell on the shoulders of the President. He had to force the pace of change within the Navy Department and co-ordinate political and military matters.[7] It was a sizeable task, even for a president of Roosevelt's knowledge and capabilities, and it was increased by the failure of naval and military policy makers to cooperate. The Joint Army and Navy Board, established in 1903 under the chairmanship of

[6] Elting E. Morison, *Admiral Sims and the Modern American Navy* (Boston, 1942), pp. 181–182.

[7] Ernest R. May, "The Development of Political-Military Consultation in the United States," *Political Science Quarterly,* 70 (June, 1955), 161–180.

Admiral Dewey, was to bring together army and navy planners to work on common problems. However, both services were inclined to pursue their own policies independently, and the Joint Board did not function well.[8] If Dewey had been a man of more intellectual breadth and political acumen, collaboration might have been better. But the elderly admiral, surrounded by war mementos and caught up in Washington's social whirl, proved to be from 1906 to 1909 a narrow and unyielding partisan of the navy's point of view.[9] Despite the many inadequacies of both the Joint Board and the General Board, Roosevelt was uncertain of his own grasp of Pacific strategy and had to rely upon them in the intricate questions which arose after 1906. He was, to be sure, increasingly dissatisfied with the performance of his army and navy planners; but, aware of the opposition to military and naval reform, Roosevelt did nothing to change the procedures within the naval and military establishments.

Less than a year after his declaration of an end to naval expansion, the President's attitude began to change. This change, apparent by late October, 1906, was not, however, a result of the emerging Japanese-American crisis. From the beginning of the school crisis until after the conclusion of the Gentlemen's Agreement, the prospects for a quick settlement and a return to normal relations seemed excellent. There was little reason for Roosevelt to alter his belief, formed during the Russo-Japanese War, that a postwar collision with Japan was unlikely. His renewed concern over the American navy stemmed, instead, from a full realization

[8] Louis Morton, "War Plan ORANGE: Evolution of a Strategy," *World Politics*, 11 (January, 1959), 221–250.

[9] The best discussion of Dewey is in Richard S. West, Jr., *Admirals of American Empire, The Combined Story of George Dewey, Alfred Thayer Mahan, Winfield Scott Schley and William Thomas Sampson* (New York, 1948). For a more recent estimate see John A. S. Grenville and George Berkeley Young, *Politics, Strategy, and American Diplomacy: Studies in Foreign Policy, 1873–1917* (New Haven, 1966), pp. 297–336.

of the revolution in battleship design brought by the *H.M.S. Dreadnought,* completed in December, 1906. This 17,900 ton ship with ten 12-inch guns and a 21-knot speed made all previous battleships obsolete and heralded a new era of naval competition.

In 1904 Roosevelt had shown an early appreciation of the all-big-gun ship, but powerful opposition within and without the American naval establishment had weakened his resolve and the issue lapsed, not to be revived until the autumn of 1906. Then a clash between Alfred Thayer Mahan and William S. Sims over the value of the dreadnought-type battleship again focused Roosevelt's attention on the issue. Mahan, at the height of his prestige, defended smaller, slower, mixed-caliber battleships on the basis of the battle of the Sea of Japan. Sims, Inspector of Target Practice and a forceful and effective advocate of naval reform, argued that the United States must build 20,000 ton all-big-gun ships or expect to fall behind in naval competition and risk its position as a great power.[10] Since 1904 Roosevelt had listened closely to Sims' critique of the American navy and in 1907 the lieutenant commander would become the President's naval aide. Sims' skillful advocacy of the dreadnought type, reinforced by the opinions of the General Board and the example of Great Britain, completely convinced Roosevelt of the superiority of this new design; never again would he doubt the need for American dreadnoughts.[11]

Though aware of the importance of the dreadnought design, Roosevelt was not yet convinced of the need for renewed naval expansion. The General Board warned that the plans of other naval powers made it imperative that the United States lay down no fewer than two large battleships for some

[10] Morison, *Admiral Sims,* pp. 158–171.
[11] George A. Converse to Roosevelt, October 19, 1906, Roosevelt Papers; Roosevelt to Sims, September 27, October 13, 1906, *Letters,* V, 427, 455.

years to come. It predicted that even with this program the nation's relative position by 1915 would be fourth, behind Great Britain, Germany, and France.[12] But Roosevelt ignored this advice, just as he had ignored it in adopting the one-ship-per-year program in 1905. He was, however, eager that the one ship Congress did authorize in 1907 should be of the most modern, powerful type, and in late October Roosevelt took the first step to secure this program by writing Senator Eugene Hale. If Hale could be won over, doubts in Congress about this expensive, revolutionary battleship could perhaps be overcome.

The President attempted to use recent troubles with Japan to frighten Senator Hale. He warned that Japanese-American tension could lead to a conflict if Japan came to accept the United States rather than Russia as its national enemy. The Japanese, Roosevelt told Hale, "are proud, sensitive, warlike, are flushed with the glory of their recent triumph, and are in my opinion bent upon establishing themselves as the leading power in the Pacific." Though Russia now stood facing Japan, its internal condition was such that "she is no longer in any way a menace to or restraint upon Japan, and probably will not be for a number of years to come." The friction with Japan made it imperative that the United States navy be "in such shape as to make it a risky thing for Japan to go to war with us"; and to be so prepared it needed dreadnought-type battleships.[13]

The senator from Maine was unimpressed with the President's letter. He did not fear war with Japan and was strongly against what he termed "monster ships" or "leviathans." Expressing contempt for the General Board, Hale predicted Congress would hold to a program of one ship

[12] Dewey to Bonaparte, October 2, 1906, General Board No. 420–422, Roosevelt Papers.
[13] Roosevelt to Hale, October 27, 1906, *Letters,* V, 473–475.

per year and that he could get one and possibly two 16,000 ton ships at the forthcoming session. But he could not secure a dreadnought. Moreover, Hale soon informed Roosevelt that when they had agreed on a one-ship-a-year program he had not conceived it would be a dreadnought and that there was "much impatience in Congress over the enormous naval expenditures." [14]

Roosevelt probably did not believe much of what he wrote Hale, for less than two months later he told British Foreign Secretary Sir Edward Grey that Japan realized "that Russia keeps steadily in mind her intention to try another throw with Japan for supremacy in easternmost Asia. . . . If Russia remains a united empire . . . Japan will need to keep herself formidable unless she expects to be overwhelmed in Manchuria." For this reason Japan had continued to prepare for war since the close of its struggle with Russia. It was possible, Roosevelt thought, that Japan had designs upon Germany, the United States, or the Philippines. On the other hand, Japan might only be "bent upon achieving and maintaining a commanding position in the Western Pacific and East Asia." But the President, though he did expect industrial competition, considered these possibilities remote and did not anticipate serious trouble in his time.[15]

Roosevelt's actions confirmed the thoughts expressed in his letter to Grey. In his annual message of December, 1906, he recommended only one dreadnought to Congress, despite the contention of Secretary of the Navy Charles Bonaparte that circumstances had changed greatly since December, 1905.[16] Roosevelt was not willing to fight for two battleships, but he did work vigorously to convince Hale and Representative

[14] Hale to Roosevelt, October 31, December 9, 1906, Roosevelt Papers.
[15] Roosevelt to Grey, December 18, 1906, *Letters*, V, 528–529.
[16] *Works*, XV, 404–405; "Report of Secretary of the Navy Bonaparte, November 28, 1906," *Annual Reports of the Navy Department for the Year 1906* (Washington, D.C., 1907).

George E. Foss of Illinois, chairman of the House Committee on Naval Affairs, of the dreadnought's value. He informed Foss that though he did not want the United States to lead in the race for big ships, it would be "well-nigh criminal for us to fall behind." [17] By the end of January, 1907, Roosevelt thought the House would stand by him, but he anticipated a battle in the Senate and ordered the new Secretary of the Navy, Victor Metcalf, to "fight to the last gasp without any compromise." [18]

If Roosevelt was actually worried about opposition in the Senate, he was perhaps pleased with the brief flurry of war rumors set off by his meeting on January 31 with the California congressional delegation. But the chances are that the President's concern about the achievement of his modest naval program was never very great. Foss and the members of his House committee were receptive to the all-big-gun ship, as they had been in 1906, and in early February they reported a bill recommending one dreadnought. The outcome never seemed to be in doubt, and on February 15 the House rejected by a margin of thirty-two votes the assault of the small-navy bloc led by Theodore E. Burton, Republican of Ohio. The Senate did not even debate the increase of the navy.[19] As Roosevelt had predicted, Hale "often refuses to stand the gaff in a fight." The administration had won its struggle for American dreadnoughts, though the Congress appropriated what would prove to be the smallest amount for the navy in the second term of Theodore Roosevelt.[20]

The tension with Japan created by the San Francisco school order had no greater effect on American strategic

[17] Roosevelt to Foss, December 19, 1906, *Letters*, V, 529.
[18] Roosevelt to Metcalf, January 27, 1907, *Letters*, V, 572.
[19] Foss to Sims, January 26, 1907, Sims Papers; *Congressional Record*, 59th Cong., 2d Sess., pp. 2589, 2603–2605, 2775, 3048–3051, 3059.
[20] Roosevelt to Metcalf, January 27, 1907, *Letters*, V, 572; *The Navy Yearbook* (Washington, D.C., 1908), p. 613.

planning than on the President's naval program. In late October, 1906, Roosevelt requested a comparison of American and Japanese naval strength and asked whether the General Board was studying a plan of operations in the event of war with Japan. The General Board's replies to both questions were reassuring. Japan posed no naval threat and the board had already completed plans for the transfer of the fleet to the Far East if war became imminent.[21] These reassurances gave a misleading impression of the General Board's preparations. It had not seriously studied the possibility of war with Japan, nor was it to do so for many months. The Russo-Japanese War had not changed the board's opinion that the main danger to American security was a German attempt to violate the Monroe Doctrine. For this reason it favored the concentration of the American fleet in the Atlantic and close relations with Great Britain. War in the Philippines was contemplated mainly as the outgrowth of such a German attack on the hemisphere. In late September, 1906, the board actually claimed Germany intended to seize colonial possessions in the Western Hemisphere when its fleet was ready.[22]

Despite the obvious unreality of such a view in the face of the bitter and growing enmity between Germany and Great Britain, the army and navy did not decide to initiate joint studies of a possible war with Japan until January, 1907. These were not undertaken with a sense of urgency, for neither Chief of Staff J. Franklin Bell, Rear Admiral Charles S. Sperry (then attached to the Naval War College), nor Chief of Naval Intelligence Raymond P. Rodgers thought Japan was inclined to fight the United States. Admiral

[21] Office of Naval Intelligence, "Report on relative naval strength of United States and Japan," October 30, 1906, Roosevelt Papers; Dewey to Newberry, October 29, 1906, Roosevelt Papers.
[22] William R. Braisted, *The United States Navy in the Pacific, 1897–1909* (Austin, Tex., 1958), pp. 170–171, 189–190, 199.

Dewey summed up the feelings of these men in voicing his own belief that the friction with Japan would not "reach a critical stage for a long time to come, probably not until trade competition accentuates the situation." [23] Reports from the American naval attaché in Tokyo indicated Japan's preoccupation with postwar problems. Financial difficulties seriously affected the operations of the Japanese navy and would prevent the inauguration of a large naval program.[24]

The studies initiated in early 1907 led the General Board to conclude that, in case of war with Japan, the United States Atlantic fleet should be sent to Asiatic waters via the Suez Canal while American armored cruisers in the Far East should fall back to join the main fleet. This voyage would take about three months, and in the meantime all American forces in the Philippines would concentrate at and try to hold Subig Bay, a fine harbor thirty miles north of Manila Bay. As things stood in early 1907, there was a strong probability Subig Bay and the Philippines would fall, "leaving the United States . . . with no point of support for its fleet, and giving to Japan the prestige of a decided initial success." [25]

The board's concern with the development of a great Far Eastern naval base dated back many years and had only been intensified by the crisis with Japan. In the autumn of 1904 the President had confirmed the board's decision to develop a large naval base at Subig Bay, despite the opposition of many army officers (including Leonard Wood), who argued that the defense of the Philippines should be focused around Manila. Congress had subsequently made small appropriations to that end, but by 1907 the base remained grossly

[23] Braisted, *United States Navy in the Pacific,* p. 199; Dewey to Brownson, January 15, 1907, Dewey Papers.

[24] Braisted, *United States Navy in the Pacific,* p. 194.

[25] Memorandum for the General Board, by Captain Sargent, June 15, 1907, General Board Papers.

inadequate for more than small repairs and was completely undefended from land or sea attack.[26] Three years earlier the General Board had warned that "the consequences of neglect or delay may be nothing less than national disaster" and in March, 1907, it reaffirmed its belief that the ability to hold Subig Bay would be the "only thing that could save us from overwhelming reverses in the early stages of war with . . . [Japan]." In order to begin the defense of this vital outpost, the General Board asked the Secretary of War to agree to allocate the entire $500,000 recently appropriated by Congress for the construction of seacoast batteries in the Philippines to Subig Bay.[27] This meager sum had been appropriated despite the concern expressed in the House over the lack of fortifications in the Philippines, and an attempt to increase it had been easily defeated. The army put up little resistance to the General Board's urgent request, perhaps because the President favored it, and in early May the War Department agreed to the proposal.[28]

In late April the General Board restated its views on the distribution of American naval forces. The entire battle fleet, the board argued, should be stationed in the Atlantic since no European nation had any battleships outside of European waters. This deployment would best protect the United States from an attack by a European power either in the Western Hemisphere or the Philippines. If Japan alone could be considered, the board would have preferred to station

[26] Braisted, *United States Navy in the Pacific*, pp. 175–178; Hagedorn, *Wood*, II, 71. For the Far Eastern naval base problem see William R. Braisted, "The Philippine Naval Base Problem, 1898–1909," *Mississippi Valley Historical Review*, 41 (June, 1954), 21–40; and Seward W. Livermore, "American Naval-Base Policy in the Far East, 1850–1914," *Pacific Historical Review*, 13 (June, 1944), 113–135.

[27] Dewey to Metcalf, March 4, 1907, No. 405, General Board Papers.

[28] *Congressional Record*, 59th Cong., 2d Sess., pp. 908–909, 1171, 1174, 1183; Arthur MacKenzie to Taft, April 3, 1907, NA, RG 94:1301687.

the fleet at Subig Bay, but the threat from Europe was primary and "it would be unwise for us to put all our battle fleet in the Pacific waters." When the United States developed a "two-ocean navy" and full bases in the Philippines and on the Pacific Coast, the fleet could then be divided. But with only a single Pacific Coast naval station adequate for large battleships and with the great Far Eastern bastion mostly a dream, the General Board adhered cautiously to its traditional policy of concentration in the North Atlantic.[29]

While the General Board reconsidered the nation's Pacific strategy, the President received a number of troublesome reports and rumors. In December, 1906, Roosevelt had asked a veteran war correspondent, James Archibald, to make a personal investigation of the defenses on the Pacific Coast and the Hawaiian Islands. In early January Archibald reported both were in a "deplorably defenseless position." Moreover, he had noticed that the recent agitation over oriental immigration had created a "somewhat restless feeling among the people regarding their defenses." While none of the "thinking people" felt any immediate danger of conflict with Japan, they did feel "that they have been left in a dangerously unprotected state" because of the concentration of the American battleship fleet in the Atlantic. Archibald concluded it was "certain that they would welcome any plan which promised an immediate strengthening of their defenses."[30]

Concern about Pacific Coast defenses, partly shared by the War and Navy Departments, was heightened by the disturbing rumors which reached Washington as 1907 progressed. Through reports from American naval attachés in Europe, Washington learned that many Frenchmen, along with the

[29] Dewey to Metcalf, April 25, 1907, No. 420–421, General Board Papers.
[30] James F. J. Archibald to Roosevelt, January 2, 1907, Roosevelt Papers.

German General Staff and the British Admiralty, believed Japan would win a war with the United States.[31] The German Emperor, William II, cornering Ambassador George von Lengerke Meyer as he returned home from Russia via Berlin, urged the fortification of Hawaii and the transfer of the fleet to the Pacific. The Japanese, he warned, had spies everywhere, and the California school question was only an excuse for bringing about a conflict.[32] Another report reaching Washington told of an important Dutchman who was convinced Japan wanted war and had deliberately manufactured an incident out of the San Francisco school order. According to his alarmist view, "through the whole Empire of the Rising Sun . . . the nerves of the little yellow men are being excited with the endless repetition that in America they are being treated like barbarians, like Chinese." From the other side of the world unsettling news came from Leonard Wood, who wrote that Japanese mapping in many areas had helped convince the people of Luzon of a threat to the Philippines.[33]

Secretary of War Taft remained unruffled by such talk. He thought Wood gave too much credence to the anti-Japanese rumors and informed the President that "reports from the army are generally less hopeful of peace in the Philippines than civilian reports." He was convinced, moreover, that within two years Manila and Subig Bay would have "formidable" defenses; he had also given orders to speed the fortification of Pearl Harbor.[34] News from outside

[31] Captain J. C. Fremont to Rodgers, February 5, 1907, NA, RG 38:ONI General Correspondence Case No. 8019; W. L. Howard to Rodgers, March 16, 1907, NA, RG 38:ONI General Correspondence Case No. 8139.

[32] Meyer, Diary, February 3, 1907, quoted in Mark A. De Wolfe Howe, *George von Lengerke Meyer: His Life and Public Service* (New York, 1920), pp. 339-341.

[33] Memorandum, February 20, 1907, apparently from Fremont in Paris, NA, RG 38:ONI General Correspondence Case No. 8019; Wood to Taft, April 13, 1907, NA, RG 350:4865/45.

[34] Taft to Roosevelt, attached to Wood to Taft, April 13, 1907, NA, RG 350:4865/45; and Taft to Roosevelt, March 9, 1907, Taft Papers.

Roosevelt's official circle reinforced Taft's calmness. British Foreign Secretary Grey felt the Japanese had been good allies and was sure they wanted "to pursue a quiet policy for some time to come," while German Ambassador Speck von Sternburg reported the German military attaché in Tokyo was certain Japan had no aggressive intentions for the immediate future.[35] This remained the President's belief. He had written William II early in 1907 that he was "always being told of Japanese or German or English spies inspecting the most unlikely places." There is no evidence that the reports of Japan's hostile intentions disturbed him, for the Gentlemen's Agreement was implemented and the troubles on the Pacific Coast seemed solved.[36]

By late May, 1907, however, the problem of keeping the peace with Japan once more became acute. The damage to Japanese businesses in San Francisco brought renewed tension to Japanese-American relations and worried the President, who doubted his ability to control the San Francisco mobs. On June 7 the cabinet held a long discussion of the Japanese situation, which prompted Secretary of the Interior James R. Garfield to write in his diary that "the general feeling is that war with Japan is inevitable before the Panama Canal is finished — not immediately for the Japanese are not ready." [37] Roosevelt himself was by now deeply concerned over the future of Japanese-American relations, though he had little fear of an immediate conflict. Henry Cabot Lodge, in a better position than most to know his friend's inner thoughts, reassured a nervous William Sturgis Bigelow that the "President does not think that they [the Japanese] have any intention of going to war," and that "the Administration

[35] Grey to Roosevelt, December 4, 1906, and February 12, 1907, Roosevelt Papers; Sternburg to Roosevelt, April 1, 1907, Roosevelt Papers.
[36] Roosevelt to Emperor William II, January 8, 1907, Letters, V, 542.
[37] Roosevelt to Henry White, June 15, 1907, Roosevelt Papers; James R. Garfield, Diary, June 7, 11, 1907, Garfield Papers.

is entirely alive to the entire situation and although it does not apprehend war or any danger of war it will not be caught unready or unprepared." Two days after the cabinet meeting, Roosevelt journeyed to Jamestown to open the exposition there and to watch a naval review. Deeply affected by the latter, he wrote his son Kermit he felt "mighty glad to think of all those battleships, now that there is this friction with Japan." [38]

On June 12 the President, following his usual habit, departed for Oyster Bay. Two days later, however, he surprised the Assistant Secretary of War by asking what plans had been made by the Joint Board in case of trouble arising between the United States and Japan and set in motion a series of important meetings and decisions on United States' defenses in the Pacific. The General Board, gathered in preparation for the Joint Board meeting called by Roosevelt, urged the dispatch of sixteen battleships to the Pacific and the rapid completion of the defense of Subig Bay, along with the creation of advanced naval bases at Pearl Harbor and Guam and the acquisition of a battleship dock at San Francisco. [39] The Joint Board, meeting on June 18, recommended a number of steps to be taken if war between the United States and Japan became imminent. These included the concentration of all land and naval forces in the Philippines at Subig Bay, the withdrawal of armored cruisers in Far Eastern waters, and, most important of all, the dispatch of the battle fleet to the Orient. [40] Carried to the President at Oyster Bay, these recommendations were considered on June 27 by Roosevelt, representatives of the General Board and General

[38] Lodge to Bigelow, June 11, 1907, Lodge Papers; Roosevelt to Kermit Roosevelt, June 13, 1907, *Letters,* V, 688.

[39] General Board Proceedings, June 17, 1907; and Dewey to Metcalf, June 18, 1907, No. 405, General Board Papers.

[40] Dewey to Taft, June 18, 1907, Roosevelt Papers.

Staff, Secretary Metcalf, and, curiously, George von Lengerke Meyer, Roosevelt's new postmaster general.

Roosevelt opened the discussion by saying that, while he did not believe there would be war with Japan, he concurred in the report of the Joint Board. He then decided the Atlantic fleet was to be moved to the Pacific sometime in October, as a "practice cruise" which would have "a strong tendency to maintain peace." Roosevelt and his advisers approved extensive measures for the defense of Subig Bay, though they significantly excluded the concentration of American troops there. All of the defensive preparations now undertaken suggested more of a long-term build-up based upon the assumption that war was not imminent. For example, the President ordered a gradual increase in the army to its authorized strength of 100,000 men, but, despite the promptings of the Joint Board, he refused to man fully Pacific Coast forts or to mine harbors there. Moreover, the army and navy were to conduct all defensive operations as quietly as possible and the War Department cautioned Leonard Wood, the Commanding General of the Philippines Division, that orders were to be carried out so as to avoid giving the impression that the nation was preparing for war.[41] Roosevelt added the only melodramatic touch to the proceedings of his war council by announcing that "if war does come after I am out of the presidency, I have decided just what sort of a regiment I shall raise of rifle men from the Rockies." [42]

The gathering of resources for the defense of a harbor in America's distant possession, the dispatch of a great fleet to the nation's west coast — these dramatic decisions excited

[41] Memorandum for the Chief of Staff, by Lieutenant Colonel W. W. Wotherspoon, June 29, 1907, and Adjutant General F. C. Ainsworth to Wood, July 6, 1907, NA, RG 94:1260092.

[42] Meyer, Diary, June 27, 1907, in Howe, *Meyer*, pp. 362–363.

Roosevelt's passion for the exercise of power. But, despite the boyish glamor with which he surrounded them, the recommendations of the Joint Board and the subsequent decisions were hardly surprises. In fact, the President knew what steps he wanted before the Joint Board convened and carefully laid down the context of its meeting so that his wishes would be met. Apparently he decided upon the most important of these measures, the voyage of the fleet to the Pacific, without consulting his cabinet or intimates such as Henry Cabot Lodge and Elihu Root.[43] Roosevelt may have been so instinctively certain of the response of the American people that he needed no advice.

The President sought a military build-up because of his deep belief that the nation should "not be caught unprepared if a war should come on." [44] However, his reasons for dispatching the battle fleet to the Pacific have been less clear to historians. Most have agreed with Howard K. Beale that Roosevelt's main object was "to impress Japan with our power so that she would not be tempted to make trouble," though a few have instead emphasized Roosevelt's desire to increase domestic support for naval construction. Historians have also mentioned a wide variety of subsidiary motives, such as a desire to impress the world with American naval power, to provide practice for the fleet, and to follow up Root's Latin American tour.[45]

[43] Roosevelt, *An Autobiography*, p. 548.

[44] Meyer, Diary, June 27, 1907, in Howe, *Meyer*, pp. 362–363.

[45] For the origins of the battle fleet's cruise, see Beale, *Theodore Roosevelt*, pp. 328–329; Thomas A. Bailey, "The World Cruise of the American Battleship Fleet, 1907–1909," *Pacific Historical Review*, 1 (December, 1932), 389–423; Braisted, *The United States Navy in the Pacific*, pp. 204–209; Harbaugh, *Power and Responsibility*, p. 300; and Robert A. Hart, *The Great White Fleet: Its Voyage Around the World, 1907–1909* (Boston, 1965), pp. 23–27. Howard K. Beale suggests that one of Roosevelt's motives for dispatching the fleet was "to give the people an object lesson that would win support for speeding up the completion of the Panama Canal." It is doubtful, however, that this was one of the President's reasons. Nei-

Whatever Roosevelt's motives may have been, they cannot be understood apart from the domestic position of his administration in the spring of 1907. The previous December the President had delivered his most radical annual message to date, and widespread fear of a new assault by the administration on the trusts in business circles contributed to a sudden break in the stock market on March 14, 1907. Since the congressional battles of 1906, business criticism of the President had been mounting and would reach a crescendo during the depression of late 1907. Moreover, in Congress conservative reaction to Roosevelt's aggressive assertion of executive power, fed by the Brownsville affair, was gaining momentum. During the second session of the 59th Congress in 1907, anti-Roosevelt feeling centered on the administration's conservation program. Without even a roll call the Senate adopted an amendment by Senator Charles W. Fulton, Republican of Oregon, to the Agricultural Appropriations Bill prohibiting the creation of further forest reserves in many Western states. In a burst of defiance, Roosevelt created twenty-one new reserves just before he signed the amended bill. The President's only important success during this session was the final acceptance by the Senate of a treaty regularizing the 1905 customs receivership with Santo Domingo.[46]

While Republican standpatters still controlled the Congress, on the Pacific Coast there was a rising challenge to

ther at the time nor later did Roosevelt mention the cruise of the fleet in connection with the Panama Canal. Moreover, there is no evidence indicating that he felt the need for increased public support. By late February, 1907, the major administrative difficulties with the canal were over and the army engineers proceeded to construct it rapidly. Beale, *Theodore Roosevelt*, pp. 328–329; Alfred D. Chandler, Jr., "Theodore Roosevelt and the Panama Canal: A Study in Administration," in *Letters*, VI, 1547–1554.

[46] Harbaugh, *Power and Responsibility*, pp. 309–312, 326–329; and Mowry, *Era of Theodore Roosevelt*, pp. 212–220.

conservative Republican dominance. That region by the spring of 1907 was still a Republican stronghold, but at least in one Western state — California — Republican rule rested on shaky foundations. California Democrats were increasing their strength while the Republican organization was being weakened by a growing reform faction. In May, 1907, the creation of the Lincoln-Roosevelt Republican League formalized the Republican split into conservative and progressive groups.[47] Long before this evidence of dissension among California Republicans, Roosevelt had been aware of the value of California and other Pacific Coast states to his party. In 1904 he had brought a California congressman, Victor H. Metcalf, into his cabinet as Secretary of Commerce and Labor, as a recognition of the West Coast's political importance. But certain of his policies had created strong opposition on the Pacific Slope. For example, from 1903 to 1906 the administration's prosecution of Oregon land-swindlers, including every member but one of the all-Republican congressional delegation, had created resentment among Northwest Republicans and made Senator Fulton a bitter foe. The President's conservation program, dedicated to the scientific and centralized development of the public domain, had from the start met with deep ambivalence in the West. During the winter of 1906–1907 important changes in the administration's public lands policy aroused strong Western opposition. The Republican governor of Washington charged that the administration's Chief Forester, Gifford Pinchot, was doing "more to retard the growth and development of the Northwest than any other man." In the summer of 1907 a convention gathered in Denver to protest the new public lands policy.[48]

[47] Mowry, *California Progressives*, pp. 67–72.

[48] Harbaugh, *Power and Responsibility*, pp. 326–330, and Samuel P. Hays, *Conservation and the Gospel of Efficiency: The Progressive Conservation Movement, 1890–1920* (Cambridge, Mass., 1959), pp. 256–257.

The administration's naval policy had also not entirely pleased the Pacific Coast for, despite its consistent support of Roosevelt's naval bills in Congress, this region did not receive a fair share of appropriations or protection. The battle fleet had always been concentrated on the eastern seaboard, where most of the navy's bases existed. In 1907 Mare Island and Bremerton were the only two bases on the Pacific Coast. The rising tension with Japan, coupled with the widespread belief in a future Japanese-American conflict, created uneasiness about the adequacy of Pacific Coast defenses. Representative William E. Humphrey, Republican of Washington, voiced such concerns during the 1907 naval debates.[49] Roosevelt was aware of conditions on the Pacific Coast and had perhaps sought to appease some of his critics by transferring Metcalf in late 1906 to the post he had originally wanted — that of the Secretary of the Navy. But the effects of this small favor had been cancelled by the widespread anger in the West over the President's initial course in the San Francisco school dispute. Roosevelt had quickly backed down and sought an expedient compromise, and the administration's friends, according to the *New York Sun*, were by the spring of 1907 content with the political situation in Washington and Oregon. In California, however, conditions were still unsatisfactory because of the effects of the Japanese question.[50]

Within the general framework of both national and California affairs, then, the cruise of the battle fleet to the Pacific Coast would serve a useful political purpose. It would be a successful and popular voyage, attracting much attention in the press of the nation and the world, thus giving Roosevelt his first widely acclaimed achievement in foreign affairs since

[49] *Los Angeles Times,* December 9, 1906; *Congressional Record,* 59th Cong., 2d Sess., p. 3063.
[50] *New York Sun,* quoted in *New Orleans Picayune,* May 20, 1907, Roosevelt Scrapbooks.

his mediation of the Russo-Japanese War. Moreover, the cruise would attract support from all Republican factions, both conservative and progressive, and California and other Pacific Coast states would appreciate the administration's determination to defend their vital interests. The cruise of the Great White Fleet to Pacific waters again indicated Roosevelt's instinctive sense of the needs of the moment.

The origins of the cruise were also related to the President's plans for the growth of the American navy. He gave no indication of his views on naval expansion after the battle over naval appropriations in 1907 until he informed Andrew Carnegie in early April that the country was no longer enlarging its navy, though the addition of one battleship per year barely enabled it to make good obsolete units. Roosevelt may have actually believed this, but it is more likely he was writing for a specific audience — a peace congress in New York City. Not until June 21 did he write, for the first time in several years, of the importance of keeping the fleet "steadily increasing in size." "If Congress will keep on building up the fleet," Roosevelt reassured Benjamin Ide Wheeler, president of the University of California, "I think I can guarantee you against a bombardment." [51]

No later than June, 1907, then, Roosevelt was determined to seek more than one ship in the next session of Congress. He knew, however, that the opposition would be formidable. In the pursuit of the modest program adopted in February, 1907, he succeeded in overcoming the growing hostility to naval appropriations. But it was not at all certain he would succeed in 1908 and 1909. Congress was restless over large naval expenditures and even Henry Cabot Lodge believed the navy was big enough.[52] In 1906 the appropriation for the single battleship authorized was delayed; in 1907 the ad-

[51] Roosevelt to Carnegie, April 5, 1907, *Letters*, V, 641; Roosevelt to Wheeler, June 21, 1907, *Letters*, V, 693.

[52] *Congressional Record*, 59th Cong., 1st Sess., pp. 7848–7849.

ministration's program won by only thirty-two votes in the House. Roosevelt complained that "in spite of the obvious uncertainty of our relations with Japan . . . I am having great difficulty in getting Congress to go ahead with the navy." [53] Nor would Congress provide adequate fortifications for Hawaii or the Philippines. This recalcitrance came at a time when the United States could not "afford to take any chances" with its navy and when, as Wood put it, "the whole problem of the East turns on sea power." [54]

Roosevelt's sudden decision to renew naval expansion reflected both his sensitivity to world naval developments and his estimate of anti-Japanese agitation in the United States. By the late spring of 1907 an increase in the navy seemed imperative if the nation was to maintain its position as a world power, for portents of an accelerated naval race drifted across the ocean from the capitals of Europe. Germany's refusal to discuss arms limitation at the forthcoming Hague Conference, along with Britain's determination to preserve its existing naval superiority over Germany, made it likely, as Roosevelt realized, that the building of the dreadnought "inaugurated a new race in the matter of size." The United States would have to make considerably larger efforts even to retain its relative naval position.[55] It was, however, the impact of the violence in San Francisco on May 20 and 21 which largely explains Roosevelt's decision to strengthen the navy. This violence came at a time when Roosevelt thought the Japanese-American crisis had largely ended, and indicated not only the vigor and persistence of the anti-Japanese agitation in California, but also the inability of San Francisco

[53] Roosevelt to Wood, December 20, 1906, Roosevelt Papers.
[54] Roosevelt to Foss, December 19, 1906, *Letters*, V, 529; Wood to Albert L. Key, December 14, 1906, Wood Papers.
[55] Jessup, *Root*, II, 70–73; Arthur J. Marder, *From the Dreadnaught to Scapa Flow: The Royal Navy in the Fisher Era, 1904–1919*, I: *The Road to War, 1904–1914* (London, 1961), 130–134; Roosevelt to Grey, February 28, 1907, *Letters*, V, 601.

authorities to control its local manifestations. The prospects for effective government in San Francisco and for any lessening of the anti-Japanese impulse now seemed bleak to the President. Thus the outbreak in San Francisco crystallized Roosevelt's doubts over his ability to control the situation in California and led him to conclude that tension between the two nations might, despite all his efforts, continue far into the future. Because of this conviction the President determined to prepare for future perils by expanding the American navy. Realizing better than anyone else just what difficulties this goal would involve, he shrewdly saw in the cruise of the battle fleet the most effective instrument of navalist propaganda since the Spanish-American War.

Strangely silent about his reasons for sending the fleet to the Pacific Coast in the period preceding the decision, Roosevelt in later years offered profuse explanations of what had become one of the most dramatic events of his second administration. The ultimate triumph of the cruise encouraged the former President to dwell upon it in his autobiography, just as the uncertainty attached to his role in the Brownsville affair led him to exclude it entirely from the same book. The main reason for the cruise given in his autobiography was the effect it would have upon the American people. "It seemed to me evident," Roosevelt wrote in 1913, "that such a voyage would . . . arouse popular interest in and enthusiasm for the navy. . . . My prime purpose was to impress the American people; and this purpose was fully achieved. . . . No single thing in the history of the new United States Navy has done as much to stimulate popular interest and belief in it as the world cruise." [56] In closing the long discussion of the fleet's voyage, Roosevelt referred

[56] Roosevelt, An Autobiography, pp. 548–550. See also Lawrence F. Abbott, Impressions of Theodore Roosevelt (New York, 1919), pp. 109–112; and André Tardieu, Notes sur les États-Unis (Paris, 1908), pp. 129–130.

to an article on the origins of the cruise in the "well-informed" London *Spectator*. Its editor, John St. Loe Strachey, wrote that the President had long contemplated the cruise and wanted a large navy because he considered it a logical consequence of the emergence of the United States as a great power. Roosevelt believed the nation needed a seagoing fleet "which has impressed itself upon the imagination of the American people." The cruise, Strachey predicted, would arouse the attention of the American people, and the "next time Mr. Roosevelt or his representatives appeal to the country for new battleships, they will do so to people whose minds have been influenced one way or another. . . . He has a policy which projects itself far into the future, but it is an entire misreading of it to suppose that it is aimed narrowly and definitely at any single power."

By December, 1907, Strachey elaborated his perceptive conclusions about the domestic origins of the cruise: "The Pacific slope constitutes one of the great divisions of the United States, and their people have recently felt themselves insufficiently protected. They have watched the development of Japan with keen attention. They know that their dislike of Asiatic immigrants constitutes perpetual provocation to Tokio, and they fancy a wave of emotion in Japan which may some day produce an attack, for which their sea-board cities are ill-prepared. The appearance of so splendid a fleet of their own upon their own coast will remove that nervousness." Moreover, Strachey was still convinced that a "powerful consideration" for the cruise was the insufficiency of the present navy to protect both coasts.[57]

[57] *Spectator*, 99 (October 12, 1907), 517, and 99 (December 21, 1907), 1037–1038. The administration's statement that the cruise to the Pacific had long been under consideration by the Navy ("Annual Report of the Secretary of the Navy, November 18, 1907," in *Annual Reports of the Navy Department for the Fiscal Year 1907* (Washington, D.C., 1908) has been generally accepted. See Bailey, *Theodore Roosevelt and the Japanese-*

Ambassador Aoki, whom Roosevelt regarded as a "singu-
larly cool-headed and wise old boy," also thought the motives
for the cruise lay in domestic politics. The cruise would
emphasize the value of the Panama Canal and the necessity
of a larger navy and adequate bases on the Pacific Coast.
With the aid of information supplied by such men as former
Assistant Secretary of State Francis B. Loomis, he concluded
that the main cause was Roosevelt's anxiety to undo the evil
effects of his pro-Japanese annual message in California.
"There is no doubt," Aoki wrote, that Roosevelt "is playing
a dangerous game [by] using the Japan[ese]-American situation to strengthen the hands of his party in the coming
presidential election." [58] Roosevelt probably did calculate
that the cruise would satisfy those critics of his Japanese
policy who claimed his course since October, 1906, had been
an ambiguous and excessively conciliatory one. He had, as
we have seen, judged in early June that public opinion would
not support the use of troops to protect Japanese rights and
felt the "utterances of the extremists in Japan" had begun to
make "an unpleasant feeling" in the United States. The
cruise of the fleet, as Roosevelt well knew, would be regarded by many as a show of strength against Japan and
thus would do much to silence the criticism of the administration's policy.

---

*American Crises* (Stanford, 1934), pp. 211–212; and Braisted, *United States
Navy in the Pacific*, p. 206. Braisted claims, without offering any docu-
mentation, that as far back as 1903 the Naval War College contemplated
sending a united fleet to the Pacific, while Roosevelt had considered
concentrating the fleet in the Pacific in 1906. This writer has found no
evidence that such a cruise was being seriously considered in naval circles
or by the President between January, 1906, and early June, 1907. The
cruise was the result of Roosevelt's rapid decision in June, and the administration's emphasis on its precedents should not be allowed to obscure
this.

[58] Roosevelt to Root, July 13, 1907, *Letters*, V, 718; Aoki to Hayashi,
June 8, 1907, Telegram Series, JA.

Roosevelt in his writings did much to encourage the interpretation of many contemporaries and historians that the cruise was a demonstration aimed at Japan. In a long letter to George Otto Trevelyan on October 1, 1911, he gave the following explanation of his decision:

I had been doing my best to be polite to the Japanese, and had finally become uncomfortably conscious of a very, very slight undertone of veiled truculence in their communications in connection with things that happened on the Pacific Slope; and I finally made up my mind that they thought I was afraid of them. Through an ex-member of the Dutch Cabinet, and, rather curiously, through two of the Austrian secretaries of Embassy—all at or from Tokyo—I found that the Japanese war party firmly believed that they could beat us, and, unlike the Elder Statesmen, thought I also believed this. Then Ian Hamilton . . . wrote me congratulating me upon my efforts to keep the peace, and adjuring me by all means to do so, and not under any circumstances to let America get drawn into war with Japan until industrialism had had time to eat out the Japanese military fiber. On receipt of this letter I definitely came to the conclusion that, if this was the way a friend of ours felt who had ample opportunities of knowing, the Japanese undoubtedly also felt that they were our superiors; and that it was time for a showdown. . . . I felt that, in any event, if the fleet was not able to get to the Pacific in first-class shape, we had better find it out; and if Japan intended to have war it was infinitely better that we should gain two or three months necessary to prepare our fleet to start to the Pacific.[59]

Years later, in 1916, Roosevelt wrote that "the voyage of the battle fleet around the world was really an answer to the very ugly war talk that had begun to spring up in Japan," and in 1918 he referred to "calling down" Japan as he had done with Germany during the Venezuelan crisis of 1902–1903. His story seemed to grow bigger as the years passed

[59] Roosevelt to Trevelyan, October 1, 1911, *Letters*, VII, 393–394.

and the political context of the decision faded from his memory.[60]

Most of the communications referred to in Roosevelt's letter to Trevelyan can still be found, and some are in their right chronological location during the months immediately preceding the President's order of June 14 convening the Joint Board. However, little evidence, aside from Roosevelt's recollections, suggests the President was deeply disturbed by the attitude of the Japanese government or by the agitation of Japanese jingoes in the early part of June, 1907. The Japanese government, as he well understood, had as much difficulty controlling journalistic sensationalism as he did, and Japan throughout the negotiations leading to the Gentlemen's Agreement had shown a conciliatory disposition and an eagerness to settle things as quietly as possible. The effects of the Gentlemen's Agreement were not noticeable by June, 1907, but it was too early to judge the agreement's performance, and Roosevelt did not become worried about the continuing immigration until later in the summer.

Roosevelt's recollections, in short, confuse what he felt several months later with his feelings at the time the decision to send the fleet to the Pacific was made. As the summer progressed, he was much more deeply impressed with the anti-American sentiment in Japan and with the estimates of American naval weakness prevalent in Europe, and he began to view the cruise as a display of American power which would preserve the peace by convincing especially the Japanese jingoes of the nation's strength and invincibility. But these were ex post facto reasons, and while they confirmed the President in his determination to dispatch the fleet, they had nothing to do with the initial decision.

Both at the time and later, Roosevelt justified the cruise

[60] Roosevelt to Hugo Münsterberg, February 8, 1916, and to Rudyard Kipling, November 30, 1918, *Letters,* VIII, 1018, 1408.

on the basis of the invaluable practice it would give the navy. In fact, this was always the official explanation offered by administration spokesmen.[61] The increase of naval efficiency was a legitimate supplementary reason, but it hardly explained why the fleet had to be sent to the Pacific rather than to European waters. The idea of a practice cruise allowed the administration to avoid giving a more truthful and more embarrassing explanation. Throughout the summer the administration carefully shielded its actual purposes, made its military preparations as quietly as possible, and went out of its way to reassure the Japanese government that the cruise was not intended as a threat.

The President knew his people were "insular, or parochial" and did not fully realize the interrelationship of nations in the modern world. To lead effectively in foreign affairs he needed to "get the facts vividly before them," and his Caribbean policy had demonstrated the great need for caution if public opinion was to be with him. "Our prime necessity," he wrote late in his presidency, "is that public opinion should be properly educated," and it was principally to effect this education that the battle fleet set sail in December, 1907.[62] The President from the start intended to bring the fleet back to the Atlantic Coast without a long stay in the Pacific, for he did not expect war with Japan. The decision to send the fleet around the world was shaped by a combination of short-term political aims and long-term naval planning. The impact on the public would aid Roosevelt and his party in the months ahead, and would at the same time allow Roosevelt to leave a more substantial naval heritage to his successor.

[61] "Annual Report of the Secretary of the Navy, November 18, 1907," in *Annual Reports of the Navy Department for the Fiscal Year 1907* (Washington, D.C., 1908).

[62] Roosevelt to Henry White, November 27, 1907, *Letters*, V, 858–859; Roosevelt to Sir Harry H. Johnston, December 4, 1908, quoted in Beale, *Theodore Roosevelt*, p. 455; Roosevelt to William Bayard Hale, December 3, 1908, *Letters*, VI, 1408.

As a grand gesture aimed at Americans and the world, the cruise would be remembered after much else about Roosevelt's presidency had been forgotten.

News of the Joint Board's recommendation to concentrate the Atlantic fleet in the Pacific began to spread in late June, and on July 2 the press confidently announced the administration's plan. This official leak, probably designed to test public opinion, was at first denied by the administration, but then confirmed by Secretary of the Navy Metcalf, who on July 4 revealed plans for the transfer of the fleet and promised the people of Oakland and San Francisco they would "see one of the finest naval spectacles ever witnessed in Pacific waters." It was, according to the Secretary of the Navy, to be a practice cruise with no strategic significance.[63] Metcalf's announcement was reinforced by a statement issued by the President's private secretary, William Loeb. The administration, Loeb claimed, had no intention of sending the fleet at once to the Pacific, and the long practice cruise which it had been planning for several years might take the fleet to some other destination. At any rate, after a few months the fleet would be brought back to the Atlantic Coast; the cruise was simply a matter of routine naval drill. The Chief of the Bureau of Navigation, Willard Brownson, expanded the official statement by explaining the importance of demonstrating to the world how quickly the United States could transfer its fighting strength from one ocean to another.[64]

These numerous official explanations of the purpose of the cruise further stimulated the intense speculation among the American press. The *New York Herald* was convinced that the new policy, shaped by weighty strategic reasons, was a

[63] *New York Herald,* July 2, 1907, Roosevelt Scrapbooks; *New York Times,* July 5, 1907.
[64] *Boston Herald,* July 5, 1907, *New York Times,* July 8, 1907.

response to the rise of Japan as a first-class power in the Far East and to the need to strengthen American influence there. The *Herald* found no desire within the administration to menace Japan and looked for more battleships at the next session of Congress. The Washington correspondents of both the *New York Times* and the *Boston Herald* thought the true cause lay in the expectation of trouble with Japan, while *The Navy*, already in the midst of its campaign for naval reform, was unable to choose among the bewildering variety of possible motives. Whatever the reason, *The Navy* protested that "our Atlantic battle fleet is no more fit to make an early appearance in battle trim on the waters of the Pacific than was the ill-fated fleet commanded by Rojestvensky." It dismissed the whole project as a "humiliating mess." And Senator Hale recorded his disbelief that the President would actually send the fleet.[65]

The eastern press was divided over the wisdom of sending the fleet to the Pacific. The conservative *New York Sun* labeled the plan as "insane" and the *New York World* became convinced Roosevelt was craftily planning the whole enterprise to secure renomination and re-election in 1908.[66] Aside from the violent opposition of such anti-administration journals, there was no general outcry, as Thomas A. Bailey has suggested, against leaving the Atlantic Coast undefended or against the tremendous cost of the voyage. Most of the papers opposed to the cruise, such as the *New York Evening Post*, emphasized the danger of further inciting public opinion in the United States and Japan, while those for the transfer either discounted war feeling or argued that because of

[65] *New York Herald*, July 2, 1907, Roosevelt Scrapbooks; *New York Times*, July 5, 1907 *Boston Herald*, July 2, 1907; *The Navy*, 1 (July, 1907), 11–12; 1 (September, 907), 11; 1 (October, 1907), 8; *New York Herald*, July 12, 1907, Roosevelt Scrapbooks.

[66] Tupper and McReynolds, *Japan in American Public Opinion*, pp. 41–42; *Literary Digest*, 35 (September 7, 1907), 313–314.

its existence the presence of the fleet would be reassuring to the American people and serve as a check upon war talk in Japan.[67] Outside the East editorial opinion was heavily in favor of the President's project. The *Baltimore Sun* thought the proposal was a declaration of the intention of the United States to defend American interests in the Pacific at any cost, and the *Chicago Inter-Ocean* predicted "the appearance in the Pacific of an American fleet . . . will temper Japanese pushfulness" and the belief it would be safe to attack the United States.[68] The Pacific Coast was greatly pleased, and some of its papers were already advocating the retention of the fleet there. Both the governors of Washington and Oregon applauded the transfer, as did Benjamin Ide Wheeler, president of the University of California. And the influential voice of Speaker Cannon joined the general approval of the President's bold act.[69] With careful management and good luck Roosevelt would be able to turn the already favorable public sentiment into a chorus of praise.

Those close to the administration shared the widespread enthusiasm over the proposed cruise of the battle fleet to the Pacific. John C. O'Laughlin, Washington correspondent of the *Chicago Tribune,* thought the Japanese were beginning to believe Americans feared them and Representative William P. Hepburn of Iowa, recently returned from Honolulu, was glad to know of the voyage to the Pacific. Henry Cabot Lodge also endorsed Roosevelt's decision.[70] The Presi-

[67] Bailey, *Theodore Roosevelt and the Japanese-American Crises,* 226–227; *Literary Digest,* 35 (July 13, 1907), 40–41.

[68] *Baltimore Sun,* July 3, 1907, Roosevelt Scrapbooks; *Literary Digest,* 35 (September 7, 1907), 313–314.

[69] *Collier's,* 39 (August 3, 1907), 15; Roosevelt later recalled—inaccurately—that popular feeling was "nearly a unit" against him at first. Roosevelt to Taft, March 3, 1909, *Letters,* VI, 1543.

[70] O'Laughlin to Roosevelt, July 7, 1907, Roosevelt Papers; Fred W. Carpenter to Taft, July 9, 1907, Taft Papers; Lodge to Roosevelt, July 13, 1907, Roosevelt Papers.

dent did not, however, take either Lodge or the Secretary of State fully into his confidence. To Lodge he explained the necessity of experimenting with such a transfer for the first time during peace and cryptically added that "before matters become more strained we had better make it evident that when it comes to visiting our own coasts on the Pacific or Atlantic and assembling the fleet in our own waters, we cannot submit to any outside protests or interference. Curiously enough, the Japs have seen this more quickly than our own people." And Roosevelt now expressed his intention of sending the battle fleet around the world. Writing to Root a few days later, he gave the same two reasons, adding that a successful voyage would have a "pacific effect." [71]

The reaction of the Japanese press to the unexpected news from Washington was strangely calm. Ambassador Wright thought it was "artificial, and that the movement of a large naval force to the Pacific just at this time . . . would tend to have an unfavorable effect upon the mind of the average Japanese." There was, as Wright suggested, a strained implausibility to the rather sparse comments of the Japanese press. Papers such as the *Asahi Shimbun, Mainichi Dempo,* and *Jiji Shimpo* generally either recognized the necessity of the United States to maneuver its naval forces together or admitted the administration's need to make its Pacific naval force commensurate with the nation's interests in that ocean.[72] Some papers hoped Japan would have a chance to welcome the armada, and the only criticism was a gentle questioning of the timeliness of the movement. Even the *Hochi Shimbun,* formerly one of the leading anti-American journals, followed the rest of the press in refusing to view the cruise as an attempt to chastize Japan, and Count Okuma

[71] Roosevelt to Lodge, July 10, 1907, and to Root, July 13, 1907, *Letters,* V, 709–710, 717–718.
[72] Wright to Root, July 10, 1907, NA, RG 59:1797/298; Beale, *Theodore Roosevelt,* pp. 543–544.

interpreted the proposed cruise as "a feature of America's newly espoused imperial policy, and as a part of her program sketched without any reference whatever to San Francisco."

The only sensational reaction in the Japanese press was from Rear Admiral Hajime Sakamoto, the chief of the Hydrographic Bureau of the Navy Department, who was reported as saying that, while it was not clear whether the United States meant to intimidate or challenge Japan, he doubted American naval officers and crews would be patriotic enough to fight if war did break out.[73] Sakamoto's interview, though exaggerated and quickly withdrawn by the *Hochi Shimbun*, was apparently an expression of the widespread contempt for American naval personnel held in Japanese naval circles.[74] But with this exception, the Japanese response made it difficult for Roosevelt's American critics to contend that his rash act had excited jingo feeling in Japan.

[73] *Japan Weekly Mail*, July 13, 1907; *Hochi Shimbun*, July 8, 1907, NA, RG 59:1797/308.
[74] Wright to Root, July 26, 1907, NA, RG 59:1797/314.

# V

# A SUMMER OF UNCERTAINTIES

As war rumors raged in June and the American military and naval bureaucracy strained to prepare the nation's feeble Philippine defenses, the State Department pondered the Japanese-American immigration problem. From the start the State Department had regarded the Gentlemen's Agreement of February, 1907, as a temporary arrangement, designed to reduce immigration, restore Japanese-American friendship, and prepare the way for a more permanent solution. Soon after its conclusion, Secretary of State Root sought to reopen negotiations for a treaty of reciprocal exclusion, but found Japan unwilling to proceed. Root did not press the Japanese government, for both he and the President were prepared to await the results of the Gentlemen's Agreement before insisting upon treaty negotiations. And both realized the American position was badly weakened by the outbreak of violence against Japanese residents in San Francisco in late May, 1907.

With the settlement of this new incident and the resumption of the normal rhythm of diplomacy, the administration once more cautiously considered a treaty of reciprocal exclusion. In the early spring of 1907 Third Assistant Secretary of State F. M. Huntington Wilson had talked with Henry W. Denison during the latter's visit to the United States. At that time Denison feared American relations with Japan might go from bad to worse if something was not done, and thought that either of two draft treaties prepared by Huntington Wilson could be negotiated. One of these treaties traded reciprocal exclusion for naturalization; the other traded it for political concessions in Korea. Both treaties had been previously discussed within the State Department, and in early June Huntington Wilson reminded the Secretary of State that either might be concluded. Apparently Root encouraged him to explore the position of the Japanese government, for on June 18 he wrote Denison asking how the recent events in San Francisco and the opposition in Tokyo had changed his views. The United States would like, Huntington Wilson said, to instruct Thomas J. O'Brien to go ahead with the treaty negotiations shortly after his arrival in September to replace Ambassador Luke Wright.[1]

While the State Department was awaiting Denison's reply, immigration continued to complicate Japanese-American relations. Weekly reports on Japanese arrivals indicated an increase over the previous year for every month since the Gentlemen's Agreement had gone into effect, and subsequent figures during the summer were to confirm the small impact of the accord. Both Huntington Wilson and Secretary of Commerce and Labor Oscar S. Straus advocated measures to reduce the illegal flow of Japanese over the Canadian and especially the Mexican borders, but curiously neither Roosevelt nor Root made moves in this direction until late August.[2]

Part of the administration's inaction was due to its hesitancy to tighten immigration restrictions unilaterally during a period of increasing tension with Japan, but perhaps more important was the vacuum of leadership in Washington.

[1] Huntington Wilson to Root, June 6, 1907, NA, RG 59:2542/105–108; Huntington Wilson to Denison, June 18, 1907, NA, RG 59:2542/428A.

[2] Straus to Root, June 11, 1907, NA, RG 59:2542/103–104; Huntington Wilson to Root, June 11, 1907, NA, RG 59:2542/109.

Roosevelt, busy at Oyster Bay, was not closely enough in touch with the complex problem of effective restriction to make the necessary decisions. Root was at Clinton and Muldoon's sanatorium in White Plains, New York, depressed by his brother's final illness and weakened physically from overwork. Throughout the summer, even Roosevelt found it difficult to consult with him over urgent matters.[3] The only important State Department officials left in Washington were F. M. Huntington Wilson and Alvey A. Adee, who could do no more than call various problems to the attention of the absent President and Secretary of State.

What attention Roosevelt and Root did give to Japanese-American relations was focused on more immediate issues, particularly the war rumors, military and naval preparations, and the refusal of the San Francisco Board of Police Commissioners on June 27 to grant licenses to certain Japanese businesses. The board, appointed by Schmitz, finally had been forced by protests of the Japanese consul to decide on the applications, and gave as its only reason for denying them the desire to grant licenses exclusively to American citizens. As the President realized, "a new San Francisco fool has cropped up to add to our difficulties with the Japanese." "The San Francisco mob bids fair," he wrote Cecil Spring Rice, "if not to embroil us with Japan, at any rate to arouse in Japan a feeling of rankling anger toward us that may at any time bear evil results; and the Japanese Jingoes are in their turn about as bad as ours." Roosevelt immediately ordered Attorney General Charles Bonaparte to investigate the matter, but he was not at all sure what the outcome would be.[4]

Ambassador Aoki, however, did not await the results of

[3] Jessup, *Root*, I, 505–506; Roosevelt to Lodge, August 23, 1907, Roosevelt Papers.
[4] Roosevelt to Root, July 2, 1907, *Letters*, V, 699–700; Roosevelt to Spring Rice, July 1, 1907, *Letters*, V, 699.

Bonaparte's investigation and on July 5 brought the new incident to Huntington Wilson's attention. Aoki also complained of the insulting articles in the San Francisco *Chronicle* and *Call*. The Third Assistant Secretary of State felt the general tone of the complaint was one of "sorrow and helplessness" and was convinced Aoki took a "broad and sentimental" view because he realized the United States was technically correct and that the board's order did not violate the treaty of 1894.[5]

The day after Aoki's visit, Huntington Wilson set down his own thoughts on Japanese-American relations. The Japanese press and publicists, he complained, were encouraging their public to believe that the regulation of laborers and of local petty trades was an indignity motivated by racial prejudice and a violation of the treaty of 1894. In ignoring United States treaty rights and the nonracial origins of the anti-Japanese agitation, the Japanese press was building up "dreams in the public mind," as it had done before the Treaty of Portsmouth. And the government now as then was unwilling to stop this for fear of placing itself at a diplomatic disadvantage. "The basis of the agitation," Huntington Wilson explained, was "purely economic" and the rioting against Japanese businesses was "incidental to the riotous conditions generally prevailing." Conditions on the Pacific Coast should clear up with a good government in San Francisco and with the diminution of Japanese immigration. Unfortunately the latter had been increasing since the Gentlemen's Agreement and thus the restriction of Japanese laborers and petty tradesmen had become more urgent than ever before.[6]

Huntington Wilson's memorandum was only one of a num-

[5] Memorandum No. 3 by Huntington Wilson, July 6, 1907, NA, RG 59:1797/385–386.

[6] Memorandum No. 2 by Huntington Wilson, July 6, 1907, NA, RG 59:1797/285–286.

ber of conflicting estimates of Japan's policy and intentions which plagued the President throughout the summer of 1907. In early July Taft forwarded a report by Major Samuel Reber of the General Staff, who had been ordered to Japan to observe conditions there. Reber found no preparations for war with the United States or hostility toward Americans, and he thought Japan's desperate need for commercial and economic prosperity would prevent it from seeking war. Reber's report confirmed Taft's views, and Roosevelt also found it persuasive.[7] But others were less certain. Representative Hepburn and John Callan O'Laughlin were suspicious of Japan; sources as diverse as the Russian military attaché in Tokyo and the Brazilian Foreign Minister viewed war between the two nations as likely.[8] And an authoritative description of Japanese opinion from Kentaro Kaneko did little to relieve the ominous flow of war speculations into Washington. "San Francisco affairs and their outcome," this Japanese friend of America wrote, "are now threatening to put the United States and Japan into a very unfortunate position." In the face of bellicose statements and rumors from the United States, the Japanese people had remained patient and reserved, but there was a limit to human patience and Kaneko feared "the Japanese will lose their temper." This, rather than war, would bring a sharp decline in America's oriental trade. The impressionable Taft now thought all Kaneko said was true and that he represented "the exact view of most Japanese."[9]

Warnings of the rising temper of the Japanese people worried the President, while the continuing diplomatic com-

[7] Reber's report, dated May 23, 1907, is in Taft to Roosevelt, July 2, 1907, Roosevelt Papers; Roosevelt to Taft, July 4, 1907, *Letters,* V, 705.

[8] Carpenter to Taft, July 9, 1907, Taft Papers; O'Laughlin to Roosevelt, July 7, 1907, Roosevelt Papers.

[9] Kaneko to George H. Lyman, April 19, 1907, in Lyman to Taft, July 6, 1907, Taft Papers; Taft to Lyman, July 9, 1907, Taft Papers.

plaints of the Japanese government, coupled with its refusal to reduce immigration, irritated him. In private he was becoming more hostile to Japan, but he was careful, as was the administration in general, to shield his feelings from the public and from Japanese diplomats. Upon the arrival of Admiral Gombei Yamamoto (a former naval minister and elder statesman) to the United States, Roosevelt took the unusual step of inviting Yamamoto and Aoki to lunch at Oyster Bay. During this luncheon, on July 12, Roosevelt emphasized the necessity of keeping Japanese laborers out of the United States. Aoki accepted the President's lecture quietly, but Yamamoto insisted that Japanese immigrants must be treated exactly as European immigrants, while Roosevelt "kept explaining to him that what we had to do was to face facts . . . that Japanese laborers must be excluded from the U[nited] S[tates] on economic grounds." [10] Apparently unable to convince Yamamoto, the President drew Aoki aside and spoke of his fear that the situation in San Francisco might become worse before it became better and told of the presence of army troops in the vicinity in case of an emergency. He also discussed at length the danger of mixing American and Japanese laborers and hoped Japan would not regard the cruise of the battle fleet as a hostile demonstration. In fact, the President suggested he and Aoki keep in touch to prevent any misunderstanding arising over the movements of the fleet.[11]

As he reassured Japan of his peaceful intentions, Roosevelt's thoughts turned to the probability of war and the means to prevent it. He was impatient with peace advocates and indifferent to the proceedings of the Second Hague Conference. "Keeping the peace with Japan" was "the instant need of things" and was made more difficult by the nation's

[10] Roosevelt to Root, July 13, 1907, *Letters,* V, 718.
[11] Aoki to Hayashi, July 17, 1907, Telegram Series, JA.

"lack of the power to look afar." [12] Though Roosevelt had faith the American people would respond in a crisis, he knew they must prepare in advance if disaster was to be averted. Because of his opposition to the fleet's cruise and to naval preparedness, Senator Hale became the prime example of the "hideous cowardice and stupidity of many of our people, which match the hideous sensationalism and offensiveness of many of the yellow press." [13] While hindering an adequate defense, Hale did nothing to rebuke those who continually insulted the Japanese, and along with others of his type gave the Japanese the impression the United States was afraid of them. The senator was a "conscienceless voluptuary," "astute" and "unscrupulous," a "physical coward" with an "utter lack of patriotism," and a "shriveled soul" — in short, a man no argument could reach.[14]

By the middle of July the President did "not believe we shall have war," though he thought Japan had about as many "prize jingo fools" as the United States. He was "more concerned over this Japanese question in all its bearings than over any other, including that of the trusts," particularly because the immigration of Japanese for May and June showed an increase over March and April and over May and June of 1906.[15] If the Gentlemen's Agreement did not begin to function properly, Roosevelt predicted "very dangerous agitation in Congress next year for their [Japanese] total exclusion by . . . law." Roosevelt seemed perplexed by the failure of Japan to end the unsettling immigration and by the motives of its statesmen in general. Aoki was "cool-headed and wise

[12] Roosevelt to Root, July 2, 1907, *Letters*, V, 699–700; Roosevelt to Carnegie, July 15, 1907, Roosevelt Papers.

[13] Roosevelt to Sternburg, July 16, 1907, *Letters*, V, 720–721; Roosevelt to Root, July 13, 1907, *Letters*, V, 717.

[14] Roosevelt to Bonaparte, July 13, 1907, *Letters*, V, 716.

[15] Roosevelt to Lodge, July 10, 1907, *Letters*, V, 710; Roosevelt to Acting Secretary of Commerce and Labor Lawrence O. Murray, July 13, 1907, *Letters*, V, 719.

. . . much more so than his fellow countrymen," and Roosevelt wrote Sternburg that "this whole Japanese business is very puzzling; I suppose because there are such deep racial differences that it is very hard for any of us of European descent to understand them or be understood by them." He saw no reason for war, nor did he believe it would come; yet the situation concerned him, "for the Japanese are a formidable military power and have unknown possibilities both as regards their power and as regards their motives and purposes." The President wanted his country to show the Japanese "every consideration and courtesy," but at the same time felt it must be made evident he was not "in the slightest degree influenced by fear of them." [16]

As July progressed, Roosevelt's efforts to maintain a balanced attitude were made more difficult by a continuing stream of alarmist reports. Chief of Staff Bell, impressed by the alleged bellicose remarks of a Japanese diplomat in St. Petersburg, thought they were representative of the feelings of that nation. "The exceptional degree of activity," Bell warned, "in seeking military information about the Pacific Coast and the Philippine Islands convinces me that the Japanese consider that there is greater possibility of trouble with us than with other nations." The President responded calmly to Bell's nervous letter and predicted existing difficulties would be surmounted, but within a few days other letters confirmed the Chief of Staff's views and weakened Roosevelt's confidence in a peaceful solution.[17] Charles Denby, American Consul General at Shanghai, was visiting Germany and had written Root that a "phase" of popular opinion in France and especially in Germany believed "Japan has defi-

---

[16] Roosevelt to Root, July 13, 1907, *Letters,* V, 718; Roosevelt to Sternburg, July 16, 1907, *Letters,* V, 720–721.

[17] Confidential Report, dated St. Petersburg, June 11, 1907, Roosevelt Papers; Bell to Roosevelt, July 18, 1907, Roosevelt Papers; Roosevelt to Bell, July 23, 1907, Roosevelt Papers.

nitely decided on war with the United States within the next few years." Moreover, military circles in Germany and Great Britain estimated Japan's chances of victory as five to four. Denby thought this information should be taken seriously because of the great vulnerability of the United States, the undecided issues of the Pacific and the unsettled state of popular opinion in Japan. Another letter from Ambassador Tower corroborated Denby's report and added that the highest government officials in Great Britain and Germany thought the Japanese-American dispute really involved "the great question of the control of the Pacific Ocean," which Japan was determined to dominate. They suspected the school question was only a ruse, used by Japan to create tension which would lead to a boycott and then to war. Military and naval observers judged Japan was only waiting for a favorable moment to open hostilities.[18]

Secretary of State Root treated both Denby's and Tower's letters with utter seriousness and told Roosevelt "we must certainly look to the basis of that [5:4] estimate & see that it is not justified." In fact, Root suggested the transmittal of Denby's letter to Governor Gillett in order to bring about its publication, which he thought might have a good effect.[19] The scheme initially appealed to Roosevelt and Taft but was fortunately never carried out. The continued troubles with Japan had made Roosevelt more careful than previously in inciting war rumors, and for this same reason he later rejected a War Department plan to transfer mortars from Narragansett Bay to Manila Bay.[20]

Denby's letter, Roosevelt informed Root, had revealed nothing he did not already know, but the effect of these alarming and authoritative communications clearly deep-

[18] Denby to Root, July 2, 1907, NA, RG 59:1797/347; Tower to Root, July 10, 1907, NA, RG 59:1797/348–349.
[19] Root to Roosevelt, July 21, 1907, Roosevelt Papers.
[20] Roosevelt to Root, July 23, 31, 1907, *Letters*, V, 725, 738.

ened the President's concern over Japanese-American relations. He now judged, "the only thing that will prevent war
is the Japanese feeling that we shall not be beaten, and this
feeling we can only excite by keeping and making our navy
efficient in the highest degree. It was evidently high time
that we should get our whole battle fleet on a practice voyage
to the Pacific." Moreover, he was prepared to warn the San
Franciscans of the effect of their policy of "insult and injury"
and was inclined to put such a warning in his message to
Congress, where it would bolster his appeal to strengthen
the army and navy.[21] The President thought foreign observers were in error about a Japanese attack on the United
States, for Japan had no reason for war unless it wanted
Hawaii, the Philippines, or Alaska. However, he realized
"these irritating articles in the newspapers and irritating actions may arouse a bitter feeling in Japan which will make
the Japanese people feel hostile to us and predispose them
to war should the occasion arise." Since their heads seemed
"to be swollen to a marvelous degree," Roosevelt judged
there was "enough uncertainty to make it evident that we
should be very much on our guard and should be ready for
anything that comes." And he was anxious to make the Japanese realize he was not afraid of them and "that the United
States will no more submit to bullying than it will bully."[22]

After the peak of the war scare had passed, Root remarked
that he believed Roosevelt at one time during the summer
"really considered a Japanese attack imminent or liable."[23]
The Secretary of State, however, was ill and depressed
throughout the summer and was not in a position to sense
accurately the President's shifting thoughts. Root himself had
not anticipated an immediate attack because of Japan's finan-

[21] Roosevelt to Root, July 23, 1907, Letters, V, 725.
[22] Roosevelt to Root, July 26, 1907, Letters, V, 729–730; Roosevelt to
Henry White, July 30, 1907, Roosevelt Papers.
[23] Meyer, Diary, September 22, 1907, in Howe, Meyer, pp. 370–371.

cial condition and its fear of appearing "barbaric" in the eyes of western civilization. "On the whole I am convinced," Root wrote Roosevelt, "that our European friends are over excited. I think the tendency is towards war — not now but in a few years. But much can be done to check or divert the tendency." [24]

Root had stated the central concern of the Roosevelt administration — how to avoid drifting into war with Japan. The President and his advisers sensed the momentum of events was carrying the two nations toward war but doubted their ability to control the powerful forces of public opinion which were primarily shaping those events. Understandably, then, the future seemed full of uncertainty; the outlook could be changed only if the most dangerous irritant — Japanese immigration to the Pacific Coast — was stopped. But by early August, 1907, no solution was in sight. The Gentlemen's Agreement was functioning poorly, and the immigration negotiations remained deadlocked. A letter from Henry W. Denison, received in late July, revealed that the Japanese government continued to insist upon naturalization as the single quid pro quo for a treaty of reciprocal exclusion. Huntington Wilson thought Denison's reply came directly from the Saionji cabinet (as in fact it did) and reflected the cabinet's "deference to present Japanese public sentiment and the exigencies of domestic politics." He did not believe the United States "should consider that we have yet received a reply made after a large view of the whole question and representing a final adverse attitude on the part of the Elder Statesmen and the ruling political powers of Japan."

But Huntington Wilson had no suggestions to offer about possible treaty negotiations. Japan had moved so quickly to absorb Korea that little was left to concede there; and if Japan continued to reject American proposals while the

[24] Root to Roosevelt, August 8, 1907, Roosevelt Papers.

administration remained unable to concede naturalization, economic coercion might be necessary. Within a few years a new treaty would have to be negotiated with Japan, and Huntington Wilson supposed the present situation could continue as long as the Californians caused no new incidents. It was unfortunate, however, that the Japanese refused to help "clear the atmosphere" by agreeing to a treaty.[25]

Instead the Japanese government throughout July had been preparing a diplomatic note on the action of the Board of Police Commissioners. It regarded the matter as more serious than the violence of late May, for Hayashi feared the board would eventually refuse licenses to all Japanese businessmen. In mid-July he instructed Aoki to express deep regret over the board's violation of Japan's treaty rights and to request that the federal government promptly intervene. The reports spread by irresponsible American journalists, in addition to the recent incidents in San Francisco, justified the belief "that not only the populace but also the authorities of San Francisco are under the domination of the anti-Japanese labor unions." Japan could "not too strongly urge" the United States government to bring pressure to bear on the San Francisco authorities. Tokyo's attitude, like Washington's, was slowly hardening.[26]

This note, if delivered, would have shaken Washington out of its summer lethargy. But Aoki insisted the federal government had no recourse other than legal action, and that the only solution was a judicial one. Before turning to diplomacy, he advised, the Japanese government should await the outcome of a suit initiated by Japanese residents in the federal courts.[27] Aoki defended the American government's inaction despite the State Department's failure to inform him

[25] Huntington Wilson to Root, July 21, 1907, Root Papers.

[26] Hayashi to Sato, July 3, 1907, to Aoki, July 13, 1907, Telegram Series, JA.

[27] Aoki to Hayashi, July 20, 1907, Telegram Series, JA.

of the investigation in progress or of its results. Huntington Wilson, who was in Washington and might have kept Japan informed, apparently saw no need to do so since he did not regard the ruling of the board as a violation of Japan's treaty rights. Roosevelt twice suggested to Root that the federal government should institute a test suit, but apparently received no reply from his ailing Secretary of State.[28]

On July 31 Aoki presented a watered-down version of Hayashi's sharp note in a *pro memoria* which merely claimed the ruling was a violation of Japan's treaty rights and expressed a hope that the federal government would maintain them. Both Second Assistant Secretary Alvey A. Adee and Huntington Wilson disagreed with the Japanese interpretation of the treaty. The latter reasoned that since the decision of the board did not discriminate against Japanese and since the federal government could not intervene, the only solution was judicial.[29] Whatever plausibility Huntington Wilson's contentions had was destroyed in early August by a statement of the United States District Attorney Robert T. Devlin that the board had intended to deprive the Japanese and not other nationalities of their business licenses. State Department officials were now hard put to see how Japan's protest could be answered, and the President was eager to go over the matter with Root before a reply was made.[30] Root probably discussed the incident with Roosevelt at Oyster Bay in mid-August, and they apparently decided immediate action was not necessary.

As August progressed the President remained uncertain

[28] Roosevelt to Root, July 26, 31, 1907, *Letters*, V, 729, 738.
[29] Adee to Root, July 31, 1907, enclosing *pro memoria* received from Aoki on July 31, 1907, NA, RG 59:1797/323; draft *Aide Mémoire* by Huntington Wilson, August 5, 1907, NA, RG 59:1797/323.
[30] Devlin to Attorney General, August 7, 1907, in Acting Attorney General Russell to Root, August 7, 1907, and Bacon to Root, August 7, 1907, both in NA, RG 59:1797/311; Roosevelt to Root, August 2, 1907, Roosevelt Papers.

of what course to follow in the immigration negotiations. The best hope of breaking the deadlock lay in the utilization of Taft's forthcoming trip to the Philippines for the opening of the General Assembly as a means of sounding out Japanese leaders. But Roosevelt doubted whether Taft ought even to stop in Japan and sought Root's advice on the subject.[31] Prior to a meeting on August 13 which finally determined Taft's itinerary, Roosevelt had a long talk with Sternburg.[32] The German ambassador saw no immediate danger of war with Japan as long as Roosevelt could control the situation in California; he viewed Japanese expansion as a future rather than a present threat. But only a combination of Christian powers could prevent Japan's eventual domination of China and the Pacific. Sternburg's opinions did not surprise Roosevelt, for they were similar to those expressed in a report from the German military attaché in Tokyo, which the German ambassador had passed on to the President in late July. Then Roosevelt had remarked that Japan's ultimate purpose was "to exercise dominion in Eastern Asia" and had concluded that Japan did not desire immediate war with the United States.[33] Now he ignored the ambassador's speculations and, passing to more military subjects, spoke of the lack of a Far Eastern naval base and the danger of the fleet's defeat if it had no harbor to return to for repairs after an engagement in those waters. Moreover, Roosevelt felt the initial thrust of a Japanese invasion of the West Coast would crush the American army. Though he had faith in an ultimate American victory, he admitted his failure to create a thoroughly trained, adequate army. And he recalled Sternburg's

---

[31] Roosevelt to Root, July 29, 1907, Roosevelt Papers.

[32] The only account is in Sternburg to Bülow, September 9, 1907, in Johannes Lepsius, Albrecht M. Bartholdy, and Friederich Thimme (eds.), *Die grosse Politik der europäischen Kabinett, 1871–1914* (40 vols.; Berlin, 1922–1927), XXV (1), 72–74.

[33] Sternburg to Roosevelt, July 29, 1907, Roosevelt Papers; Roosevelt to Sternburg, August 3, 1907, Roosevelt Papers.

words at the close of the Spanish-American War: "Even the best racehorse will surely fail in a big race for the want of thorough training."

Having satisfied his penchant for dramatic speculation, the President conferred with Root, Taft, and Meyer on August 13 at Oyster Bay.[34] A thorough canvas of the Japanese situation revealed Root's displeasure with the prolonged negotiations with Japan over the killing of seal-poachers in the Pribilof Islands. Hayashi was pressing for a full investigation of the circumstances of the killing instead of taking the steps which Root considered necessary to prevent a repetition of the incident, and the prospect of a satisfactory settlement seemed remote.[35] Root also believed Japan had made some arrangement with Colombia for a base in case of war with the United States. Rumors of an understanding had first reached the State Department in late July, and Root showed little caution in accepting such unsubstantiated tales.[36] At any rate, he felt that from now on the administration should show a courteous but firm attitude toward Japan or it would misunderstand and think the United States was afraid of its power. The council decided to send Taft to Japan, where he would undertake conversations on the immigration problem only if the Japanese wanted them. Otherwise, his visit would be a mere courtesy call. Taft was to return via the Trans-Siberian Railway and convey to the German Emperor the President's personal gratitude for an offer to furnish the

[34] Meyer, Diary, August 13, 1907, in Howe, *Meyer,* pp. 365–366, gives a summary of the meeting.

[35] The course of the fur seal controversy can be followed in NA, RG 59: cases 290 and 13097.

[36] The rumor was inspired by President Rafael Reyes, who hoped to frighten the United States into a favorable settlement of the Panama dispute. During the winter of 1907–1908 Reyes may have sought an alliance; if so, Japan was not interested. On May 26, 1908, Japan and Colombia signed the Takahira–Cortes Treaty, which merely established diplomatic relations. Not until late in 1908 did reports from Colombia prove the falsity of the rumor. The episode can be followed in NA, RG 59: case 7804.

United States with a base of supplies in case of war with Japan. Finally, Roosevelt congratulated himself upon the decision of last June, for the announcement of the cruise to the Pacific had stopped the war talk.

Since the end of July, Roosevelt's attention had turned increasingly to preparations for the great cruise. Wright's doubts about the effect it would have on Japan, along with Hale's continued public opposition, intensified Roosevelt's determination to watch the fleet leave Hampton Roads in early December. On August 1 Loeb publicly reaffirmed the administration's plan to dispatch the fleet, and Roosevelt insisted privately to Assistant Secretary of the Navy Truman H. Newberry that every possible battleship and armored cruiser must join the battle fleet.[37] Three possible routes existed: the first from Hampton Roads to San Francisco via the Straits of Magellan, with the fleet returning the same way; the second via the Straits of Magellan, with the fleet returning through the Suez Canal; and the third from Hampton Roads through Suez, with the fleet returning via the Straits of Magellan. Roosevelt favored the second route, though he was willing to accept the third if Rear Admiral Willard H. Brownson, chief of the Bureau of Navigation, and Admiral Robley D. Evans, commander-in-chief of the Atlantic fleet, urged it.[38] Brownson opposed sending the fleet around the world after it reached San Francisco, for he thought it would gain little additional experience by such a voyage. Evans, however, refused to take the fleet through the straits during the winter and in effect this meant it would have to proceed from San Francisco back to the Atlantic via Suez.[39]

[37] *New York Times*, August 2, 1907; Roosevelt to Newberry, August 6, 1907, *Letters*, V, 743–744.
[38] Newberry to Roosevelt, August 1, 1907, Roosevelt Papers; Roosevelt to Newberry, August 10, 1907, *Letters*, V, 745.
[39] Brownson to Roosevelt, August 17, 1907, Evans to Brownson, August 17, 1907, Roosevelt Papers.

Brownson concurred in Evans' estimate and only the formal decision remained to be made at a conference called by Roosevelt at Oyster Bay on August 23. Meeting with the President, Newberry, Brownson, and Evans confirmed the Straits of Magellan–Suez Canal route, though publicly the administration claimed it had not decided upon the return route of the fleet.[40] The admirals' reluctance to have newspaper men along was overridden by the President, who argued the cruise was "a striking thing" in which the people would be greatly interested. With the final route decided, preparations began in earnest, the commander-in-chief warning that it would "be a very unfortunate thing" if the fleet failed to start in early December.[41]

While plans for the cruise matured, efforts to prepare defenses for Subig Bay and the Philippines proceeded with painful slowness. By late June not a single gun defended Subig Bay, nor would any for several months to come.[42] Bell, Wood, and other army officers disliked the decision to concentrate all forces there in case of war, and Wood thought it would be a "death trap" for American forces defending it. Moreover, Wood deplored the lack of intelligent cooperation among the different staff departments in Washington and the absence of definite information there. No topographical maps of the terrain around Subig Bay existed, and the torpedo company which arrived in late August came without any explosives. "I believe, without exception," Wood confided in his diary, "conditions are worse now than before the Spanish-American War." And a year later he was still able to write Roosevelt that "we are not ready," for the army

[40] Brownson to Roosevelt, August 19, 1907, Roosevelt Papers; *New York Times*, August 24, September 5, 1907.
[41] Roosevelt to Newberry, August 10, 17, 1907, *Letters*, V, 745, 759.
[42] Braisted, *United States Navy in the Pacific*, p. 202; Rear Admiral J. N. Hemphill to Metcalf, June 21, 1907, NA, RG 45: area ten file. See also Louis Morton, "Preparations for the Defense of the Philippines During the War Scare of 1907," *Military Affairs*, 13 (Summer 1949), 95–104.

lacked artillery, vigorous officers and many other supplies.[43] In the autumn of 1907 Wood was so disturbed by the lack of preparedness in the Philippines and by the continuing war rumors there that he urged W. Cameron Forbes "to join him in getting hold of the Secretary [Taft] and telling him some plain truths as to conditions here." Whatever Wood's worries, Taft displayed no sign of nervousness over the state of America's readiness for war. His main concern seemed to be formulating plans to get adequate fortifications for Manila and Hawaii from the next Congress, and he was willing to wager that Manila would be fortified "long before we have a Japanese war." [44]

The uncertainties of the summer made an increase in the country's naval program, and thus the cruise of the fleet, more imperative than ever. Roosevelt had written off any attempt to cooperate with Hale and no longer sought to avoid an open rupture over the naval program. But fearing that Hale and others would make a fight in the Senate over the voyage, the President began to build a basis of support among Western senators and congressmen.[45] Roosevelt's chief ally was Jonathan Bourne, Jr., a progressive Republican elected to the Senate from Oregon in 1906 and an enthusiastic advocate of the cruise. Bourne was confident the "movement will be an increasingly popular one" and that the Pacific Coast and Rocky Mountain senators would be united in their support. Moreover, he predicted it would only be a "matter of time when we will have trouble with Japan, unless we anticipate same by practical demonstrations of our superiority in event of war." The voyage would increase the efficiency of the

[43] Bell to Roosevelt, July 18, 1907, Roosevelt Papers; Wood, Diary, September 5, 1907, and Wood to Roosevelt, August 6, 1908, both quoted in Hagedorn, *Wood*, II, 81, 86–87.

[44] Journal of W. Cameron Forbes, July 21, 1907, Forbes Papers; Taft to Roosevelt, July 26, 1907, Roosevelt Papers.

[45] Roosevelt to Root, July 31, 1907, *Letters*, V, 738; Roosevelt to Bourne, August 13, 1907, Roosevelt Papers.

navy, strengthen the Monroe Doctrine, elevate the status of
the United States among nations, increase the nation's trade
and "be of direct benefit in aerating our national blood and
stimulating our patriotism." [46]

Lawrence Abbott, son of Lyman Abbott and president of
the *Outlook,* joined Bourne in predicting the cruise would
be a popular one, and Roosevelt himself cast aside his own
doubts. "My impression," he wrote Lodge, "is that the people
as a whole have been extremely well pleased at my sending
the fleet to the Pacific, for a good many different reasons. I
need hardly say to alter the decision now would be ruin-
ous." [47] The cruise, in Roosevelt's view, was "good from every
standpoint," and it was only by experiencing the difficulties
involved in the transfer "that we shall be able to force the
creatures of the Hale type into providing what the navy
actually needs." Aside from the domestic advantages, the
mere statement that the fleet was going to the Pacific had
been useful "in preventing clamor for hostilities against us
by the Japanese yellow press." [48]

By late August rumors were current that the administration might ask for as many as four battleships when Congress
convened.[49] Roosevelt did not reveal what number he intended to seek, but the summer's tension had obviously
strengthened his determination of the late spring to increase
again the American navy. And the troubles with Japan had
also sharpened Roosevelt's realization of the difficulties of
America's position in the Far East. The American people, he
wrote, were clearly not prepared to assume a continuous and
active responsibility for the Philippines. The islands had been

[46] Bourne to Roosevelt, August 9, 17, 25, 1907, Roosevelt Papers.
[47] Lawrence Abbott to Roosevelt, September 20, 1907, Roosevelt Papers;
Roosevelt to Lodge, September 2, 1907, *Letters,* V, 779.
[48] Roosevelt to Taft, August 21, 1907, *Letters,* V, 762; Roosevelt to Albert
Shaw, September 3, 1907, Roosevelt Papers.
[49] *New York Times,* August 27, 1907.

taken in the heat of war, and it was now difficult to awaken public interest in their proper defense. If attacked, the nation would defend them vigorously but to no avail, and the resulting defeat would create "such utter disgust that at the first opportunity the islands would be cut adrift or handed over to anyone." Roosevelt, of course, did not approve of the people's attitude but realized it had to be faced. And "just as in connection with the Californians and Japanese, while I partly altered my own convictions on the subject, I partly simply had to recognize that the convictions of the great mass of our people on the Pacific Slope were unalterable," so now he must re-evaluate his attitude toward the Philippines. In a letter to Taft which marked the depth of his despair over the nation's preparedness, he wrote:

> I think we shall have to be prepared for giving the islands independence of a more or less complete type much sooner than I think advisable from their own standpoint, or than I would think advisable if this country were prepared to look ahead fifty years and to build the navy and erect the fortifications which in my judgment it should. The Philippines form our heel of Achilles. They are all that makes the present situation with Japan dangerous. . . . You should state to them that if they handle themselves wisely in their legislative assembly we shall at the earliest possible moment give them a nearly complete independence. . . . My point is that we must very seriously consider both domestic and foreign conditions as regards the retention of the islands. To have Hale at the head of the naval committee . . . while the possession of the Philippines renders us vulnerable in Asia for lack of a great fleet is a veritable national calamity. To keep the islands without treating them generously and at the same time without adequately fortifying them and without building up a navy second only to that of Great Britain, would be disastrous in the extreme. Yet there is danger of just this being done. . . . I do not believe our people will permanently accept the Philippines simply as an unremunerative and indeed expensive duty. I think that to have some pretty clear avowal of our

intention not to permanently keep them and to give them independence would remove a temptation from Japan's way and would render our task at home easier.[50]

Taft opposed any public declaration on the future of the Philippines until he returned with his report, nor was he as discouraged as the President about their fortification. He thought the chances of Congress voting considerable funds were good because of the large budgetary surplus and the Japanese scare.[51] With hasty action delayed by Taft's caution, Roosevelt's mood passed as relations with Japan eased in the following months. But the vivid accuracy of his prophecy remained.

Roosevelt undoubtedly understood the difficulty of achieving a two-ocean navy during his presidency and realized the maintenance of the United States navy in second place would be an arduous task. But he was not a man to step aside when faced with a challenge, and he planned to do what he could to leave a strong naval legacy to his successor. Just as he would fight for an advanced program of reform legislation without any chance of getting it, so with more hope would he fight for an enlarged navy. "I do want to leave certain things to my successor," he wrote in September, "in such shape that the work I have done won't be undone. . . . I want to put the navy on such a basis that it cannot be shaken from it." [52]

The cruise of the battle fleet, as Roosevelt had intended from the start, would lay the basis of popular support for his augmented naval program. This was badly needed, since he expected to have an "awful time" with the next Congress.[53] But the purpose of the voyage, originally domestic, had

[50] Roosevelt to Taft, August 21, 1907, *Letters,* V, 761–762.
[51] Taft to Roosevelt, August 31, 1907, Roosevelt Papers.
[52] Roosevelt to Anna Cabot Mills Lodge, September 20, 1907, *Letters,* V, 801.
[53] *Ibid.*

gradually broadened during the tense summer as Roosevelt's confidence in his ability to keep the peace weakened and as his suspicion of the Japanese government grew. If Japan had any intention of precipitating war, Roosevelt believed only American naval preparedness could prevent hostilities, and thus he came to see the cruise as a means of impressing the Japanese government and jingoes with the strength and efficiency of the American navy.[54] And at the same time, he hoped the major European powers would be forced to revise their low estimate of America's ability to defend its Far Eastern interests. A brilliant symbol of America's naval potency, the voyage of the battle fleet would delay or prevent a dangerous encounter in the far Pacific until the nation's defenses were complete.

[54] Roosevelt to Melville Stone, July 26, 1907, *Letters*, V, 728.

# VI

## TAFT AND AOKI

As August, 1907, drew to a close, the President turned with renewed energy to problems with Japan. Throughout most of the summer he had seemed indecisive as relations between the two nations deteriorated. In fact, Roosevelt's own view of Japan had grown more somber as he observed the activities of Japanese jingoes and tried to fathom the intentions of the Saionji cabinet. Nevertheless, he still wanted to restore amity between the two nations, and late in the month he sought a breakthrough in the immigration negotiations by instructing William Howard Taft, during his stay in Tokyo, to concede naturalization in return for a treaty of reciprocal exclusion.[1] Since the autumn of 1906 Roosevelt had refused to make this concession because of an unwillingness to offend West Coast Republicans and a belief that Japan would settle for less. Now he suddenly reversed his position. Apparently he felt something had to be done to solve the immigration problem and that the political repercussions of naturalization would be worth sustaining if a treaty of reciprocal exclusion brought an end to Japanese immigration. He must also have been impressed with the tenacity of the Japanese government and convinced of the need to treat it more generously. Without a cessation of Japanese immigra-

[1] Taft to E. A. Hayes, September 11, 1907, Taft Papers.

tion, Roosevelt predicted an effort would be made in the forthcoming Congress to pass Asiatic exclusion legislation and that "the temper of the country about such legislation will be wholly different from a year ago." [2] Thus Taft's trip assumed considerable importance. If the administration's chief diplomatic messenger could not clear the path for a settlement, then some of Roosevelt's gloomy summer thoughts about the future of Japanese-American relations might prove correct. As Taft, without exaggeration, wrote his brother, "I shall leave here at a quarter past seven to begin a fateful political trip around the world." [3]

No doubt the thought of Taft's mission to Japan buoyed the President. The Secretary of War was a trusted and experienced adviser who had performed many important diplomatic tasks in the past. Taft's impression of the situation in Japan would be worth far more to Roosevelt than the reports of former Ambassador Wright or of the new ambassador, Thomas J. O'Brien. As if anticipating a favorable outcome, Roosevelt drafted the Japanese portion of his forthcoming annual message in which he praised Japan nearly as lavishly as in December, 1906.[4] The President soon discovered, however, that two advisers on Far Eastern policy, F. M. Huntington Wilson and Luke Wright, did not like what they read. "In general," the Third Assistant Secretary of State wrote Roosevelt, "all Japanese excepting those of the broadest and best type, are already too 'cocky,'" and he disapproved of further flattery. The whole trouble with Japan was "one of 'face' . . . [and] as a matter of 'face' the thing they now most desire is naturalization, for they regard the lack of the right as an insinuation of inferiority." Huntington Wilson could see no prospect of a formal settlement in the next few

[2] Roosevelt to Root, September 26, 1907, *Letters*, V, 808–809.
[3] Taft to Charles Taft, August 18, 1907, Taft Papers.
[4] Memorandum for speech, no date, Roosevelt Papers.

years because of the exigencies of Japanese politics.[5] Advice against praising the Japanese also came from Luke Wright, who feared some Americans might feel the President was encouraging their "cocky feeling" and was apologizing for the position he had taken on immigration restriction.[6]

Apparently the objections of Huntington Wilson and Wright made some impression on the President, for the proposed draft never became a part of his annual message. But he did not succumb to Huntington Wilson's pessimism, for Taft's journey to Japan as well as several other events encouraged his belief that a friendly settlement could be reached. One of these events occurred on September 8 in Vancouver, British Columbia, where smoldering discontent against increased Japanese immigration erupted in a dangerous anti-oriental riot. Coming only a few days after demonstrations against Hindu laborers at Bellingham, Washington, the Vancouver riots dramatically emphasized the common immigration problem of the whole Pacific Coast. Henry Cabot Lodge was quick to see the connection between American and Canadian immigration difficulties, as was the President, who thought the Vancouver incident would "do good" by bringing "sharply home to the British public" the similar attitudes held all along the Pacific Coast. He also believed Japan would be easier to deal with now that it faced the same feeling in the British Empire as in the United States.[7] Elihu Root, back in Washington with renewed health, found the "fix" of the British press "amusing" and sensed in a conversation with Aoki a different atmosphere which indicated that "the strain is off." [8] The State Department did not con-

[5] Huntington Wilson, *Memoirs*, pp. 162–163; and memorandum by Huntington Wilson for the President, September 1, 1907, NA, RG 59:1797/387.
[6] Wright to Roosevelt, September 25, 1907, Roosevelt Papers.
[7] Lodge to Roosevelt, September 10, 1907, Roosevelt Papers; Roosevelt to Lodge, September 11, 1907, *Letters*, V, 790.
[8] Root to Roosevelt, September 25, 1907, quoted in Jessup, *Root*, II, 24–25.

ceal its more optimistic view of the immigration negotiations with Japan, while some American journalists thought the ground was swept out from under Japan's position.[9]

The President and State Department were also encouraged by the situation in San Francisco, which was improving under the reform administration of Mayor Edward Taylor. In late September Root finally intervened in the employment bureau controversy and ordered District Attorney Devlin to urge the Board of Police Commissioners to grant the licenses.[10] At the same time he reassured Aoki that the federal government was using all its influence to settle the problem. Root's concern, along with the encouraging remarks of Taylor and the new board to Consul Matsubara, persuaded the Japanese government to await patiently a reversal of the order. Not until December, 1907, was its patience rewarded.[11]

The easing of tension with Japan felt by the administration was not apparent throughout the country. By September a national debate over America's Philippine policy, precipitated by the summer's war rumors, reached a crescendo. The *New York Herald* urged the sale of the islands and found in a nationwide poll of congressional opinion that most Democrats agreed. Many Republicans also preferred relinquishing the burden of the Philippines if only a face-saving method could be found.[12] Most Pacific Coast Republicans, however, spoke out strongly in favor of the administration's Philippine policy, as did Admiral George Dewey. "Every one concedes," the hero of Manila Bay argued, "that the Orient is the future great field for the principal commercial

[9] *New York Times,* September 11, 1907; *Collier's,* 40 (September 28, 1907), 23.

[10] Root to Bonaparte, September 23, 1907, NA, RG 59:1797/325a.

[11] Aoki to Hayashi, September 27, 1907, Telegram Series, JA; Matsubara to Hayashi, September 16, 19, 27, 1907, Telegram Series, JA.

[12] *New York Herald,* September 8, 1907, Roosevelt Scrapbooks.

nations of the world." Without control of the Philippines, the United States could not expect to gain its share of the East's commerce.[13] Neither Dewey's appeal nor the appeals of other imperialists aroused much enthusiasm across the nation. The President correctly sensed that by the autumn of 1907 Republican policy toward the Philippines, begun with such high hopes of imperial glory in 1898, was politically more of a handicap than an advantage.

Some opponents of the administration were also trying to turn the cruise of the battle fleet into a political liability for the President. The *New York World* and *New York Sun* both claimed Roosevelt hoped to gain personal political benefits from the voyage, and the *Sun* went so far as to suggest that he planned to force war upon Japan in order to gain re-election.[14] This implausible theory made little headway against the growing tendency to interpret the fleet's transfer as a demonstration aimed at Japan. The *Atlanta Georgian* thought the cruise had already changed the war spirit in Japan, and the *Washington Herald* reported that military and naval circles in Washington strongly believed the transfer of the fleet was the result of anti-American agitation in Japan. The *New York Times'* Washington correspondent was convinced that the "hectoring," "pinpricking" diplomatic tactics of Japan first suggested the cruise, which had already brought a noticeable change in Japan's attitude.[15] Even supporters of the administration were finding it hard to sustain the official interpretation of the battle fleet's voyage. The *Outlook* now thought the main purpose was to reveal naval weaknesses and needs to the public, while the *World's*

[13] *Brooklyn Eagle,* September 22, 1907, Roosevelt Scrapbooks.
[14] *Literary Digest,* 35 (September 7, 1907), 313–314, and *Chicago Record Herald,* October 18, 1907, Roosevelt Scrapbooks.
[15] *Atlanta Georgian,* September 18, 1907, Roosevelt Scrapbooks; *Washington Herald,* October 25, 1907, Roosevelt Scrapbooks; *New York Times,* September 21 and 27, 1907.

*Work* argued the cruise would remind the American people of important interests in the Pacific.[16]

The swirl of speculation and controversy over the transfer of the battle fleet seemed only to make the President more determined to carry out his bold plan. Amid rumors that the administration planned to break away from its static naval program, the *New York Times* authoritatively announced that the fleet would circle the globe.[17] During a trip down the Mississippi River in late September and early October Roosevelt delighted big-navy men in Washington by departing from several prepared speeches to emphasize the importance of a "great fighting Navy." Secretary Metcalf went further than the President in suggesting that Congress might be asked to authorize four battleships in the coming session. And while Roosevelt restated his determination to dispatch the fleet and hinted at large naval increases, he corrected the widespread impression on the Pacific Coast that the fleet would spend some time there. The fleet would stay, the President said, only if Congress failed to appropriate enough money to bring it back to the Atlantic.[18]

In the midst of such speculation, Taft arrived in Yokohama on September 28, accompanied by Thomas J. O'Brien, the new American ambassador to Japan. The warm reception by the Japanese press and government officials pleased the Secretary of War, particularly because "there was an evident desire on the part of the Japanese government" to avoid war.[19] Taft responded with a frank speech at Tokyo, praising Japan's policy in Korea and denouncing a war between the two nations as "a crime against modern civilization." Taft

---

[16] *Outlook,* 87 (September 28, 1907), 140; *World's Work,* 14 (October, 1907), 9392.

[17] Roosevelt to Shaw, September 3, 1907, Roosevelt Papers; *New York Times,* September 5 and 27, 1907.

[18] *New York Times,* October 2–4 and 25, 1907.

[19] Taft to Charles Taft, Mischler's Diaries, October 10, 1907, Taft Papers.

admitted that "for a moment . . . a little cloud came over the sunshine of the fast friendship of fifty years," but it had passed quickly and he was confident the San Francisco affair could be settled by diplomacy. The *New York Times* reported that the speech had a buoyant effect on the Japanese business community, and all sections of the Tokyo press enthusiastically applauded Taft's friendly utterances.[20] In the United States, too, Taft's speech received widespread editorial praise. The *Literary Digest* labeled him America's "Secretary of Peace," and the Republican *New York Evening Mail* remarked that Taft had "sat upon the irresponsible purveyors of war talk so hard that it will be a long time before they recover their breath." [21]

By far the most important aspects of Taft's visit were the conferences he held with Japanese government leaders. Foreign Minister Hayashi displayed no reticence in opening discussions on the stalemated immigration negotiations. He explained to Taft that the Japanese people would be satisfied with the complete restriction of immigration by treaty only if it was applied equally to all countries. Popular interest had been aroused, Hayashi said, because the emigration companies had succeeded in exploiting "patriotic self conceit" through the use of their political influences. Reciprocal exclusion was fair only on its face; and while Japan would welcome naturalization as a friendly concession, it was not acceptable as a quid pro quo. It was impossible, Hayashi thought, "in the temper of the Japanese people," to consent to a treaty of reciprocal exclusion; the only way to deal with the excessive immigration was administratively through the Japanese Foreign Office. Japan would be "most discreet" in issuing passports, and Hayashi felt the Foreign Office could

[20] *New York Times,* October 2, 1907; *Japan Weekly Mail,* October 5, 1907.
[21] *Literary Digest,* 35 (October 12, 1907), 516.

reduce immigration sufficiently to prevent further trouble. Hayashi agreed with Taft's impression that Japan seemed willing to restrict immigration so long as it did not involve open treaty concessions. Japan's idea, Taft thought, was to maintain the status quo until the situation became less acute. Then a formal solution might be found.[22]

In more general talks with Prime Minister Saionji, Taft explained the determination of the United States to retain the Philippines and fulfill its obligation to them. He also reminded Saionji of Katsura's statement of Japan's attitude toward the Philippines given in July, 1905. Saionji knew of the conversation and reaffirmed the opinion expressed by Katsura at that time. As Hayashi had said several days before, Japan would become concerned with the Philippines only if the United States sold them to a third power. Though Japan would be conciliatory in its negotiations with the United States, Saionji informed Taft, "he wished to have it clearly understood that Japan could not possibly agree to any arrangement that would require of her any concession incompatible with her dignity as a nation in an absolutely equal footing with other powers." [23]

The position of the Japanese government deeply impressed Roosevelt's diplomatic agent. "I am convinced," he telegraphed the President, "that we cannot secure a treaty such as you and I would like to have but that we can obtain practically the same exclusion by administrative measures." Japan did not want war with the United States, because of its financial condition and its involvement in Korea and China. In China, Taft thought, Japan was "determined to secure predominance . . . and to obtain every commercial

[22] Taft to Roosevelt, dictated October 4, apparently sent October 18, 1907, NA, RG 59:1797/383; O'Brien agreed with Taft's estimate of Japan's position. O'Brien to Root, October 3, 1907, NA, RG 59:2542/147.

[23] Memorandum by Taft of conversation with Saionji, October 1, 1907, Mischler's Diaries, Taft Papers.

concession possible." Taft accepted Hayashi's estimate that the Japanese people would bitterly resent concessions in the immigration dispute which suggested the Japanese were not the equal of other races. Such concessions would destroy the present cabinet. Moreover, Taft felt the "popular voice is now so strong in Japan that the government could with difficulty resist pressure of war by the people" if Congress passed exclusion legislation. He had reassured Hayashi that radical action was unlikely, though agitation on the Pacific Coast was strong.[24] Taft and O'Brien both concluded that the United States could secure its purpose through administrative action without a treaty. After many months of deadlocked negotiations, Taft's mission to Japan pointed the way toward a peaceful settlement of the immigration imbroglio.

From Tokyo Taft journeyed to Shanghai, where he was received by Chinese merchants and officials with an enthusiasm sharply in contrast to his reception in the summer of 1905. Taft found American businessmen there suspicious of the intentions of Japan and Russia and anxious over the willingness of the United States to maintain the Open Door.[25] He also found Thomas F. Millard, Far Eastern correspondent of the *New York Herald* and a bitter critic of Japan's China policy, eager for the United States to adopt a hard line in Asia. Millard informed Taft that businessmen in China "firmly believe that Japan and Russia intend to retain Manchuria," and he urged the Secretary of War to declare America's determination to protect its interests in China.[26] Apparently influenced by Millard, Taft did just that in a speech before the American Association of Shanghai on October 8. Speaking as a private citizen, Taft stated that the government would listen to any complaints about injuries to

---

[24] Taft to Roosevelt, October 18, 1907, NA, RG 59:1797/383.
[25] Taft to Roosevelt, October 10, 1907, Roosevelt Papers.
[26] Vevier, *United States and China,* pp. 58–59.

America's China trade and would respond to political obstacles placed before its expansion. Taft's remarks encouraged American businessmen in the Far East and convinced one American journal, the *Overland Monthly*, that his visit marked a new era of American prosperity in that region.[27] The experiences at Shanghai strengthened Taft's conviction that the Chinese were more friendly to the United States than ever before, because of their fear of Japan and Russia and their knowledge that the United States did not want territory or exclusive privileges. "There seems to be a general impression," he warned Root, "that Japan is determined to secure some undue privileges in China. . . . It is quite possible that you will have to assert with considerable stiffness the determination of America to insist on the Open Door policy and not to allow it to be set aside by underhanded methods." [28]

Events in Washington suggested that Roosevelt did not take the Secretary of War's concern over the Open Door seriously. On October 24, 1907, or shortly before, Ambassador Aoki sounded the President on the possibility of concluding an agreement with the United States and received a favorable response. For some time Aoki had been concerned over the growing feeling in the United States that diplomatic tension existed between America and Japan. Not only in the United States but in Europe, he thought, "a general belief has begun to prevail that the two nations are drifting rapidly to inevitable conflict." One manifestation of this feeling was the widespread interpretation that the cruise of the battle fleet was a demonstration meant for Japan; another was the popular feeling that Japan was "pushing herself forward in disregard of the interest . . . of others"

[27] *New York Times,* October 9, 1907; *Overland Monthly,* 51 (January, 1908), 34–41.
[28] Taft to Roosevelt, October 10, 1907, Roosevelt Papers; Taft to Root, October 10, 1907, Mischler's Diaries, Taft Papers.

and that she needed to be reminded of the power of the United States. Aoki hoped his proposed agreement would quiet the "ill-temper" of the American public and allow a continuation of the status quo in immigration matters. The danger of exclusion legislation would be removed and the Pacific cruise would lose all of its "demonstrative character." Japan could then invite the fleet to visit its own shores and turn its reception into a "cordial celebration of [an] entente cordiale." [29]

Aoki approached the President through John C. O'Laughlin, the Washington correspondent of the *Chicago Tribune*, who was as enthusiastic as the Japanese ambassador about the proposed agreement. He predicted it would remove apprehension of Japan's designs upon the nation's Far Eastern possessions, justify Roosevelt's decision to send the fleet to the Pacific, and generally ease the international situation. And by ending speculation in Japan over the battle fleet's cruise, it would improve the prospect of negotiating a satisfactory immigration treaty when the treaty of 1894 expired in 1911. "You know better than I," Roosevelt's friend confided, "the importance of keeping Japan quiescent until the Panama Canal shall have been completed. Then we will be in a position, provided your successor carries out your admirable naval policy, to do what we please, irrespective of Japan." [30]

Roosevelt thought the agreement was an "excellent idea" and invited Aoki to lunch on October 25 to discuss its details. They quickly concluded that the Japanese-American understanding should begin with a preamble declaring each power's friendly intentions and include the following clauses: (1) one which would deny either nation's intention of seeking exclusive control of the Pacific by declaring that ocean to be an "international highway of commerce"; (2) a second,

[29] Aoki to Hayashi, October 27, November 6, 1907, Telegram Series, JA.
[30] O'Laughlin to Roosevelt, October 25, 1907, Roosevelt Papers.

pledging each nation "to respect [the] territorial rights of the other and to maintain the existing order of things on the Pacific"; and (3) a final clause affirming the "principles of territorial integrity and Open Door in China." Roosevelt also urged that the names of Hawaii, the Philippines, and Formosa be written into the agreement. Aoki, however, was reluctant to become so specific. Neither suggested the immigration question be included. With the final phase of the immigration negotiations just beginning, it clearly would have been unwise to mention that delicate subject. However, Roosevelt warned Aoki that if Japanese immigration did not diminish, Congress might act; and he hoped Japan would conclude some understanding through an exchange of notes before the meeting of Congress in December. Aoki was eager for Japan to do so, for, as he warned the President, should Congress pass exclusion legislation both governments would face a situation "incomparably graver" than the present one.[31]

The result of Aoki's labors came as an unpleasant surprise to the Tokyo Foreign Office. Hayashi was annoyed that Aoki, by proceeding on such an important matter without authorization, had placed Japan in an embarrassing position. All the members of the Saionji ministry disapproved of any agreement at this time. And two powerful figures outside the government, Hirobumi Ito and Taro Katsura, believed that such a declaration would be useless as long as the immigration question, the main obstacle to Japanese-American friendship, remained unsolved.[32] Thus Hayashi informed Roosevelt that, while Japan accepted the substance of the proposed declaration, the government feared that by leaving the immigration question untouched the agreement "would provoke

[31] Aoki to Hayashi, October 27 and 28, 1907, Telegram Series, JA.
[32] A. M. Pooley (ed.), *The Secret Memoirs of Count Tadasu Hayashi* (New York and London, 1915), pp. 243–244.

popular disappointment, instead of inspiring confidence."
And the Japanese government was convinced that an attempt
"at a definitive adjustment of the immigration problem will
be not only futile, but extremely inadvisable and even
dangerous in view of the undue importance which appears
to be placed by the public on that question." It preferred
to continue to restrict Japanese emigation to the continental
United States and let time soothe popular feelings. In the
meantime, the Foreign Minister hoped Roosevelt could
prevent "premature action" by Congress.[33] When Ambassador
O'Brien pointed out that Hayashi's protests had magnified
the importance of discriminatory acts against the Japanese
in the United States, the Foreign Minister reminded him
that "at this time he was being subjected to cross-fires from
his own people which he could hardly withstand, and that
he was compelled to do something to allay the agitation." [34]

Aoki's arguments against his government's policy proved
unavailing, and on November 4 he carried its refusal to the
President. Roosevelt again emphasized the dangerous state
of public opinion against Japan and feared that Congress
might reflect that sentiment. If an agreement had been concluded, Roosevelt said, he had intended to say in his annual
message that there was "absolutely no Japanese situation"
and to recommend some congressional "action." Aoki inferred
that the President had planned to take advantage of the
favorable impression made by the agreement by recommending a Japanese naturalization law. But with the American public so excited, Roosevelt felt he could not make any
such recommendation.[35]

O'Laughlin found Aoki deeply chagrined over the action

[33] Hayashi to Aoki, November 2, 1907, Telegram Series, JA; and "Views
of Hayashi called forth by Aoki's message," November 2, 1907, NA, RG
59:2542/210.
[34] O'Brien to Root, November 4, 1907, NA, RG 59:2542/210.
[35] Aoki to Hayashi, November 6, 1907, Telegram Series, JA.

of his government. The Japanese ambassador spoke of resigning, and indicated, according to O'Laughlin, that his government's refusal was open to suspicion and justified the concentration of American naval strength in the Pacific. The Japanese government had rejected his proposal, Aoki speculated, because it feared Japanese public opinion would disapprove an exchange of assurances with the United States while the immigration question remained unresolved. Aoki had hoped a settlement could be reached in the atmosphere of good feeling created by the agreement; now he could only reassure O'Laughlin that Japan was friendly and would abide by the present immigration arrangement. O'Laughlin, however, was not certain of Japan's friendship, and he asked the President why Japan was willing to make agreements with France and Russia but not with the United States. Japan clearly wanted to keep its hands free, and the United States ought to be prepared for any possibility. Instead of reducing Japanese-American tension, the negotiations with Aoki had, in O'Laughlin's view, confirmed the wisdom of the administration's decision to dispatch the battle fleet to the Pacific.[36]

The course of the Japanese government puzzled Washington. In late July, 1907, Hayashi had indicated through Denison that Japan would accept naturalization as a quid pro quo for a treaty of reciprocal exclusion; by early October Hayashi had changed his mind and rejected Taft's offer. Less than a month later he refused to support the policy advocated by Ambassador Aoki, a former foreign minister and one of the nation's most experienced diplomats. What evidence exists suggests that the policy of the Saionji cabinet was shaped both by domestic considerations and by a limited understanding of conditions in the United States. Weak since its formation in January, 1906, the cabinet had successfully

[36] O'Laughlin to Roosevelt, November 4, 1907, Roosevelt Papers.

weathered the first year and a half in office, but by the autumn of 1907 Saionji faced a severe budgetary crisis which consumed most of his energies and precluded taking any risks in foreign affairs. Heavy postwar outlays for military and naval expansion and for the nationalization of the railways had produced a large deficit which was increased by a financial depression. The *genro,* especially Kaoru Inoue and Masayoshi Matsukata, became alarmed and demanded reduced expenditures and higher taxes. Lengthy negotiations between the ministry and the *genro* extended from late October to early December, when a solution was reached. The dissatisfaction of the *genro* with the ministry's financial policy did not end, however, and was to be one of the main causes for Saionji's resignation in July, 1908.[37]

In the realm of foreign affairs the Saionji cabinet had, with the support of the *genro,* seemingly been more successful, concluding ententes with France and Russia and pursuing an active policy in Korea. In July, 1907, the Korean king was forced to abdicate and the Japanese governor general became a virtual regent. Nevertheless, the ministry was criticized for its conduct of foreign affairs by members of the political parties, particularly by Count Okuma and his followers within the *Kenseihonto.* Since the summer of 1907 Okuma had continually attacked Hayashi's allegedly weak and dilatory policy in the immigration dispute with the United States and, along with some other politicians, criticized the foreign minister's failure to settle outstanding questions with China.[38] Both the cabinet and the *genro* were sensitive to these criticisms from men generally considered

[37] For the domestic situation of the Saionji cabinet see Lawrence A. Olson, Jr., "Hara Kei, A Political Biography" (unpublished Ph.D. dissertation, Harvard University, 1954), pp. 180–187; Hackett, "Yamagata," 372; Bailey, "Saionji," 151–153, 157; *Japan Times,* November 27, 1907, NA, RG 59:4592/37; O'Brien to Root, December 23, 1907, NA, RG 59:4592/37.

[38] *Nichi Nichi Shimbun,* December 20, 1907, NA, RG 59:2542/287; *New York Times,* October 6, 1907.

in touch with popular feeling. The most powerful *genro,* Aritomo Yamagata, was deeply concerned with the growing social unrest and radicalism of the postwar period. And Foreign Minister Hayashi feared the effect the public's restlessness might have on foreign questions. After both the Sino-Japanese and Russo-Japanese Wars the public and the political parties had demanded more than the leaders of Japan thought it wise to take, and the terms of the Portsmouth Treaty had provoked violent riots. These disturbances must have been vivid in the minds of Japanese leaders, who possibly believed they could occur again.[39]

Within this domestic context the policy of the Saionji cabinet in the autumn of 1907 becomes more clear. Both the cabinet and the *genro* were less willing in October than in July, 1907, to risk a sharp popular reaction to an immigration treaty with the United States. They were probably influenced by the rising tension of the summer of 1907, exemplified by feverish defensive preparations in the Philippines and by Roosevelt's decision to send the fleet to the Pacific. By the autumn of 1907 the cruise seemed certain and was widely viewed in both the United States and Europe as a demonstration against Japan. Despite Aoki's interpretation of its origins, his government was probably uneasy over the President's motives for dispatching the fleet and of his intentions once it reached the Pacific.[40] Nor was it completely convinced that if a treaty of reciprocal exclusion was signed Roosevelt would fulfill his part of the bargain and secure a Japanese naturalization act from Congress.[41]

[39] For evidence of the attitude of the cabinet and *genro* toward public opinion see Hayashi, *Secret Memoirs,* pp. 226–229; Olson, "Hara Kei," 144, 192; Hackett, "Yamagata," 356, 368, 370–371.

[40] On October 25 O'Brien wrote Root that members of the government sometimes doubted the real intentions of the United States, though they generally thought they were pacific. However, rumors put out by Hearst and the *New York Sun* created concern in government circles; O'Brien to Root, October 25, 1907, NA, RG 59:1797/140.

[41] Hayashi to Aoki, September 9, 1907, MT 3.8.2.21, JA.

It was, however, the Japanese government's view of conditions in the United States which best explains its reluctance to act. The government could, after all, have weathered a popular protest and endured considerable national humiliation if an immigration treaty had seemed essential for good relations with the United States. But Saionji, Hayashi, and the *genro*, while uneasy over Roosevelt's intentions, continued, as they had from the beginning of the Japanese-American crisis, to underestimate the breadth and depth of anti-Japanese feeling in the United States and the difficulty of Roosevelt's political predicament. Apparently they viewed the anti-Japanese agitation as a somewhat artificial creation of labor leaders and ambitious politicians, and thus failed to respond to Roosevelt's growing sense of urgency by reducing emigration as rapidly as the President wished.[42] Instead, Japan's leaders hoped to retain the status quo in the immigration negotiations with the United States while quietly applying and refining restrictions of their own. In justifying this policy to the American government, they emphasized the strength of public opinion, an explanation which Americans could easily appreciate. But the Saionji ministry was far more immune from public opinion than was the Roosevelt administration. The Japanese political structure was a curious blend of authoritarian and democratic elements, with a restricted electorate, a Diet of limited powers, and powerful elites such as the *genro*, the civil bureaucracy, and the armed services. The ministry could, if enough was at stake, rule without the support of a majority of the Diet's lower house. Thus the government had considerable insulation from public opinion and could have made more concessions, more quickly, if it had judged the situation differently. Not until late 1907 did it finally realize that only immediate action would avert a far more serious crisis.

[42] Hayashi to the *genro*, November, 1907, PVM 1–18, JA.

All those considerations which impelled the government to defer a settlement of the immigration question encouraged it to reject Aoki's proposed understanding. If the situation was not critical enough for an immigration treaty, there was no need for a political agreement which might offend some segments of public opinion and place the government in a potentially embarrassing position. Japanese leaders probably discounted the power of exclusion forces in the Congress, but they were surely disturbed by Roosevelt's threatening attitude and realized he might capitulate to demands for exclusion legislation if the Gentlemen's Agreement did not quickly become effective. Japan could not be certain a political agreement would not be followed by exclusion legislation. In the general confusion over the administration's policy prevalent in both the United States and Japan in late 1907, such doubts over Roosevelt's intentions would not have been unreasonable. For in the course of the dispute touched off by the San Francisco school crisis, the President had shown himself receptive on more than one occasion to pressures from the Pacific Coast. Tokyo's lessening confidence in Roosevelt made it more cautious in diplomatic dealings with the United States and encouraged it to pursue a course which seemed to promise gradual reconciliation between the two nations at little domestic cost.

# VII

## COMPLETION OF THE GENTLEMEN'S AGREEMENT

The President was disappointed by the refusal of the Japanese government to endorse Aoki's proposal. By quieting doubts in both nations, the agreement might have encouraged a rapid settlement of the immigration controversy and better relations between the United States and Japan. The failure to effect a rapprochement increased the uncertainty in each nation about the policy of the other and stiffened the administration's determination to achieve a solution to the immigration dispute.

A few days after Roosevelt learned of Japan's refusal to conclude an agreement, the German government moved to capitalize on the unabated friction between the United States and Japan. From the very start of the San Francisco school crisis William II had displayed an active interest in the rising tension between the two nations, forwarding a bewildering variety of reports to the President along with his own alarmist views. Germany itself had been a constant and fertile source of war rumors. In early November Ambassador Tower reported the views of an important official close to the Emperor, who claimed Japan was "almost ready . . . to go to war." Tower believed the highest German naval and military authorities thought Japan would strike before the completion of the Panama Canal. "The impression is," he wrote, "that war is almost inevitable." [1]

Many of these officially inspired war rumors were intended to further the German government's aim of an American-German-Chinese Entente. William II had first suggested such an arrangement to the Chinese minister in Berlin in the autumn of 1906, but the Chinese had been slow to act upon the Emperor's proposal despite their increasing disillusionment with Japan's policy in Manchuria. It was only after the conclusion of agreements between France and Japan, Japan and Russia, and Russia and Great Britain in the summer of 1907 that the Chinese government became so fearful of the aims of those powers that it decided to seek an understanding with the two excluded from the agreements, the United States and Germany.[2] The unusually friendly greeting given Taft may have reflected this intention. In October, 1907, the German minister in Peking, Count Artur von Rex, reported that the Chinese ministers in Berlin and Washington had been instructed to sound each government on the possibility of an alliance.[3] This seemed a propitious time for Germany to broach the subject to Roosevelt, for the diplomatic agreements of the summer of 1907 had further isolated the German Empire and had increased the need for some countermeasure. A Far Eastern understanding with the United States and China would be a brilliant achievement with strong repercussions in Europe.

In early November Sternburg informed the President of China's intention and told him that Germany would probably be ready to go hand in hand with the United States. The Chinese minister, however, had not yet approached Roose-

[1] Tower to Roosevelt, November 2, 1907, Roosevelt Papers.
[2] Werner Levi, *Modern China's Foreign Policy* (Minneapolis, 1953), pp. 89–90, 99–102.
[3] *Grosse Politik*, XXV (1), 67–71, 74–77.

velt. He doubted that sufficient motivation for such an alliance existed and thought a declaration favoring the integrity
of China and the Open Door might do harm at the present
time. A better occasion, Roosevelt suggested, might be the
cruise of the battle fleet to Asiatic waters, and he again
promised to cooperate with William II in the great questions
of the Far East. Then the President and his German friend
went on to indulge in dramatic speculations over the future.
According to Sternburg's report, Roosevelt said he placed
little faith in the declarations of Japan to respect the integrity of China and predicted that Japan, Great Britain,
Russia, and France would in time attempt to dismember the
Chinese Empire. Looking into the future, he saw the probability of the cooperation of the German and American fleets
against Japan. Sternburg asked if German troops would be
needed to protect the United States in the event of a Japanese
invasion. Roosevelt appreciated the offer but believed that
only through an initial defeat could he achieve a fundamental
reorganization of the American army. Once reorganized, he
had confidence the army would eventually be victorious.[4] A
few days later, Roosevelt reassured William II through
Tower of his agreement with the Emperor's position on
China. The President favored the maintenance of the Chinese
Empire and the system of the Open Door but thought nothing
would be gained at the moment "by an open statement to
this effect." Later, in early December, Roosevelt pointed out
that while a formal alliance was impossible, an understanding for joint action would be possible.[5]

Berlin soon learned, however, that its move had been premature. Rex's information was incorrect, for the Chinese
ministers had only been instructed to report on the general

---

[4] *Grosse Politik*, XXV (1), 78–79.
[5] Roosevelt to Tower, November 19, 1907, Roosevelt Papers; *Grosse Politik*, XXV (1), 80.

feeling in Germany and the United States toward an alliance. Much to the vexation of William II, China actually delayed any diplomatic move until the summer of 1908. Nevertheless, the Emperor was optimistic over the prospects for such an agreement, and by early January, 1908, Germany had decided to await China's initiative in proposing an exchange of declarations. China must aim, Bernhard von Bülow telegraphed Rex, at gaining America's support for the idea so that the United States and not Germany would appear to the world as the driving force. This could be easily managed, the German Chancellor blandly predicted, if China paid enough attention to Roosevelt's self-esteem and desire for action.[6]

The German government was badly misled by its own poor judgment and by Roosevelt's shrewdness. Though impressed by some of the information forwarded through Tower, the President did not anticipate war with Japan in the immediate future.[7] He hoped to avoid further estrangement and for that reason responded eagerly to Aoki's proposal for a joint declaration. As long as any prospect remained for a peaceful settlement of America's dispute with Japan, the German proposal made no sense. An American-German-Chinese understanding would have multiplied tension with Japan and probably would have made any further negotiations impossible. Moreover, the United States would have been associated with Germany in its growing rivalry with Great Britain and the Triple Entente. From every point of view, including that of domestic politics, the proposed declaration was dangerous for the administration. Only if war with Japan had been imminent would it have been useful as a desperate measure to gain last-minute support. Because of his uncertainty over the future and his desire to maintain cordial

---

[6] *Grosse Politik,* XXV (1), 80–90.

[7] Roosevelt to Theodore Roosevelt, Jr., October 29, 1907, *Letters,* V, 824. Roosevelt also probably realized that much of the information forwarded by the Germans was intended to further their own ends.

relations with Germany, Roosevelt did not openly reject the German overture, but instead encouraged William II to think that some declaration might be agreed upon. Throughout the early months of 1908 the Emperor continued to advance his proposal, and it was not until the signing of the Root-Takahira Agreement in November, 1908, that he realized how misplaced his hope had been.[8]

Roosevelt's reaction to Taft's report from Tokyo revealed his eagerness to reduce Japanese-American tension through the settlement of the immigration dispute. The Secretary of War had said little that was new. His description of the domestic difficulties of the Saionji cabinet was similar to that contained in previous dispatches from Ambassador Wright, and his advocacy of an informal, administrative solution simply re-emphasized a proposal suggested by Hayashi before the conclusion of the Gentlemen's Agreement of February, 1907. While Roosevelt disregarded Wright's dispatches and Hayashi's suggestion, however, Taft's first-hand impression, along with his own sense that time was running out, led him to move quickly to achieve an administrative solution to the problem of Japanese immigration.

By late October, 1907, the outlook for success appeared clouded. On the one hand, the administration was encouraged by signs the Japanese government was tightening the regulation of the emigration companies and was watching more closely emigration to Mexico and Hawaii.[9] And it was also pleased by the departure of Rodolphe Lemieux, Canadian Postmaster General and Minister of Labor and Immigration, on October 28 for Tokyo, where he was to discuss more effective immigration restrictions. Lemieux's mission raised the prospect of cooperation with Great Britain during the

[8] For a more detailed treatment of the episode, see Luella J. Hall, "The Abortive German-American-Chinese Entente of 1907–8," *Journal of Modern History*, 1 (June, 1929), 219–235.

[9] Huntington Wilson to Root, October 26, 1907, NA, RG 59:2542/260.

final stages of the immigration negotiations. Despite these signs of hope, other information suggested the negotiations might be long and tedious. In early October Huntington Wilson talked with Kikujiro Ishii, Chief of the Commercial Bureau of the Japanese Foreign Office, who had been investigating conditions among Japanese residents in the United States and Canada. Ishii thought employers in need of Japanese labor would not let the labor unions dictate American immigration policy; he saw no need for any further action by Japan. Huntington Wilson attempted to discourage Ishii's optimism by stressing the danger of exclusion legislation; he left these discussions with the impression that the Japanese government would have to be convinced of the need for action.[10] Taft's conversations in Tokyo, along with other assurances given by Hayashi, indicated Japan's willingness to continue restrictive measures; but the question of what further measures Japan would take to make its restrictions more effective remained unanswered, as did the related question of how quickly the Japanese government would act.

For Washington these had become the crucial issues by late October, 1907. Since the President's executive order implementing the Gentlemen's Agreement, Japanese immigration had averaged over one thousand per month, and for the twelve months ending October 1, 1907, immigration had been double that of the preceding twelve months.[11] Moreover, the flow of illegal immigration over the Mexican border continued, as did the abuse of transit rights, and many Japanese who entered the United States legally as non-

[10] Memorandum No. 2 by Huntington Wilson to Root, October 12, 1907, NA, RG 59:2542/170.

[11] "Report of the Commissioner-General of Immigration, July 1, 1907," in *Reports of the Department of Commerce and Labor, 1907* (Washington, D.C., 1907), p. 150; "Report of the Commissioner-General of Immigration, July 1, 1908," in *Reports of the Department of Commerce and Labor, 1908* (Washington, D.C., 1909), p. 186.

laborers soon became actual laborers. On October 25, during a cabinet discussion of the discouraging immigration situation, the President impressed Oscar Straus as being very much annoyed.[12] A few days later, in talks with Aoki over the proposed Japanese-American agreement, Roosevelt spoke at great length about the immigration question and the danger of congressional action if immigration was not stringently controlled. By asking for the conclusion of an agreement before Congress opened, Roosevelt intimated that the sentiment for exclusion legislation was nearly out of control. Root, too, explained to Aoki the inadequacy of present Japanese restrictive measures and voiced his fear that unless closer control was exercised Congress would take "legislative measures." The efforts of the President and Secretary of State were not wasted on Aoki. He placed great weight upon the influence of labor in American politics and upon the apparent suspicion of the American government that Japan was not attempting to restrict immigration to the United States. "In order to avoid drifting into a critical position," the Japanese Ambassador urged that effective steps be taken to prevent direct and indirect immigration to the United States.[13]

Roosevelt and Root were not content with issuing warnings to the Japanese government through Ambassador Aoki. In early November Root informed Hayashi that pressure for exclusion legislation in the forthcoming Congress could be forestalled only if voluntary restriction became effective. The increase in Japanese immigration since March, 1907, proved that the present arrangement was not working, and Root warned that unless Japan "adopts very stringent and effective measures, it will be regarded as a failure." A week and a half later Root suggested a number of administrative measures

[12] Oscar S. Straus, *Under Four Administrations, From Cleveland to Taft* (Boston and New York, 1922), p. 226.

[13] Aoki to Hayashi, October 27, 29, November 6, 1907, Telegram Series, JA.

dealing with the content and form of passports, the revocation of passports violated by their holders, the registration
of laborers legally within the United States, the exclusion of
laborers and potential laborers from the American mainland,
and the limitation of their emigration to Hawaii. Japan had
promised in February, 1907, Root pointed out, to consider a
treaty if the President's executive order did not work. The
existing arrangements had failed; and while the United States
did not wish any formal agreement, it did ask Japan to cooperate promptly in enforcing effective administrative measures, "which alone may make the alternative, legislation by
Congress, unnecessary." [14]

A few days before Root sent this message to Hayashi,
Roosevelt called in Aoki and personally emphasized the
urgent need for more rigorous measures. The President explained "that the situation was becoming extremely embarrassing for him as the Pacific Coast States uncompromisingly
demanded exclusion of Japanese," and he read to the Japanese Ambassador passages from letters he had received
demanding action. The President's apparent dilemma deeply
impressed Aoki, who telegraphed Tokyo that "diplomatic
steps should be taken without delay to keep the President
committed to the policy of maintaining a sympathetic attitude towards Japan." [15] Aoki, as he had often done, took the
President too seriously, for little evidence remains suggesting
Roosevelt would soon have been forced to agree to exclusion
legislation. Representative Hayes of California was about to
introduce a Japanese exclusion bill, but it had no more
chance than in the past of getting onto the floor of Congress
as long as Speaker Cannon and the administration continued
to oppose it. Support for such legislation did not come uni-

[14] Root to O'Brien, November 9, 18, 1907, NA, RG 59:2542/161A and
164A.
[15] Aoki to Hayashi, November 13, 1907, Telegram Series, JA.

formly from all sections of the coast, but mainly from California, and even there advocates of exclusion varied in their intensity.[16] Representatives Hayes and Kahn, who had long been advocates of Japanese exclusion, were from San Francisco districts where the influence of the Union Labor party was strong. Other Californians in the House and Senate, particularly Senator Flint, seemed more immune to labor's demands and more willing to cooperate with Roosevelt in his efforts to induce Japan to limit its own emigration. If the situation did not eventually improve, as Roosevelt realized, the demand for exclusion from the Pacific Coast might become much more widespread and compelling. But there was no immediate danger of exclusion legislation, as Taft had truthfully told Hayashi in Tokyo. Roosevelt, Root, and Huntington Wilson exaggerated this danger in order to force Japan to restrict immigration effectively and quickly.

Even before the administration had begun to insist upon reduced immigration, the Japanese government had tightened its own restrictive measures. By early October the semiofficial *Japan Times* reflected the more forceful attitude of the government in arguing that the emigration companies should be suppressed.[17] The ominous warnings from Root and Roosevelt further increased the efforts of the Japanese government, and in early November Hayashi publicly announced that Japan intended to control emigration for its own benefit and to conform to the wishes of the United States. The government also reduced the monthly quota of emigrants to Hawaii.[18]

[16] O'Laughlin to Aoki, December 27, 1907, O'Laughlin Papers. On April 17, 1908, Representative Duncan E. McKinley of California admitted that neither California nor other Pacific Coast congressmen intended to press for exclusion legislation at the present session. McKinley said such agitation would interfere with the administration's diplomatic negotiations with Japan (*Los Angeles Times,* April 18, 1908).

[17] *Japan Times,* October 9, 1907, NA, RG 59:1797/374.

[18] *New York Times,* November 8, 17, 1907.

At the same time Hayashi moved to replace Ambassador Aoki, whose conduct of negotiations in Washington had long irritated the Foreign Office. Hayashi had never regarded Aoki as fit for his post, and kept him only because he was already there when Hayashi became Foreign Minister in January, 1906. Personal animosities had existed between the two men since the 1890's, but these probably would not have resulted in Aoki's recall if it had not been for his tendency to act independently and to adopt the American point of view in the immigration dispute. Hayashi suspected that Aoki had first suggested to the United States a reciprocal exclusion treaty, a proposal which had long delayed a less formal settlement.[19] Aoki's attempt to begin negotiations for a Japanese-American agreement without authorization from Tokyo was the last straw, and in mid-November Japan inquired if Kogoro Takahira, then ambassador to Italy, would be an acceptable replacement. Root was reluctant to see Aoki leave, for he thought the recall might be regarded as a consequence of the Ambassador's friendliness to the United States. But Hayashi was insistent and Washington gave its consent.[20] The Japanese government ran the risk of exciting considerable press speculation by removing Aoki at such a delicate moment. However, reassurances by semi-official Japanese newspapers that Aoki's recall indicated no change of policy, plus the swift announcement of Takahira's appointment, combined to reduce the significance of the change.[21]

Foreign Minister Hayashi received the detailed American proposals for more effective restriction in a friendly fashion. He promised to reply as soon as certain statistics were collected and assured O'Brien of his willingness to establish

[19] Hayashi, *Secret Memoirs*, pp. 10, 15, and O'Brien to Root, December 5, 1907, NA, RG 59:2542/259.

[20] O'Brien to Root, November 16, 1907, and Root to O'Brien, December 4, 1907, NA, RG 59:6429/7–8.

[21] *Literary Digest*, 31 (December 14, 1907), 899–900.

satisfactory regulations. In fact, he intended to apply the same restrictive measures to emigration to British Columbia as to the United States. But errors of judgment would still be made, Hayashi explained, and he reminded O'Brien that the Japanese people were sensitive on the matter of discrimination. O'Brien thought Hayashi intended to reduce immigration, though not to the extent urged by Roosevelt and Root.[22] Apparently Hayashi was delaying a reply to the American note until the return of Ishii and until the end of the negotiations in progress with Lemieux and the British ambassador, Claude MacDonald. He may have feared that simultaneous negotiations with Canada and the United States would encourage the creation of a common front against Japan and bring a less favorable final settlement. Deferring the negotiations with the United States also gave Hayashi more time to prepare the Japanese people to accept the concessions which the government must inevitably make. On December 4 Hayashi told a committee from the emigration societies that he had the power to restrict emigration and would do so for the best interests of the nation. The committee left angry, and Hayashi expected trouble from some of its members in the Diet.[23] A day later Ishii, having returned from the United States, spoke of the need to restrict the flow of Japanese laborers over the Canadian and Mexican borders into the United States.[24] And the *Kokumin Shimbun* argued that emigration to Korea was more hopeful than emigration to the United States or Canada, where Japanese could not enjoy peace. However, the *Hochi Shimbun* complained that the settlement being reached with the United States meant almost a complete prohibition of emigration. "We are amazed," the *Hochi* editorialized, "at the weak

[22] O'Brien to Root, November 27, 29, 1907, NA, RG 59:2542/233 and 262.
[23] O'Brien to Root, December 5, 1907, NA, RG 59:2542/259.
[24] *Japan Weekly Mail,* December 7, 1907.

policy of our diplomatic authorities." [25] Count Okuma regarded any written restriction as a disgrace and thought the government was withholding information from the people because of its embarrassment over the immigration negotiations. And a national convention of those engaged in emigration demanded that the Diet confirm the right of the Japanese people to move to other lands.[26]

Hayashi dared not put off an agreement with the United States too long, for he finally recognized the growing impatience in Washington and feared the troubles it might bring. By December 20 he had largely concluded negotiations with Canada and was ready to give more detailed assurances to the United States. Aoki was instructed to inform Root that passports were now granted only to: (1) laborers who had been in the United States and were returning there; (2) parents, wives, or children of Japanese laborers who were actually in the United States; and (3) men who were bona fide partners of Japanese farmers settled in the United States. Hayashi had, in addition, instructed provincial governors to issue passports only to emigrants who would not, because of insufficient funds, become laborers once in the United States.[27]

The Japanese proposal arrived in Washington at an inopportune time. Evidence accumulating there indicated that

[25] *Kokumin Shimbun,* December 19, 1907, NA, RG 59:2542/287; *Hochi Shimbun,* December 7, 1907, NA, RG 59:6429/15.

[26] *Nichi Nichi Shimbun,* December 20, 1907, NA, RG 59:2542/287; *Jiji Shimpo,* December 6, 1907, NA, RG 59:2542/266.

[27] Hayashi to Aoki, December 19, 1907, NA, RG 59:2542/240; the nature of the Foreign Office's restrictions on the emigration of laborers between March, 1907, and January, 1908, is not clear. Hayashi claimed in his dispatch to Aoki that the United States already knew that passports were being issued to these three classes. Yet in a dispatch to Komura in London he said that Japan was adopting these regulations to limit emigration to the United States. Hayashi had never formally communicated the first two of the three categories to the United States, and Huntington Wilson was surprised to learn that Washington was supposed to know of their existence.

Japan was still issuing passports to laborers for the continental United States and that restrictions on the emigration of farmers were being evaded. Moreover, total Japanese immigration did not show any signs of diminishing, and the regulations suggested by Hayashi seemed unlikely to change the situation rapidly. Huntington Wilson reminded Root that the American government had never agreed to have passports granted to the first two categories, and he regarded the third category as dangerously vague. In late December Root informed Hayashi that immigration restriction would be futile until the issuance of passports was highly centralized and based upon detailed regulations. "Unless there is a very speedy change in the course of emigration," Root warned Hayashi, "it will be impossible to prevent the passage of exclusion legislation by Congress and the Executive Department . . . will not feel justified in continuing a hopeless opposition to such legislation." [28] Washington's patience was clearly running out.

Before Root's stiff telegram reached Tokyo, Hayashi conceded some of the American demands. While not admitting that previous restrictions had failed so completely as Root claimed, Japan did agree that past measures had been too lax and that additional measures were needed. Hayashi now gave satisfactory assurances regarding the contents and form of passports and the exclusion of laborers and potential laborers from the American mainland and the limitation of their emigration to Hawaii. He also promised, of his own accord, to limit the emigration of laborers to foreign territory adjacent to the United States. However, Hayashi did not agree to the revocation of passports violated by their holders or to the registration of laborers within the United States. He

[28] Memorandum by Huntington Wilson to Root, December 24, 1907, NA, RG 59:2542/240; Root to O'Brien, December 31, 1907, NA, RG 59:2542/256.

particularly resented this last suggestion because it would subject Japanese in the United States to indignities and humiliations.[29]

The American government had good reason to be pleased with Japan's response, despite the existence of some unresolved points. O'Brien believed Hayashi had failed to regulate provincial governors closely enough in the past but that the Japanese restrictions would prove more effective in the future.[30] Root was generally satisfied, though he insisted in a note to Hayashi in late January that Japan could either concur or devise effective alternatives to the two regulations it had rejected. Root suspected that considerable fraud had been practiced against Japan's passport system and instructed O'Brien to seek a clarification of a number of small but unsettled points. The most important remaining issue, Root privately indicated to O'Brien, was to devise a system for the registration of Japanese laborers legally within the United States, so that those immigrants who had become laborers after entering the country could be detected.[31]

By late January, 1908, Japan's important concessions to the United States, along with a sharp drop in Japanese immigration for December, 1907 (from an average of about 1,100 for previous months to 717), eased tension between the two nations.[32] At the same time, the American government was reassured by signs of the Japanese Foreign Office's determination to fulfill the American demands despite attacks from some members of the *Kenseihonto*. The *Japan Weekly Mail* thought many Japanese "were more or less indignant about

[29] Memorandum from the Japanese Foreign Office, December 30, 1907, and note from the Japanese Foreign Office, December 31, 1907, NA, RG 59:2542/331.

[30] O'Brien to Root, January 2, 1908, NA, RG 59:2542/331.

[31] Root to O'Brien, January 23, 29, 1908, NA, RG 59:2542/258 and 345.

[32] "Report of the Commissioner-General of Immigration, July 1, 1908," in *Reports of the Department of Commerce and Labor, 1908* (Washington, D.C., 1909), p. 186.

the course that emigration affairs have taken" but did not see any alternative to the policy of the Foreign Office. The *Weekly Mail* hoped the *Kenseihonto* would not make an issue of foreign policy, for a strong reaction had set in against Japan in the West and "at no time during the Meiji era has greater circumspection been needed in the field of diplomacy." [33]

On February 20, 1908, Hayashi sent Ambassador O'Brien memoranda granting further concessions to the United States. He now agreed to establish a system of registration for Japanese residents in the United States and to warn emigrants against misuse of their passports, though he refused to invalidate the passports of those who violated their terms. The Foreign Minister also gave satisfactory assurances on a number of less important points, and informed Root that the Foreign Office was further centralizing the issuance of passports and would not revoke its suspension of emigration to Hawaii without consulting the United States.[34] Root had now achieved most of his original demands and could only await the results. O'Brien thought the United States had obtained as much as could reasonably be expected "in view of the weak condition of the cabinet and the threat to censure . . . Hayashi for yielding in emigration matters." Hayashi had shown "manliness and courage" in resisting pressure from some politicians and from the emigration companies.[35] Both Roosevelt and Root were reasonably content with Japan's reply. But as Root pointed out to O'Brien, Japanese who were in effect laborers were still arriving with passports good for the continental United States. Unless the new administrative measures soon proved their effectiveness, O'Brien was to inform Hayashi, exclusion legislation would be enacted. Not

[33] *Japan Weekly Mail,* January 25, February 1 and 22, 1908.
[34] Memorandum from Japanese Foreign Office, February 18, 23, 1908, NA, RG 59:2542/453-455.
[35] O'Brien to Root, February 25, 26, 1908, NA, RG 59:2542/471 and 438.

only the number of nominal laborers but also the total number of Japanese coming to the United States must "promptly and materially decrease." [36]

As the negotiations with Japan drew to a close, the State Department was attempting to stop the flow of illegal Japanese immigration over the Mexican border. Cooperation with Mexico had been contemplated for some time, but it was not until February, 1908, that Root decided to dispatch American experts to negotiate an agreement with the Mexican government and with Mexican transportation lines. The State Department hoped Mexico would allow American immigration inspectors to process Japanese immigrants at ports of arrival and at interior transportation centers, thereby preventing many unqualified immigrants from illegally crossing the border. The Diaz government, however, proved to be unexpectedly sensitive over allowing any infringement of Mexican sovereignty while critics of the regime were denouncing the presence of the American fleet in Magdalena Bay. Moreover, Diaz and Foreign Minister Ignacio Mariscal were offended by discussions in the American press of the acquisition of Baja California, as were some Mexican nationalists. Ambassador David E. Thompson advised against negotiations with Mexico for the time being, and Washington concurred. The result was a failure to secure any significant cooperation from the Diaz government. In March, 1908, Root attempted to secure Japan's cooperation in suppressing the smuggling of Japanese immigrants across the border. Japan had already prohibited the emigration of Japanese laborers to Mexico and was willing to aid American officials, but the problem of other Asiatics crossing the border remained unsolved when Roosevelt left office. [37]

[36] Root to O'Brien, February 25, March 9, 1908, NA, RG 59:2542/411 and 456.
[37] The negotiations with Mexico can be followed in NA, RG 59:223.

The agreement concluded by late February, 1908, represented the second and final stage of the negotiations begun in the latter part of 1906. The first stage, completed a year earlier, had attempted, unsuccessfully, to end the direct and indirect immigration of Japanese laborers to the United States. Now the United States and Japan adopted detailed provisions designed to end once and for all the flow of Japanese laborers to American shores. Passports were to be issued only to merchants, students, and tourists and (1) to laborers who were former residents of the United States; (2) to those who were partners of Japanese farmers in the United States (settled agriculturists); and (3) to the parents, wives, and children of Japanese laborers living in the United States. Japan also consented to reform its passport system and to take great care in the issuance of passports, to establish a system of consular registration in the United States, to limit the emigration of laborers to adjacent territory, and to suspend emigration to Hawaii. The Gentlemen's Agreement promised largely to end Japanese immigration to the United States and thus to remove the most troublesome irritant to Japanese-American amity.

About a month after the completion of the negotiations, President Roosevelt had a long talk with Ambassador Takahira, who had arrived to take up his duties in Washington. Roosevelt had come to trust Takahira during the negotiations ending the Russo-Japanese War, and now the President reaffirmed to the new Ambassador his friendship for Japan. Despite his own good will, however, Roosevelt predicted that some time would have to pass before Japanese immigrants would be welcome in the United States. Japan had taken the place of Germany in the popular mind as a potential enemy, and even some congressmen believed in eventual war with Japan, as did some prominent men in Great Britain, France, and Germany. Roosevelt wished to leave office with relations between the United States and Japan in the best possible shape, and for that reason no more laborers must enter the country. He was also eager for the conclusion of the Japanese-American arbitration treaty which Root had suggested to Takahira on February 25. Along with the invitation of Japan to the American fleet, it would help quiet anti-Japanese sentiment in the United States.[38]

The President was not, however, as confident of the future of Japanese-American relations as his talk with Takahira suggested. In early April he was still concerned over the rate of Japanese arrivals to the United States (five hundred per month) and believed that "no one can tell when the situation will grow acute." [39] But his apparent uneasiness did not prevent a growing rapprochement between the two nations. An arbitration treaty was signed on May 5 and quickly approved by the Senate. Its conclusion, remarked the *Nation,* "comes like a west wind blowing away the fog." [40] Until well into the summer Roosevelt and Root remained disappointed in the size of the decrease in Japanese immigration and continued to remind the Japanese government of the legislation this immigration might provoke. But the long and tedious negotiations with Japan were ended. The way seemed clear for statesmen of good will in both nations to rebuild Japanese-American friendship.

[38] Takahira to Hayashi, March 26, 1908, Telegram Series, JA; negotiations over the arbitration treaty can be followed in NA, RG 59:11991. Takahira was eager for Japan to accept Root's proposal of February 25, 1908. He thought a Japanese-American arbitration treaty would quiet nervousness within the Roosevelt administration and among the public. Both Bryce and Jusserand advised Takahira to sign a treaty (Takahira to Hayashi, March 15, April 28, 1908, Telegram Series, JA).

[39] Roosevelt to Arthur Lee, April 8, 1908, *Letters,* VI, 995.

[40] *Nation,* 86 (May 14, 1908), 433.

# VIII

## Coalition Against Japan

Although in January, 1908, the immigration negotiations with Japan seemed to be entering their final phase, the mood of the Roosevelt administration was somber. The President and Secretary of State lacked confidence in the Japanese government and were uncertain it would enforce regulations agreed upon by the two nations. Both men felt Japan could control its emigration and were impatiently awaiting results. Both also sensed that time was running out. If Japanese immigration did not soon diminish, the administration foresaw a serious weakening of Republican forces in California and possibly a Democratic victory there. In order to avoid such distasteful developments, the President might have accepted exclusion if Japanese immigration had not fallen off in 1908. Such a policy, with all its pitfalls, was more attractive than the mob violence in San Francisco which Roosevelt feared continued immigration would provoke. And it would have been politically expedient, pleasing the Pacific Coast and perhaps preventing another outbreak of anti-Japanese feeling in the California Legislature.

Foreign speculation about Japan's intentions further stirred the uneasiness of the President and Secretary of State. The President's English friend, Cecil Spring Rice, wrote of the imminence of a great racial conflict in the Pacific. Another old acquaintance, General James H. Wilson, passed on information indicating that the *genro*, while eager for peace, were disturbed by the dispatch of the battle fleet to the Pacific.[1] Chancellor Bülow confirmed the peaceful inclinations of the *genro*, though he apparently shared the feelings of the German ambassador in Tokyo, Baron Mumm von Schwarzenstein, that anti-American sentiment was widespread among the Japanese people. Ambassador Tower reported that Schwarzenstein and Bülow envisaged no immediate attack upon the United States but regarded the future as full of uncertainty.[2]

Other prominent men warned that the immigration question had reached a critical stage. Merriman C. Harris, Methodist Bishop of Japan and Korea, felt Japan had suffered deep humiliation in the immigration negotiations and urged that the situation "be handled with very great delicacy."[3] An American adviser to the Korean government, Durham W. Stevens, predicted exclusion legislation would end Japan's friendship with the United States and replace it with a "wall of chilly reserve which . . . will last for many years to come."[4] And Senator Flint of California, viewing events from a different perspective, nervously informed Root that unless business conditions improved further Asiatic immigration would bring trouble in California.[5]

It is difficult to measure the impact of such diverse information upon the President and Secretary of State. Clearly neither believed in the inevitability of a Japanese-American

---

[1] Spring Rice to Roosevelt, December 4, 1907, Roosevelt Papers; James H. Wilson to Huntington Wilson, January 7, 1908, NA, RG 59:8258/77.

[2] Tower to Roosevelt, January 8, 10, 1908, Roosevelt Papers.

[3] Bishop M. C. Harris to Taft, January 2, 1908, Mischler's Diaries, Taft Papers; and extract of letter from Harris to Bishop Earl Cranston, in Cranston to Roosevelt, January 24, 1908, NA, RG 59:2542/341.

[4] Durham W. Stevens to Brownson, December 24, 1907, NA, RG 59:12611/4.

[5] Frank P. Flint to Root, January 8, 1908, NA, RG 59:2542/276.

conflict, and both realized that the rulers of Japan, heavily preoccupied with domestic problems, were not inclined to challenge the United States. In fact, Roosevelt calculated that the Japanese government was susceptible to dipolmatic coercion and would, after a sharp protest, probably accept American exclusion legislation. Yet he had, since the Peace of Portsmouth, been impressed with the turbulence and instability of Japanese public opinion and could not be certain exclusion legislation or some incident in the United States might not bring an upheaval which the Saionji ministry and the *genro* would find irresistible.[6]

Thus in January, 1908, Roosevelt and Root knew any course pursued by the American government would be risky. Exclusion legislation would satisfy the Pacific Coast but perhaps inflame Japanese public opinion. On the other hand, maintenance of the ineffectual Gentlemen's Agreement might have the opposite effect. The safest policy was to press Japan for tighter immigration restrictions while at the same time creating an Anglo-American coalition against Japanese immigration, and this was the path Roosevelt followed in the early months of 1908.

The United States had first approached Great Britain for assistance during Lemieux's negotiations in Tokyo in late 1907. Acting on instructions from Washington, O'Brien sounded Ambassador MacDonald on the possibility of the two embassies working together on the immigration question. MacDonald put off O'Brien, for he thought joint action would have a bad effect on the Japanese government. Moreover, the Canadian immigration commissioners were strongly opposed to cooperation with the United States.[7] This failure,

[6] For indications of the attitude of Roosevelt and Root see Roosevelt to Spring Rice, December 21, 1907, *Letters,* VI, 869–871; and Root to Huntington Wilson, January 8, 1908, NA, RG 59:8258/77.

[7] MacDonald to Grey, March 17, 1908, *British Documents,* VIII, 457–458.

however, did not diminish Roosevelt's desire to construct a common front with Great Britain and Canada against Japan. In early January, 1908, he encouraged Colonel John J. McCook, a New York lawyer and conservative Republican, to invite William L. Mackenzie King, Deputy Minister of Labor and Immigration, to Washington to discuss "matters of common interest." [8] After the Vancouver riots King had conducted an extensive inquiry into the immigration to Canada of laborers from Japan, China, and India. As Roosevelt realized, the Deputy Minister knew more about the problems of oriental immigration than anyone else in the Canadian government, and he was also a promising young protégé of Prime Minister Wilfrid Laurier.

With Laurier's approval King arrived in Washington on January 25 to meet the President, whom he found in a belligerent and frank mood. Roosevelt's remarks, as preserved in King's diary, indicate the President was worried about the continued flow of Japanese immigration into the United States and irritated over the course of negotiations with Japan. He told King that "we have been doing some pretty plain talking the last few days. We have allowed these people to go too far thro' being too polite to them. I made up my mind that they were simply taking advantage of our politeness. I though they had done this, and I decided to send the fleet into the Pacific; it may help them to understand that we want a definite arrangement. They have been telling us right along that they will restrict, they have not done so, the numbers have been increasing. Now they tell us they cannot control their people, or prevent them emigrating. On this we will demand a positive guaranty." [9]

[8] John J. McCook to King, January 9, 1908, King Papers; a different interpretation of King's conversations in Washington is in Esthus, *Theodore Roosevelt and Japan*, pp. 221–226.

[9] King's Diary, January 25, 1908, in R. MacGregor Dawson, *William Lyon Mackenzie King: A Political Biography* (Toronto, 1958), I, 152.

Roosevelt believed that "England's interests and ours are one in this matter," and that it was important to recognize this unity of interests because of Japan's attempt, during the immigration negotiations, to play off Great Britain and the United States. Moreover, if both nations were to remain indifferent to the popular feeling in British Columbia and California, the whole area west of the Rockies might unite and form a Pacific republic to protect its interests. King's purpose was to serve as a means of communication with the British government, for Roosevelt felt that Bryce, whom he regarded as a "fine old boy . . . fonder of books than . . . of active politics," had not conveyed the serious and immediate nature of the question to his superiors. The President wanted King to go to Great Britain to do so. Sir Edward Grey, Roosevelt thought, could "do much for the cause of peace, not that we want to ask the help of the British, but the Japanese must learn that they will have to keep their people in their own country. Britain is her ally, a word thro' her ambassador, spoken in a friendly way to an ally, assuring her of the feeling might go far. I cannot write for that would be misunderstood." [10]

After giving his own views, Roosevelt sent King to Secretary of State Root, who took a somewhat different approach. He questioned King about the details of the Lemieux Agreement and suggested that a Canadian-American understanding on Japanese immigration might be helpful. Root then revealed that initially he had "a strong feeling of sympathy and admiration for the Japanese, but little by little, I have come around to the opinion that we are face to face with a very serious situation. In this country we have gone too far in the number of foreigners we have permitted to enter." "This silent invasion by foreign people," Root warned, "is as

[10] *Ibid.*, pp. 152–153.

effective as that of the Huns and Goths in the days of the Roman Empire." [11]

As if to emphasize the perilous condition of Japanese-American relations, Roosevelt and Root delivered speeches which "amazed" King at a Gridiron Club dinner the same evening. Politeness was all right up to a certain point, Roosevelt stormed, but if advantage was taken of your attitude, then the time had come to send the fleet to the Pacific. Root spoke too, and though he asked for press restraint in commenting on foreign relations, he suggested that war with Japan was possible. King saw the United States "on the very verge of war. The whole tone of the President's talk with me today was we must have absolutely what we are demanding or war. His speech tonight was be prepared for war, & be ready for it on a moment's notice. . . . It was plain to me . . . that . . . [Root also] fears the possibility of war in the immediate future. There will be war for sure if the Japanese do not see what this country wishes done and do it quickly." [12]

While King mostly listened during his brief stay in Washington, he did provide information which sharpened the President's suspicions of Japan. During his investigation of oriental immigration he had discovered documents which proved the Japanese government had been aware of violations of its understanding with Canada. In fact, King claimed that the Japanese had deliberately over-issued by two or three times the number of passports they said they were issuing, and that immigration was completely under the government's control. Finally, King told Roosevelt of a dinner given him by two Japanese, at which one of his hosts described a dream in which Japan had taken control of the

[11] Memorandum by W. L. Mackenzie King on conversations in Washington, PRO, FO 371/471.
[12] King's Diary, January 25, 1908, in Dawson, King, I, p. 154.

Pacific, of western Canada, and of the western United States.[13]

In significant ways the President's account of his first conversation with King differed from the account recorded in King's voluminous diaries. Writing Arthur Lee on February 2, Roosevelt explained that Laurier had sent King down to Washington to sound him, because the Canadians were concerned over Japanese immigration. The President was impressed with King but surprised when the Canadian told him that if Japanese were not excluded from western Canada that section would secede and set up a republic along with America's Pacific Coast. Roosevelt asked King to repeat this, then laughed and said no such republic would be formed. King thanked the President for sending the fleet to the Pacific and expressed the wish that London could be awakened to the strong feeling in these western regions. The President agreed and told King that America and Great Britain ought to work together on the immigration question.[14] Roosevelt's account had, in short, reversed King's by placing the Canadian government and King in an active role while relegating himself to a passive one.

King returned to Ottawa to report his conversations to his surprised superiors, Laurier and Governor General Earl Grey. Neither had realized the extent of Japanese-American tension nor anticipated such a direct overture for Canadian-American cooperation against Japanese immigration. Laurier had bitter memories of the President's conduct in the Alaskan boundary dispute and was suspicious of Roosevelt's motives. Calling Roosevelt's belligerent speech before the Gridiron Club "all flam," he was personally inclined not to cooperate with the United States.[15] At the same time, however, Laurier

[13] Dawson, *King*, I, 176–177; and Roosevelt to Lee, February 2, 1908, *Letters*, VI, 918–921.

[14] Roosevelt to Lee, February 2, 1908, *Letters*, VI, 918–921.

[15] Dawson, *King*, I, 154.

realized the United States and Canada had a common interest "in keeping the yellow men out" and that the imperatives of national interest and political survival must overrule his own personal feelings.[16]

The Prime Minister's receptivity to Roosevelt's overture can be understood only in the light of Canada's own difficulties with Japanese immigration, which had begun nearly a year after those of the United States.[17] In 1907 a sharp and unexpected increase in Japanese immigration to British Columbia incited racial tension which Laurier underestimated until dangerous riots erupted at Vancouver on September 8. Then Laurier and his cabinet colleagues began to grasp the seriousness of the situation. Petitions for the immediate exclusion of Japanese immigrants poured in from Pacific Coast trade and labor organizations, as did predictions from provincial Liberals that the fate of the party in British Columbia was closely tied to the immediate restriction of Japanese immigration.[18] William L. Mackenzie King, reporting from Vancouver in early November, conveyed to Laurier his astonishment at the extent to which anti-Japanese feeling overrode economic self-interest. King had arrived in British Columbia thinking the agitation was confined to laborers, but soon realized that it was broadly spread through all classes of the population and that its intensity equaled that of the anti-Japanese agitation in California. Laurier,

[16] Memorandum by W. L. Mackenzie King on conversations in Washington, PRO, FO 371/471.

[17] For the background of Japanese immigration into Canada see Charles J. Woodsworth, *Canada and the Orient* (Toronto, 1941), pp. 60–73; and W. L. Mackenzie King, *Report of the Royal Commission Appointed to Inquire into the Methods by Which Oriental Laborers Have Been Induced to Come to Canada* (Ottawa, 1908).

[18] For examples see Ralph Smith to Laurier, August 2, 1907, Trades and Labor Congress of Canada, Winnipeg, Manitoba, to Laurier, September 17, 1907, Canadian Public Archives: R.G. 7 (Governor General's Office), G. 21/332; J. A. MacDonald to Laurier, October 11, 1907, Laurier Papers.

like King, came to see the Vancouver riots as symbolic of a
deep, widespread, and unchangeable racial prejudice.[19]

The Prime Minister, however, resisted the cries from
British Columbia for Asiatic exclusion legislation. To impatient critics Laurier spoke of the significance of commercial
ties with Japan and of the importance of imperial interests
and warned that "the day is passed when we can treat Japan
as we can treat China and other Oriental powers." He hoped
a reasonable solution could be worked out with Japan which
would obviate the need for exclusion legislation.[20] But the
longer such a solution took the more its achievement might
be imperiled, for excessive delay might bring renewed rioting in Vancouver and intolerable pressure from Liberals in
British Columbia. Laurier knew that the Asiatic Exclusion
League of Vancouver was transforming itself into a potentially powerful political organization, and he was also aware
of the Conservative party's exploitation of the immigration
question.[21]

Despite these pressures for decisive action, Laurier proceeded cautiously, within the framework of past relations
with Japan. The position of Canada was somewhat peculiar,
for in 1906 it had adhered to the Anglo-Japanese Treaty of
Commerce and Navigation of 1894 without reserving the
right to limit immigration. Parliament had accepted this arrangement because of renewed assurances from the Japanese
consul general in Ottawa, T. Nossé, that Japan would continue to restrict voluntarily emigration to Canada, as it had
done since 1900. The arrangement had worked until the
spring of 1907, when an increase of emigration from Hawaii

---

[19] King to Laurier, November 9, 1907, Laurier Papers, and King to Richard
Jebb, October 30, 1907, King Papers; Laurier to Claude MacDonald, October 11, 1907, PRO, CO 42/913.

[20] Laurier to J. A. MacDonald, October 29, 1907, Laurier Papers.

[21] W. E. McInnes to Frank Oliver, October 2, 1907, PRO, FO 371/274.

along with a relaxation of restrictions by the Japanese government had brought an unwelcomed influx of immigrants to British Columbia. By the autumn of 1907 the solution to racial tension in British Columbia seemed to be a confirmation of Nossé's assurances, which would satisfy domestic needs, protect Japan's pride, and preserve imperial interests.[22]

Laurier, however, expected substantial concessions from Japan. Since the turn of the century he had gone out of his way to void anti-Japanese laws passed by the British Columbia legislature and, after the Vancouver riots, he had quickly apologized and offered compensation. Now, with British Columbia fearing a "quiet, persistent, systematic Japanese invasion," Laurier hoped the Japanese government would appreciate his domestic position and cooperate fully with the special mission he dispatched to Japan under the leadership of his Postmaster General, Rodolphe Lemieux.[23] Lemieux arrived in Tokyo in late October, 1907, instructed to secure an agreement which would set a specific limit on the emigration of Japanese laborers to Canada and give the Canadian government permission to reject Japanese emigrants lacking a passport or permit.[24] By obtaining a numerical limit, the Canadian commissioners hoped to avoid tedious and time-consuming negotiations over the details of immigration restriction; by obtaining a formal agreement, they calculated that the position of the Laurier ministry could be successfully defended in Parliament.

When Lemieux, with the assistance of Ambassador Claude MacDonald, opened negotiations with Foreign Minister Hayashi, he found the Japanese position unexpectedly firm.

[22] Laurier to L. D. Taylor, October 13, 1907, Laurier Papers.
[23] Governor General Earl Grey to the Earl of Elgin, December 9, 1907, PRO, FO 371/274.
[24] Memorandum presented by Rodolphe Lemieux to Count Hayashi, November 25, 1907, Lemieux Papers.

Hayashi insisted that the Saionji ministry had difficulties of its own stemming from the "high spirited and sensitive" qualities of the Japanese people. While he was willing to place detailed restrictions on Japanese emigration, he dared not give Canada the right to turn back Japanese emigrants, for that would require an act of the Diet and engender political controversy; nor would he agree to a numerical limit which would politically embarrass the Saionji ministry. Hayashi, just as in his dealings with the American government, wanted to keep the details of the arrangement private.[25]

Impressed by the intensive agitation in Japan over the emigration question, Lemieux finally softened many of the Canadian demands. By sacrificing some of the forms which Laurier had desired, he reached in late November, 1907, an agreement which he believed achieved their substance. It placed detailed but private restrictions upon the movement of Japanese laborers to Canada, while a public letter from Hayashi to Ambassador MacDonald stated in general terms the willingness of the Japanese government to cooperate. Through the application of its Alien Labor Law Canada could prohibit the emigration of Japanese laborers from Hawaii to British Columbia, and Hayashi agreed confidentially and unofficially that the objectionable classes would not exceed four hundred per year. Aside from its numerical limitation, the substance of the agreement was almost identical to that which the United States and Japan would soon conclude. To both Lemieux and MacDonald it seemed to satisfy the needs of the Laurier ministry.[26]

Lemieux and MacDonald, however, were momentarily out of touch with the political calculations of the Prime

[25] Précis of interview with Count Hayashi, November 25, 1907, Lemieux Papers; MacDonald to Grey, November 27, 1907, PRO, FO 371/274.
[26] Lemieux to Laurier, December 10, 1907, Lemieux Papers.

Minister. Laurier's cabinet had been in power since 1896 and still ruled both houses of Parliament with ample majorities. But while most Canadians regarded Laurier as Canada's first statesman, many thought his regime was old and tired. Perhaps Laurier's sense that his Liberal government was losing its momentum sharpened his awareness of the political implications of Japanese immigration.[27] At any rate, by late 1907 the Prime Minister was deeply concerned over the plight of Liberals in British Columbia and over the attacks of Conservatives on the government's immigration policy. Whatever agreement was signed would have to be vigorously defended in Parliament. Also, by late 1907 Laurier had considerable doubts over the good faith of Japan, due to William L. Mackenzie King's contention that the Japanese government had knowingly permitted an increase in emigration to British Columbia in 1907. Upon learning of Lemieux's arrangement, Laurier insisted on both a numerical limit and "the fullest possible statement of Japanese policy to lay before parliament." Otherwise, he warned, "the pressure to denounce the treaty will be hard to resist."[28] Since Lemieux and MacDonald felt there was no chance of securing such terms from the Saionji ministry, Laurier ordered Lemieux to break off negotiations and return to Ottawa. After reaching Ottawa, Lemieux convinced Laurier and his cabinet that the agreement was all that could be hoped for. It was finally concluded just before King arrived on his first visit to Washington on January 25, 1908.[29]

In many ways Laurier had been more fortunate than Theodore Roosevelt. Though confronted with a similar racial feeling, his political dilemma had been simpler. The

[27] Governor General Grey to Earl Crewe, June 17 and September 16, 1908, PRO, CO 42/919 and 920; John W. Dafoe, *Laurier, A Study in Canadian Politics*, 2nd ed. (Toronto, 1963), pp. 44, 81–82, 84.

[28] Laurier to Lemieux, December 19, 1907, Lemieux Papers.

[29] Lemieux to W. T. R. Preston, January 14, 1908, Lemieux Papers.

Vancouver riots occurred in a much less unsettled national atmosphere and had less complex repercussions than the anti-Japanese agitation in California. In addition, Laurier was dealing with a Japanese government already awakened to the importance of emigration restriction by its difficulties with the United States, and he had the advantage of seeking to enforce an old understanding rather than create a new one. It was not surprising, therefore, that success came more quickly to Canada than to the United States.

The apparent victory of the Laurier ministry, however, did not quiet the opposition in Parliament. The Conservative party, led by Robert Borden, attacked the government for signing the Anglo-Japanese commercial treaty without reserving the right to limit immigration. It promised to keep British Columbia a white man's country. Lemieux's report on the agreement with Japan on January 21 stirred more heated debate and brought the charge that he had surrendered the nation's control of its own immigration and sacrificed British Columbia to imperial interests.[30] In defending his policy and the tie between Great Britain and Japan, Laurier went so far as to point out that the same people whom the Conservatives were so eager to exclude might one day send ships to join with those of Great Britain in defending vital Canadian and British interests in the north Pacific against a common enemy.[31]

As expected, Parliament sustained the understanding with Japan, but British Columbia distrusted the agreement. Even Laurier was not certain, after the influx of Japanese laborers in 1907, that Japan would effectively control emigration in the future.[32] He realized, moreover, that his immigration

[30] Woodsworth, *Canada and the Orient,* pp. 84–94; *Ottawa Citizen,* January 29, 1908.

[31] *Debates of the Canadian House of Commons,* 10th Parliament, 4th Sess., LXXXIII (Ottawa, 1907–1908), 2090–2101.

[32] See, for example, Frederick Peters to Laurier, February 8, 1908, Laurier Papers.

policy might be costly to the Liberal party in British Columbia in the general elections in the autumn of 1908, as in fact
it was. He was determined, therefore, to restrict Japanese
immigration swiftly without damaging imperial policy.
Theodore Roosevelt's suggestion of Canadian-American cooperation to secure British intervention in Tokyo seemed
attractive, timely, and likely to encourage the Canadian-
American rapprochement which Secretary of State Root had
been seeking since May, 1906. Thus Laurier's primary motives in collaborating with the American President were his
sense of the political situation in Canada, his distrust of
Japan, and his belief that the United States and Canada had
common interests in the Pacific.

King returned to Washington on January 31 with a promise
of cooperation from Laurier. Pleased with Laurier's response,
the President proceeded to give King more details of the
American position. From several incidents, Roosevelt said,
he decided Japan had been trifling with the United States
on the immigration problem. The moving of the fleet had
been necessary to show Japan the United States was serious
and wanted immediate action. He was willing to let Japan
find its own solution as long as the flow of laborers ceased.
Japan had, since King's last visit, made promises which
were all the United States could expect. Yet Roosevelt still
regarded King's trip as urgent, for his role was to help Japan
realize, through its ally Great Britain, that agreements must
be kept and immigration restricted. According to King, the
President did not want to send a formal communication on
this subject to Great Britain; nor did he wish anything about
King's mission to be among state papers.[33]

Though Roosevelt may not have wanted to send a formal
communication to the British government, he clearly did not

[33] Dawson, *King*, I, 154–155; memorandum by W. L. Mackenzie King on
conversations in Washington, PRO, FO 371/471.

mind sending an informal one. During King's second visit Roosevelt, Root, King, and Bryce lunched together, and the President repeated much of what he had already said to King. If the arrangements proposed by Japan were not carried out, Roosevelt told Bryce, measures would be taken to exclude Japanese laborers by law. The President thought the policy of Great Britain and the United States toward Japanese immigration ought to be similar, and he believed Great Britain could help bring a friendly settlement by explaining the attitude of the United States to Japan. Root informed Bryce that the United States had "spoken very plainly" to Japan, and Roosevelt repeated his most recent reason for the dispatch of the fleet. The cruise of the battle fleet seemed to acquire a new purpose in the President's mind with each new phase of Japanese-American relations.[34]

Ambassador Bryce was surprised by the President's disclosures and at times amused by his behavior. He had not sensed the uneasiness within the administration over Japanese immigration, nor supposed Roosevelt would actually suggest that King, while in London, should see leading members of the Conservative opposition. Yet Bryce thought much good had come from these conversations, and reported privately to Grey that they had impressed him "with the nearness of risks which seemed previously too remote to be worth regarding. His impulsiveness is a danger. I don't, & can't, believe, that the Japanese would be such fools . . . as to provoke serious trouble with the U.S. But the President, & even Root, think this possible . . . it is right to remember the possibility of a moment's coming in which a warning from you might save the situation." [35] Once again Roosevelt's account as written to Arthur Lee differed from King's,

[34] Bryce to Grey, February 2, 1908 and February 5, 1908, PRO, FO 371/473 and 471.
[35] Bryce to Grey, February 6, 1908, Grey Papers, FO 800/80.

primarily by casting the Canadians in the role of initiators. King had been sent by Laurier on a second visit, according to Roosevelt, to discuss the advisability of a trip to Great Britain to further Anglo-American collaboration on the Japanese immigration problem. Roosevelt agreed that King should go, as did Ambassador Bryce.[36]

The results of King's second visit heartened the President. "I believe we have now," he wrote Lee on February 2, "got our negotiations with Japan in good shape, which, together with Japan's agreement with Canada, will probably bring about a peaceable and satisfactory solution." Everything depended on the effectiveness with which Japan carried out its agreements. If Japanese immigration did not substantially diminish, Roosevelt regarded trouble as inevitable.[37] But he did not think trouble was likely, though in his talks with Bryce and King he naturally emphasized all of the uncertainties in Japanese-American relations. Since Hayashi had conceded many of the American demands, and since Canada had promised to cooperate with the United States, Japanese-American relations would probably improve. Moreover, Japanese immigration for December had dropped sharply — from an average of about 1,100 for previous months to 717. This was not enough, but at least the trend was in the right direction.[38]

After King departed for Ottawa, Roosevelt wrote Laurier implying that the initiative for King's trip both to Washington and to London had come from the Canadian Prime Minister. Though containing more subtle distortions than his message to Lee the next day, this letter understandably annoyed King, Laurier, and Governor General Grey. They had no

[36] Roosevelt to Lee, February 2, 1908, *Letters,* VI, 918–921.
[37] *Ibid.*
[38] Report of the Commissioner General of Immigration, July 1, 1908, in *Reports of the Department of Commerce and Labor, 1908* (Washington, D.C., 1909), p. 86.

doubt that King originally went to Washington at Roosevelt's request and that he was going to Great Britain for the same reason. Grey thought Roosevelt was trying "to pull Canada into his quarrel with Japan," and King wrote that "every sentence in the letter had the twist of a smart politician." Laurier regarded the letter as a "Yankee trick" but was willing to overlook the President's misrepresentations, and toward the end of February he sent King on a third trip to Washington to complete arrangements for his mission to Great Britain.[39]

The reasons for Roosevelt's prevarications about King's visits to Washington and his mission to Great Britain are difficult to understand. He had, after all, told the British through Bryce that he wanted them to influence Japan, and he certainly could not have supposed the British government would be unaware of the origins of King's mission. Perhaps Roosevelt was only providing against the contingency of a future public debate over King's mission and his role in it. Then, of course, the letters to Laurier and Lee would be supremely useful in setting the record straight, as similar letters had proved useful in other controversies.[40]

Roosevelt soon learned that his bid for British support had failed. On February 6, 1908, Bryce conveyed to Root Foreign Secretary Grey's rejection of the American request for assistance. Grey declared that Japan had never mentioned to Great Britain its immigration difficulties with the United States, and for Britain to approach Japan on behalf of the United States would imply doubt whether Japan intended to keep its assurances. If Japan raised the subject with Great Britain or if further difficulties arose, Grey would then "bear

[39] Roosevelt to Laurier, February 1, 1908, *Letters*, VI, 917–918; Dawson, *King*, pp. 155–157.

[40] In a letter to Whitelaw Reid on March 30 Roosevelt mentioned he had the "record" in mind when writing Laurier. Roosevelt to Reid, March 30, 1908, *Letters*, VI, 985.

in mind" the views of the President. Either possibility seemed unlikely, since the United States was settling its difficulties with Japan on about the same terms as Canada had reached.[41]

Britain's rejection of Roosevelt's overture for Anglo-American cooperation was, on the face of it, a surprising development. Since the late 1890's the British had come to realize the vast power and international importance of the United States, and they had made many sacrifices to achieve an Anglo-American rapprochement. Roosevelt, too, had done much to encourage closer relations between the two nations and had probably anticipated prompt British assistance against Japan. He knew, as did the British government, that any clear choice between the Anglo-Japanese Alliance and Anglo-American friendship could only be decided in favor of the latter.[42] For a variety of reasons, however, the British government did not see itself confronting that choice in the early months of 1908. Since the summer of 1907 Bryce had been out of touch with the growing anxiety in Washington over Japanese-American relations. It was not until late November that he reported the inadequacy of the Gentlemen's Agreement and the beginning of new negotiations. Even then he thought the Roosevelt administration was optimistic over the outcome.[43] He simply failed to perceive the President's and Secretary of State's distrust of the Japanese government and their determination to solve the problem of Japanese immigration within the near future. Thus both Bryce and Grey were startled by Roosevelt's revelations to King, particularly because they knew the United States and Japan were concluding an agreement similar to the one Lemieux had reached in Tokyo.[44]

[41] Grey to Bryce, February 5, 1908, *British Documents*, VIII, 455.
[42] Marder, *From the Dreadnought to Scapa Flow*, I, 184.
[43] Bryce to Grey, November 28, 1907, PRO, FO 371/269.
[44] Bryce to Grey, January 13, 1908, and Grey's note on letter, Grey Papers, FO 800/80.

The British Foreign Office also discounted Roosevelt's words because of the image which it held of the President. Most members of the new Liberal government, including Sir Edward Grey, did not know Roosevelt and had formed their impressions of him at second hand. They seemed to regard him as a popular, masterful politician, impulsive in speech but astute and cautious in action.[45] Through Bryce's dispatches, Grey knew that domestic political motives had figured prominently in Roosevelt's decision to send the battle fleet to the Pacific.[46] By February, 1908, the Foreign Office was worried that Roosevelt's blustering and threatening attitude would precipitate a real crisis between the United States and Japan. Charles Hardinge, Permanent Under-Secretary of State, expressed the feelings of the Foreign Office when he noted that "the President is playing a very dangerous game, and it is fortunate that he has such cool-headed people as the Japanese to deal with." [47] The British felt it was Washington, not Tokyo, which stood in need of a warning. Thus Roosevelt's dark portrayal of Japanese-American relations, designed in part to impress the British government, actually tended to defeat his own purpose of an Anglo-American coalition against Japan.

At the same time, the British Foreign Office had a somewhat different estimate of Japan's intentions than did President Roosevelt. Along with Ambassador MacDonald, Grey thought Japan was engaged in the difficult task of postwar consolidation and that the aim of its foreign policy was to provide security for peaceful development. For Japanese leaders, conflict with the United States was unthinkable. Japan had recently concluded a satisfactory immigration

[45] Bryce to Grey, September 2, 1907, PRO, FO 371/357.
[46] Bryce to Grey, September 16, 1907, PRO, FO 371/360.
[47] Minute by Charles Hardinge on Bryce to Grey, March 18, 1908, PRO, FO 371/475.

agreement with Canada and would surely soon reach a similar accord with the United States.[48]

Finally, the delicate state of Anglo-Japanese relations heightened the British government's sense of caution. The leaders of the Liberal ministry which took office in December, 1905, were unenthusiastic about the tie with Japan. In contrast to their Conservative predecessors, they were more concerned with the continental balance of power than with imperial problems, and they feared the alliance might draw Great Britain into unwanted adventures in the Far East. From the start, Sir Henry Campbell-Bannerman and Grey emphasized the defensive aspect of the alliance, and intimate contact between the two governments ended.[49] Nonetheless, Grey wanted to maintain the tie with Japan and to conceal the new attitude of the British government from Japanese leaders. As Grey pointed out to the Committee of Imperial Defense in 1911, Great Britain could not end the alliance and then find itself "in just the same position as if the Alliance had never existed." Japan might search elsewhere for security and Great Britain would have to consider Japan as a potential foe, further straining the naval budget and perhaps forcing a redistribution of British naval strength.[50]

Grey had every reason to avoid these developments, for much of his predominance over British foreign policy in the early years of Liberal rule came from policies which had permitted the fulfillment of his party's program of social reform.[51] For these negative reasons the Japanese alliance

[48] Minute by Grey on memorandum on Japanese-American relations by Beilby F. Alston, January 10, 1908, PRO, FO 371/471.

[49] George Monger, *The End of Isolation: British Foreign Policy, 1900–1907* (London, 1963), p. 286, and Ian H. Nish, *The Anglo-Japanese Alliance: The Diplomacy of Two Island Empires, 1894–1907* (London, 1966), pp. 343, 363.

[50] Minutes of the Committee of Imperial Defense, May 26, 1911, PRO, Cab. 2/2/2.

[51] Monger, *The End of Isolation*, pp. 309–310.

was worth preserving. But given the ambivalent position of
the British government, it was important to place no unnecessary burden upon it. There had already been some
strain upon the alliance over trade conditions in Manchuria,
and Grey feared that Japan would soon begin to seek Anglo-
Japanese cooperation in the regeneration of China. By January, 1908, Foreign Minister Hayashi, aware of British aloofness, bitterly complained to Ambassador MacDonald that the
Liberal government had become "inimical to the alliance"
since the conclusion of the Anglo-Russian Agreement.[52] Eager
to remove Japan's doubts, Grey was unwilling to advise
Britain's sensitive ally unless convinced that a real crisis in
Japanese-American relations was at hand. He was, in fact,
extraordinarily cautious, for when Bryce, before Roosevelt's
first talk with King, suggested that Great Britain might
volunteer to help smooth out issues between the United
States and Japan and give the United States the details of
the Lemieux Agreement, Grey warned that it would be
"dangerous for us to interfere." [53] Grey's estimate of Japanese-American relations, different from President Roosevelt's, permitted him to place temporarily the imperatives of
the Anglo-Japanese Alliance ahead of those of Anglo-American understanding.

Roosevelt did not seem discouraged by the rejection of
his overture. Soon after receiving Grey's reply, he learned
of the battle fleet's successful passage through the Straits of
Magellan. Pleased by the fleet's success, Roosevelt told visiting members of the Canadian House of Commons that it was

[52] MacDonald to Grey, January 31, 1908, telegram, PRO, FO 371/472.
Hayashi's complaint to MacDonald was deliberately exaggerated. Though
the Foreign Minister felt the Anglo-Russian entente made Great Britain less
dependent upon its alliance with Japan, he still thought the British government had nothing to lose and everything to gain by continuing it. Hayashi
to the *genro*, November, 1907, PVM 1–18, JA.
[53] Grey to MacDonald, February 1, 1908, telegram, PRO, FO 371/472;
note by Grey on Bryce to Grey, January 13, 1908, Grey Papers, FO 800/80.

in the Pacific in the interests of western Canada, the Pacific Coast states, and Australia. The President now thought the Monroe Doctrine applied not only to Latin America but to Australia and the Pacific Coast as well.[54] By early February, 1908, Roosevelt seemed less concerned over Japanese-American relations, though there was a certain amount of inconsistency in his point of view. When William II approved the dispatch of the battle fleet as "one of the wisest steps that you could have taken possibly" to avert an immediate Japanese attack, Roosevelt disparagingly referred to the Emperor's fears as an "imperial pipe dream."[55] Yet twice during February, 1908, the President's cabinet pondered the meaning of recent increases in Japan's army. Root was impressed by the crushing military and naval burdens carried by the Japanese people and predicted that sooner or later they would force either a revolution or a foreign war. The President was angry at certain "sublimated sweetbreads" who failed to recognize the possibility of trouble with Japan. It was possible, he thought, that Japan intended inroads on China, though its treaties with France, Great Britain, and Russia upheld the integrity of the Chinese Empire. The President also speculated upon possible dangers to the fleet in Far Eastern waters. He had instructed the battle fleet to be on its guard against a torpedo or mine attack, though any such attempt by Japan was "extremely improbable." China, he predicted, was much more likely to be the scene of any war than America's Pacific Coast.[56]

On February 14 Roosevelt had a long talk with Ambassador Bryce in which he tried, despite his own sense of a

[54] Roosevelt to Edward VII, February 12, 1908, *Letters,* VI, 940–941; memorandum by Ralph Smith on interview with President Roosevelt, February 10, 1908, PRO, FO 371/471.

[55] Tower to Roosevelt, January 28, 1908, Roosevelt Papers; and Roosevelt to Root, February 17, 1908, *Letters,* VI, 946.

[56] Meyer, Diary, February 14 and February 21, 1908, in Howe, *Meyer,* pp. 383–385; and Garfield's Diary, February 14, 1908, Garfield Papers.

diminishing crisis, to convince the British government of the need for action. Roosevelt said he agreed with Grey's views that a British attempt to influence Japan might be harmful. What he really desired, Roosevelt confided, was "a complete understanding between the two countries on the subject of their relations to Japan and the adoption of a similar attitude on the question of Asiatic immigration." Roosevelt did not suggest doing anything at that time, but he thought that "if a moment arrived when the position became critical, or the necessity arose of telling the Japanese Government in a direct and forcible way that the immigration of their laborers could not be allowed to go on, His Majesty's Government and his own should speak in the same sense and with equal decision." Bryce asked when such a crisis might arise, and Roosevelt replied at about the beginning of June. The President did not believe Japan wanted war; nevertheless he went on to speculate that a conflict might be provoked by an anti-Japanese riot on the Pacific Coast or an outbreak of popular feeling in Japan resulting from exclusion legislation in the United States. Germany, France, and Russia all believed there would be war. Roosevelt did not; he thought the tremendous Japanese military and naval efforts were probably directed against China, "for the sake of establishing control there." But if the risk of war did arise, it could be averted "by the simultaneous use of firm warnings by the two Governments." Bryce perceptively concluded that Roosevelt "entertains some doubt of the *bona-fides* of the Japanese Government, believing that the Emigration Companies interested in keeping up the outflow of Japanese labour are very powerful in Japan, and that without attributing to that Government an intention so obviously wild and hazardous as that of provoking a war, he thinks the contingency of a breach not too remote to be provided against." [57]

[57] Bryce to Grey, February 14, 1908, *British Documents*, VIII, 455–456.

In effect the President had swiftly adjusted to Great Britain's refusal to act and now sought to pave the way for future collaboration if Japanese-American relations deteriorated. Such an occurrence was unlikely, but worth providing for. By giving a specific date for a possible crisis, Roosevelt perhaps hoped further to impress the British government with the seriousness of the situation. At any rate, he certainly puzzled Bryce, who speculated that June was the latest date that Congress could pass an exclusion law before next December and that it was also just before the Republican National Convention.[58]

About a week after Roosevelt's conversation with Bryce, King appeared on his third and final visit to Washington. He bore a friendly letter from Laurier which accepted Roosevelt's opinions on the exclusion of Asiatic laborers and announced that King would soon proceed to London. The President was invited to make suggestions. Roosevelt again emphasized the importance of convincing British statesmen how uncertain the future was. The immigration question was not settled, and Japan seemed to be preparing for an eventual war with the United States. Only if Japan understood the common interest of the United States and Great Britain in the Pacific would there be peace. Then, Root added, the influence of the wise old men who were determining Japan's present policy would be preserved.[59] By this time, however, Roosevelt and Root realized that not all of the original purposes of King's mission could be fulfilled. Great Britain was unwilling to open the subject of immigration with Japan as long as no new difficulties arose, and King's arguments were unlikely to change the British position. Roosevelt attempted, therefore, to broaden the scope of King's mission so that it

[58] *Ibid.*
[59] Laurier to Roosevelt, February 20, 1908, Roosevelt Papers; memorandum by W. L. Mackenzie King on conversations in Washington, PRO, FO 371/471.

would further the Anglo-American understanding on Asiatic immigration he had outlined to Bryce. "What I would like to accomplish," Roosevelt told King, "is not merely an understanding for to-day, but some kind of a convention between the English-speaking peoples, whereby . . . it would be understood on all sides that the Asiatic peoples were not to come to the English-speaking countries to settle, and that our people were not to go to theirs." [60]

The President now saw the cruise of the fleet in the Pacific as furthering this aim. In early February Ambassador Whitelaw Reid had received a letter from Prime Minister Alfred Deakin, expressing the hope that the fleet could visit Australia. Both Roosevelt and Root were eager that it should, for such a visit would symbolize the unity of the English-speaking peoples of the Pacific. Roosevelt asked King whether he wanted the fleet to visit Vancouver and Victoria, but King avoided the question. The President concluded by offering to do whatever the Canadians wished.[61] King left Washington convinced of Roosevelt's determination to settle the problem of Asiatic immigration once and for all. He would prefer to do so by a convention of the English-speaking peoples, but if that failed, he was prepared to settle it by war.[62] King took Roosevelt too literally. In reality, the President was willing to settle for much less than a final solution to the problem of Japanese immigration.

Despite the administration's lessening apprehension over the future of Japanese-American relations, information continued to reach the President suggesting that the future would be filled more with turmoil than with peace. A secretary of the Austro-Hungarian Embassy in Tokyo, Otto Franz, described to a receptive Huntington Wilson the hatred of

[60] Dawson, *King*, I, 157–158.
[61] *Ibid.*
[62] Dawson, *King*, I, 158.

the Japanese government and people toward the United States. They had, Franz prophetically explained, a presentiment that the United States would try to block Japan's ambitions in China. Taft's Tokyo speech and the cruise of the battle fleet had shown the Japanese they could not "take a domineering attitude" toward the United States. Both discouraged the common feeling in Japan that the United States, faced with Japan's seizure of Hawaii and the Philippines and with a landing on the California coast, would pay an indemnity rather than fight a long war.[63] Leonard Wood, about to leave the Philippines in late January, 1908, also poured out his distrust of Japan. The feeling was widespread among the Filipinos and white men in the Far East, Wood thought, that Japan intended to make trouble for the United States at the first favorable moment. Japan's policy was "Asia for the Asiatics," and it intended to proclaim a "Monroe Doctrine" for Asia. Wood urged an agreement with Great Britain which would provide for the maintenance of a naval force in the western Pacific superior to that of Japan; he also warned against losing control of the Pacific by withdrawing the battle fleet.[64]

Roosevelt did not seem too concerned by this new information. Most reliable reports suggested, contrary to Franz's view, that the Japanese government was not hostile to the United States; and Leonard Wood, for all his excellence as a military officer, was an extreme Japanophobe who did not understand Roosevelt's Far Eastern policy. In mid-March, when Roosevelt discussed Japanese-American relations with Ambassador Bryce, he did not show the "same eagerness to discuss the subject as when he had introduced it a month ago; and he referred to it with much more calmness." How-

[63] Notes by Huntington Wilson on conversation with Otto Franz, March 1, 1908, NA, RG 59:12611/1.

[64] Wood to Root, January 25, 1908, Root Papers; and Wood to Roosevelt, January 30, 1908, Roosevelt Papers.

ever, more Japanese immigrants had entered the United States in January than Roosevelt liked, and he dwelt upon the possibility of a dangerous situation arising out of an "insult" to an American girl in San Francisco by a Japanese.[65] But these speculations were becoming increasingly unreal, for a day later Japan invited the battle fleet to visit its shores. Within two days the cabinet accepted the invitation.

The President's interest in King's mission to London waned as relations with Japan improved. Roosevelt still wanted a united front against Japan, but there was nothing more he could do to create it. He had repeatedly explained the American position to King and to the British government; he could now only await some British initiative. The Canadians, too, proved less interested as the date for King's departure neared. Laurier mistrusted Roosevelt and began to regret being drawn into the whole project. But it was too late to back out and on March 18 King arrived in London.[66]

The British cabinet was interested in King's views on the immigration problem with Japan and in his account of his conversations with Roosevelt. Both the American government and the people of British Columbia, King revealed, regarded the interests of the Canadian and American west as identical and believed the United States could best defend them. King thought this was actually true but saw no reason to demonstrate the identity of interests to the world by concluding an agreement with the United States.[67] After listening to King, Foreign Secretary Grey believed "the Pacific slope is in a state of high fever" and feared the people there would come to feel that "when the pinch comes, we shall not support them in resisting Japanese immigration." He reas-

---

[65] Bryce to Grey, March 19, 1908, *British Documents*, VIII, 458–459.
[66] Dawson, *King*, I, 158–159.
[67] *Ibid.*, 160–163.

sured King that such a suspicion was unfounded and twice promised that Great Britain would see that Japan observed the immigration arrangement made through Lemieux. Later, in July, 1908, Grey did remind Japan of the importance of restricting immigration to Canada. Grey did not believe Japan wanted to place its emigrants on the American continent or that Japan wanted war with the United States.[68] The British ministers generally felt Roosevelt was too bellicose and might precipitate trouble which could otherwise be avoided. Everyone with whom King came into contact thought aggression by Japan against the United States would inevitably arouse Britain's sympathy for America.[69] The Anglo-Japanese Alliance had little popular support in Great Britain and even less in the Dominions. The tension between the United States and Japan emphasized the potential conflict between the alliance and the widespread feeling in Britain that war with the United States was impossible. In a showdown between the United States and Japan, Great Britain could only side with the great power across the Atlantic whose aid might be crucial in maintaining Europe's increasingly precarious balance of power.[70]

According to Arthur Lee, King was successful and created a good impression in London. King had found no disagreement with Roosevelt's belief that the immigration of Japanese laborers to English-speaking countries should be stopped and that if necessary these countries should cooperate to make

[68] Grey to Bryce, March 30, 1908, quoted in George M. Trevelyan, *Grey of Fallodon* (Boston, 1937), p. 230; memorandum by Grey on conversations with King, March, 1908, PRO, FO 371/471; King to Bryce, May 2, 1908, King Papers.

[69] Dawson, *King*, I, 164–165.

[70] So strong was the British aversion to war with the United States that the Admiralty in 1909 excluded the American navy from British naval calculations. When the Anglo-Japanese Alliance was extended in 1911, Grey demanded and received a provision in effect relieving Britain of any obligation to support Japan in a war against the United States. Marder, *From the Dreadnought to Scapa Flow*, I, 182–185, 233–239.

the exclusion effective. In fact, Grey told Lee he was eager to cooperate with the President. Apparently the Foreign Secretary meant to do so only if Japanese immigration did not continue to decrease, for he informed John R. Carter, First Secretary of the American Embassy, that Japan would not make trouble and would carry out its promises.[71] Roosevelt heard nothing of the form British cooperation would take, nor did King or Laurier inform him of the results of the mission to London. Nonetheless, the President seemed satisfied. While he still hoped to secure unity of action between the United States and the British Empire, he also claimed King's visit had achieved just what he had wanted and that nothing more could be done at the moment.[72]

Actually Roosevelt had not achieved the immediate aims of his overtures to Great Britain and Canada. He had hoped to create a coalition against Japanese immigration and to persuade the British government to warn Tokyo of the need for prompt restriction. In these objectives he had failed. The President's efforts, however, had convinced British leaders of the seriousness of the immigration problem and perhaps prepared the way for further collaboration if a crisis came with Japan. But even here Roosevelt was less successful than he hoped. Foreign Secretary Grey found it impossible to believe there was any danger of a Japanese-American conflict, even if the United States and Canada enacted exclusion legislation. Roosevelt conceded that Japan would probably keep its immigration agreement and that, if it did not, the nation would accept exclusion legislation. But he thought there was an outside chance another pattern of events could develop — that an exclusion act or some other incident might provoke a popular outcry in Japan which would overwhelm

[71] Lee to Roosevelt, February 21, March 31, 1908, Roosevelt Papers; John R. Carter to Roosevelt, April 3, 1908, Roosevelt Papers.
[72] Roosevelt to Lee, April 8, 1908, *Letters*, VI, 995–996.

that nation's conservative and far-sighted rulers. Then an Anglo-American coalition would be crucial in stiffening the backs of Japan's leaders and preventing war. In effect, Roosevelt was shaping his view of Japanese politics in terms of the American experience of 1898, when William McKinley had been forced by public opinion, against his better judgment, to lead the nation into war. Roosevelt and Root felt this could happen again not only in the United States but also in other nations. Understandably, the British Foreign Office viewed the situation in Japan from a different perspective. It saw the danger of war not in Japan's actions but in the impetuousness of Theodore Roosevelt. Given Grey's belief in the wisdom of the Japanese government and his uneasiness over the state of the Anglo-Japanese Alliance, there was little point in a diplomatic coalition against Japan which seemed so full of peril.

# IX

## STRATEGY IN THE PACIFIC

The continuing uncertainty over Japanese-American relations during the autumn of 1907 had strengthened Roosevelt's intention to seek substantial naval increases. Both the President and his naval advisers had become acutely conscious of the inadequacy of the nation's forces for meeting defensive demands in two oceans. In late September the General Board pointed out the need for a fleet in each ocean; it also recommended a large building program including four battleships.[1] Rumors of the administration's plan to ask for large naval increases appeared in the press and brought a strong plea from Andrew Carnegie to Roosevelt not to alter his previous policy. Carnegie feared the President's new program would "spread alarm thruout the country and the world." "Great leaders," he warned, "cannot reverse their policies suddenly without their astonisht people asking why." Despite its fervor, Carnegie's appeal had no apparent effect on Roosevelt. "I cannot imagine," he replied, "how anyone . . . can fail to back me up."[2] On December 3, 1907, he asked the Congress for a broad range of military and naval measures, including improved coastal fortifications

[1] Dewey to Metcalf, September 26, 1907, No. 420–2, General Board Papers.
[2] Carnegie to Roosevelt, November 18, 1907, Roosevelt Papers; Roosevelt to Carnegie, November 19, 1907, *Letters*, V, 852.

and, most important, four battleships. The Hague Conference had failed to deal with the limitation of armaments, the President announced, and therefore keeping the navy at its present size by building one battleship a year was not sufficient.[3] The President's naval program met with a mixed response, but speculation over its fate in the new Congress was soon overshadowed by the departure of the battle fleet.[4]

The battleships had been readied to sail only after feverish preparations, such as a *New York Times* reporter had not seen in the New York naval yard since the Spanish-American War. Excitement among officers and crews was widespread.[5] The fleet's commander, Admiral Robley D. "Fighting Bob" Evans, was an able and popular officer with a gift for colorful overstatement. Roosevelt had confidence in Evans, but Root apparently doubted the Admiral's discretion. As if to confirm Root's fears, Evans announced shortly before the departure of the fleet that his men would give a good account of themselves "whether it be a fight or a frolic."[6]

By December 16 the battle fleet had gathered in Hampton Roads, ready to leave at the President's command. The storm clouds of the previous day had disappeared and the morning dawned brilliantly clear on the large crowd gathered to witness the historic departure. A homespun peanut-grower from the interior had not seen "so many folks out since the day the *Monitor* fought the *Merrimac*." Early in the day the officers gathered on the President's yacht, the *Mayflower*, where Roosevelt told Evans the cruise would be a peaceful one, though he should be prepared at all times to fight. The Admiral was also informed that after a few months' stay on the Pacific Coast the battle fleet would come home via the

---

[3] *Works*, XV, 466–481.
[4] *Literary Digest*, 36 (February 22, 1908), 253–254.
[5] *New York Times*, December 8, 1907.
[6] Sperry to Edith Sperry, April 6, 1909, Sperry Papers; *New York Times*, November 3, 1907.

Suez Canal.[7] The officers then returned to their ships and led them past the President, who stood alone on the bridge of the *Mayflower* watching the great armada file out of the Roads into the Atlantic. Roosevelt later told Admiral Alfred von Tirpitz, German Minister of Marine, that at the fleet's departure he was certain his course would be justified. If Japan unexpectedly precipitated war, the United States would have gained three months in dispatching the fleet to the Pacific; if Japan became peaceful, the wisdom of his decision would also be confirmed.[8]

The departure of the fleet excited the nation and rekindled speculation over the meaning of the cruise. Despite the lessening of tension with Japan, some journalists and politicians continued to view the cruise as a demonstration aimed at that nation. An increasing number of Americans now thought of the fleet as an agent which would aid the United States in fulfilling its destiny in the Pacific. *Harper's Weekly* predicted the voyage would prove America was a great power in the Far East and would encourage China to resist the encroachments of Japan.[9] William Howard Taft believed the influence of the navy would encourage the maintenance of the Open Door in China, the most important American interest in the Far East. "The eye of the Oriental," the future president announced, "is that organ through which he sees and thinks." Not all public figures favoring the cruise endowed it with such great meaning. Alfred Thayer Mahan wrote that the training effect alone justified the transfer to the Pacific, which

[7] *New York Times,* December 16, 17, 1907; Robley D. Evans, *An Admiral's Log* (New York and London, 1910), pp. 411–414.

[8] Roosevelt to George O. Trevelyan, October 1, 1911, *Letters,* VII, 393–394. Francis B. Loomis told Howard K. Beale in 1940 that after the fleet sailed Roosevelt had misgivings about the wisdom of sending it. This writer has found no evidence to support Loomis' recollection. Beale, *Theodore Roosevelt,* p. 332.

[9] *New York Times,* December 17, 1907; *Harper's Weekly,* 52 (January 4, 1908), 7.

he thought should be an annual event. Even Mahan, however, felt that for the near future the Pacific was a greater center of world interest than the Atlantic, and an area of greater danger for the United States.[10]

Considerable doubt still existed about the wisdom of the fleet's cruise. Roosevelt later recalled that the great New York dailies issued frantic appeals to Congress to stop the battleships from sailing.[11] While there is no proof of this, the *Literary Digest* did report mystification and uneasiness in parts of the eastern press over the purpose of the voyage. According to one malicious eastern rumor, the President hoped to use the fleet to precipitate war with Japan, and already had a gorgeous uniform which he planned to wear at the front.[12] The *Nation,* still opposed to the voyage, thought part of its purpose lay in extorting more battleships from Congress. And the Boston *Advocate of Peace* predicted "immense mischief" from the cruise because it would "excite the imagination of the masses . . . [and] kindle their fighting patriotism." [13]

Though the President's bold project divided the American press, the Japanese press continued to view the transfer of the fleet calmly. Some papers, such as the influential *Jiji Shimpo,* hoped the fleet would visit Japan, and the *Kokumin Shimbun* believed the cruise and the expansion of the American navy indicated a tendency in the United States to ally with Japan.[14] Neither the press nor politicians in Japan attempted to probe deeply into Roosevelt's motives. If the

[10] *New York Times,* January 15, 1908; Alfred Thayer Mahan, "The True Significance of the Pacific Cruise," *Scientific American,* 97 (December 7, 1907), 407.

[11] Roosevelt, *An Autobiography,* p. 552.

[12] *Literary Digest,* 35 (December 21, 1907), 946–947; *Chicago Record Herald,* March 19, 1908, Roosevelt Scrapbooks.

[13] *Nation,* 85 (December 5, 1907), 505; *Literary Digest,* 36 (February 29, 1908), 292.

[14] *Jiji Shimpo,* October 5, November 4, 1907, and *Kokumin Shimbun,* October 11, 1907, NA, RG 59:1797/368 and 378.

battle fleet did awe Japan, that fact was carefully concealed. Nor did the cruise have any visible effect upon the immigration negotiations. The British ambassador at Tokyo, Claude MacDonald, felt that the voyage did not impress Japan and that, if it was intended as a menace, it left the Japanese government "absolutely cold." [15]

In Europe comment on Japanese-American relations was widespread well before the departure of the fleet. Taft's trip through Russia and conversation with the tsar had created the impression that his visit had political significance, and led some Russian papers to speculate on a possible Russo-American agreement. The American embassy in St. Petersburg was embarrassed by calls from Russian officers volunteering for service in the Philippines in case of a Japanese-American War.[16] The semi-official *Novoe Vremya* felt that the United States was challenging Japan for the mastery of the Pacific and warned Russian diplomats to be prepared. Other Russian papers also saw far-reaching effects from the shifting of American naval strength to the Pacific. Admiral Zinovi P. Rozhestvensky, commander of the ill-fated Baltic fleet during the Russo-Japanese War, predicted the voyage would quiet Japanese chauvinism.[17]

The German press, like the Russian, was pro-American, but at the same time concerned that a confrontation with Japan in the Pacific would find the United States unprepared. A noted German naval critic, Count Ernst von Reventlow, felt the American navy was inferior to Japan's in personnel and experience, but he did not think Japan would precipitate an immediate showdown.[18] Shortly before the fleet left, Ad-

[15] MacDonald to Grey, March 17, 1908, *British Documents*, VIII, 457–458.

[16] Montgomery Schuyler to Root, December 7, 1907, NA, RG 59:8422/62.

[17] *Current Literature*, 44 (January, 1908), 18–22; *New York Times*, December 18, 1907.

[18] *Literary Digest*, 35 (October 19, 1907), 561; *New York Times*, August 4, 1907.

miral Tirpitz urged Roosevelt to risk the move to the Pacific, though several years later he told the former President that he had not believed the cruise could be made successfully and that he had expected Japan to attack. If Roosevelt's memory was accurate, the fears of Tirpitz far exceeded those of William II, who thought Japan was unprepared for war. The Kaiser rejoiced over the battle fleet's cruise, which he interpreted as overthrowing British and Japanese naval calculations in the Far East.[19]

Though less impressed with the timeliness of the cruise, British journalists also regarded it as full of significance. The *London Observer* viewed the voyage as a demonstration of American power in the Pacific and of America's determination to defend its interests there, in response to the rise of Japan. A noted British journalist, Sydney Brooks, wrote that the cruise symbolized the passing of America's chief interests from the Atlantic to the Pacific. It was, according to Brooks, a necessary result of America's imperial expansion.[20] In France the departure of the fleet set off intense speculation over a Japanese-American war.[21] There, as in the rest of the European press, interpretations differed as to its meaning, but most commentators agreed it was an event of great importance in American foreign relations. Roosevelt's hope of drawing the attention of the major powers to the United States had been largely fulfilled.

The substance of American naval power was less potent than the symbol, for the fleet was in many ways unprepared for battle when it left Hampton Roads. In addition, troublesome doubts were being cast on Pacific strategy, which had

[19] Alfred von Tirpitz, *My Memoirs* (2 vols., London, 1919), I, 187, and Roosevelt to Trevelyan, October 1, 1911, *Letters*, VII, 393–394; William II to Bülow, December 30, 1907, *Grosse Politik*, XXV (1), 87–88.

[20] *London Observer*, December 15, 1907, Roosevelt Scrapbooks; *Literary Digest*, 36 (February 29, 1908), 293.

[21] *New York Times*, December 22, 1907.

seemed so settled in June, 1907. Chief of Staff J. Franklin
Bell and other army officers had acquiesced in the Joint
Board's decision to speed the defenses of Subig Bay and to
concentrate all defensive resources there in case of war with
Japan only because they believed an emergency defense could
be erected more quickly at Subig Bay than at Manila Bay.
What the General Board regarded as a final decision, the
army regarded as a temporary one, and by the autumn of
1907 Bell began to press the army's point of view.[22] Just before Taft's departure for the Far East, Bell told the Secretary
of War that only Grande Island in the mouth of Subig Bay
should be fortified, and that the naval base and main defensive force should be concentrated at Manila. He asked Taft
to examine the terrain surrounding Subig Bay when in the
Philippines and instructed Wood to inform Taft fully during
his visit.[23] In late October, before Taft arrived in the Philippines, the army succeeded in convincing the President that
the Joint Board should study further the naval base problem,
giving consideration to defense from both land and sea attack. Until new conclusions were reached, the President ordered the suspension of all work on permanent fortifications
at Subig Bay.[24]

Leonard Wood had no trouble convincing Taft that it was
impossible to defend Subig Bay by land and that the naval
base should be located behind the fortifications of Manila
Bay. The Secretary of War ordered a concentration on the
defenses of Manila Bay as soon as the temporary fortifications on Grande Island were completed.[25] By November
Wood had new evidence to support his conclusions — the

[22] Memorandum by Bell for Adjutant General F. C. Ainsworth, September 30, 1907, NA, RG 94:1260092.
[23] Braisted, *United States Navy in the Pacific*, p. 217; Taft to Bell,
September 11, 1907, Mischler's Diaries, Taft Papers.
[24] Robert Shaw Oliver, Acting Secretary of War, to Wood, October 28,
1907, Roosevelt Papers.
[25] Wood to Ainsworth, November 1, 1907, NA, RG 94:1260092.

first topographical maps of the area surrounding Subig Bay. Wood now informed Washington that the ring of mountains around Subig Bay would have to be defended by 80,000 to 120,000 men, depending on whether permanent or temporary fortifications were installed along the thirty-mile perimeter. Otherwise, enemy troops would be able to shell American ships in the bay from these heights. At present a force of only 14,000 troops could be mustered, and that force was short of officers and of essential materials. A strong attack, Wood believed, would come swiftly after Japan had begun war and destroyed whatever fleet the United States had in Asiatic waters. With defensive forces gathered at Subig Bay, the Philippines would soon fall; with those same forces gathered behind the shorter lines of Manila Bay, ready to withdraw to Corregidor Island, the chances of prolonged resistance would be much better. Moreover, the defense of the political capital, Manila, would preserve American prestige among the Filipinos. The urgent need, as Wood pointed out, was for the army and navy to reach an agreement over the protection of America's Far Eastern possession.[26]

Studies by the Army War College and the General Staff supported Wood's views.[27] Bell was firmly convinced the United States would never have sufficient troops in the Philippines to defend Subig Bay by land until the fleet arrived from the Atlantic. With the naval station at Subig Bay, he concluded, "there would be a practical certainty of its loss; at Manila, probability of its loss; at Cavite, possibility of its salvation; whilst at Corregidor there would be a practical certainty of holding it until our fleet arrived." Bell had also reached new conclusions about the nature and location

[26] Wood to Ainsworth, November 2, December 23, 1907, NA, RG 94:1260092; and Wood to Roosevelt, December 13, 1907, Roosevelt Papers.
[27] Wood, "Attitude of Army officers on subject of location of naval base in Philippine waters," no date, in Report No. 2041, October 21, 1909, NA, RG 165.

of the fortifications protecting Manila and Subig Bays. With American forces facing the very real possibility of retreat to Corregidor until the fleet arrived, permanent fortifications on the mainland would be useless, as would guns on the islands in Manila Bay that were not protected from overhead fire.[28] Major General William P. Duvall, assistant to the Chief of Staff, felt the need for overhead cover the more he contemplated "the desperate situation of this mere handful of troops." The army's plans for the fortifications of Manila and Subig Bays, however, had only considered attack from the sea, and the problem of protecting these fortifications from enemy forces on the mainland found both the Chief of Ordnance and the Chief of Engineers without ready answers. In late January, 1908, Taft convened a special board of army officers to consider the effect of new developments upon Philippine defenses. This board confirmed Bell's beliefs and ordered a special study of the problems of overhead cover. The army was realistically adjusting to America's weakness in the Philippines.[29]

The General Board, however, continued to resist the overwhelming evidence gathered by Bell and his subordinates. Admiral Dewey refused to let die his long-cherished hope of a great naval base at Subig Bay. The General Board concluded on January 29, 1908, that no location in Manila Bay was suitable for a naval base without unreasonably large expenditures, and it doubted the army could create a gun and mine defense for Manila Bay as strong as for Subig Bay. The General Board suggested the army undertake further studies of the defensibility of each location. But Bell was

[28] Memorandum on location of naval stations, Philippine Islands, by Bell for Taft, December 21, 1907, and memorandum on Philippine fortifications, by Bell for Taft, December 21, 1907, NA, RG 94:1330258.
[29] Memorandum by Major General William P. Duvall for Bell, December 28, 1907, NA, RG 94:1330258; Proceedings of Board of Officers appointed by Taft, January 23, 1908, NA, RG 94:1330258.

not to be shaken from his position; on the same day he re-affirmed before the Joint Board his belief that Subig Bay could not be defended from a serious land attack with any forces likely to be available.[30] The navy finally capitulated, and on January 31 the Joint Board resolved that the major Far Eastern naval base, essential to sustain American policy in the Orient, would have to be located in Manila Bay. But the board also agreed that prior to the establishment of the base in Manila Bay, all the military resources in the Philippines would be used to defend the temporary naval base if war became imminent. With the General Board members bitter over their defeat, the process of agreeing upon a naval base site in Manila Bay would prove long and tedious.[31]

The President was annoyed by the reversal of the policy long advocated by his naval and military experts. "Such vacillation and one-sided consideration," he believed, had done "grave harm" to both services and had led many senators and congressmen to express their disbelief in the general staff system. Convinced that some defect existed in the strategic planning methods of the army and navy, Roosevelt ordered an investigation of the Subig Bay controversy.[32] The picture of policy-making revealed in long reports by the Joint Board and by the Secretary of War did nothing to restore the President's faith in his naval and military planners. From 1901, when the General Board first advocated the development of Subig Bay, until the spring of 1907, neither the General Board nor the Joint Board had seriously considered defense against land attack. The army regarded the selection of naval base sites as a purely naval matter and concerned itself only with establishing defenses against attack from the sea. Moreover, prior to late 1906 American planners

[30] Memorandum by General Board, January 29, 1908, Roosevelt Papers; Minutes of Joint Board, January 29, 1908, NA, RG 225.

[31] Dewey to Taft, January 31, 1908, Joint Board, NA, RG 225.

[32] Roosevelt to Metcalf, February 11, 1908, *Letters*, VI, 937–939.

looked upon Japan as a warm friend of the United States. The impact of the siege of Port Arthur, together with the changed attitude of Japan toward the United States, led the war colleges of the army and navy in January, 1907, to reconsider American defense policy in the Pacific. In March, 1907, prior to the conclusion of the study, the navy brought up the problem of defending Subig Bay. Chief of Staff Bell, who had actually seen the terrain surrounding Subig Bay, doubted it could be defended against land attack and hurried those army studies which led, along with Wood's reports, to the Joint Board's decision of late January, 1908, to establish the naval base at Manila Bay.[33]

Two years after the fall of Port Arthur the nation's strategic planners were only beginning to adjust to the dominance of Japanese military power in the Far East. The Secretary of War was not apprehensive over this record of sluggish and inadequate planning, and assured the President that the Joint Board was now aware of the scope of its obligation. But by the time of Taft's report, mid-April, 1908, Roosevelt had little reason to be reassured. No agreement had been reached on the location of a naval base in Manila Bay, nor did Taft and Bell any longer believe that in the event of war, prior to the completion of the defenses of Manila Bay and prior to the establishment of the naval base there, all resources should be used to defend the temporary naval base. They preferred to tow the floating dry dock *Dewey* to Manila Bay and submerge it.[34] American military and naval strategists had, in effect, agreed on neither the location of the Philippine naval base nor on measures for its defense.

The reassessment of the nation's Pacific defenses led naval planners to urge the development of secondary bases in the Pacific. In early October, 1907, the General Board recom-

[33] Taft to Roosevelt, April 14, 1908, Roosevelt Papers.
[34] *Ibid.*

mended the erection of a coaling plant at Guam and of a naval station at Pearl Harbor. Three months later the General Board elaborated on its plans for Pearl Harbor. A fortified naval station there would provide a stopping point for American ships on their way to the Far East and would aid in the protection of the Pacific Coast.[35] Such a base, the Joint Board later pointed out, was essential if the United States was to maintain control over its insular possessions and its Pacific Coast. Pearl Harbor, moreover, had unusual natural advantages.[36] Neither the General nor Joint Board contemplated in early 1908 making Pearl Harbor the nation's principal Pacific base. Both the army and navy still planned to establish the primary one in the Philippines.

The President was eager to locate a naval base at Pearl Harbor and on January 17 repeated the arguments of the General Board to the chairmen of several congressional committees.[37] From almost the start of the San Francisco school crisis Roosevelt had been sensitive to the demands of the Pacific Coast for more adequate defenses, yet by early 1908 little had been done to strengthen them. Probably the most important point to defend was the Bremerton naval yard on Puget Sound, which had the only government dry dock on

[35] Dewey to Metcalf, October 3, 1907, No. 405, General Board Papers; General Board memorandum on Pearl Harbor, January 17, 1908, Roosevelt Papers.

[36] Dewey to Metcalf, March 5, 1908, Joint Board, NA, RG 225. After the decision to develop Pearl Harbor, the army became increasingly concerned over the protection of this potentially vital naval base. The small number of troops in the Hawaiian Islands (less than 150 men) would be hopelessly inadequate in the face of a Japanese attack or an uprising by the Japanese population in the islands. Thus the army decided in the autumn of 1908 to reinforce the Hawaiian garrison, to increase the Hawaiian National Guard, and to arrange for the dispatch of additional troops from the mainland in an emergency. The last two steps were necessary because the regular army was too small to keep the Hawaiian garrison at full war strength. See NA, RG 165, Report No. 3195.

[37] Roosevelt to Francis E. Warren, January 17, 1907, Letters, VI, 912–914.

the entire coast capable of taking battleships. But the defenses of Puget Sound were deficient in almost every way. One report compared their condition to that existing at the outbreak of the Spanish-American War.[38] In the Puget Sound region, as along the rest of the Pacific Coast, uneasiness existed over the inadequacy of coastal fortifications and the activities of Japanese residents. The mayor of Port Townsend, Washington, called these matters to the attention of the War Department and the Tacoma, Washington, Chamber of Commerce petitioned for improved protection.[39] In Los Angeles, an organization called the Southern California Rifles was formed to defend the coast in case of war.[40]

Senators and congressmen from the Pacific Coast, particularly Representative William E. Humphrey and Senator Levi Ankney, Republicans of Washington, and Senator Flint of California, strove to secure in Congress larger fortification appropriations. In late December Roosevelt asked Humphrey, in conjunction with his Pacific Coast colleagues, to prepare a report on what defenses were needed. For four years Humphrey had been urging the Atlantic fleet be concentrated on the Pacific Coast, and now he was convinced that Puget Sound was nearly defenseless. Torpedo boats and submarines, the alarmed congressman argued, were the only weapons with which to defend the wide and deep channels leading to the Bremerton naval yard and to Seattle.[41] Secretary of the Navy Metcalf thought the interests of the Pacific Coast were being taken care of, and the Joint Board, while admitting the inadequacy of Puget Sound defenses, con-

[38] "Report on Puget Sound Defenses," by Major H. L. Hawthorne, October 16–18, 1907, NA, RG 94:1308492.
[39] Memorandum for Oliver by Duvall, March 26, 1908, NA, RG 94:1343373; Tacoma, Washington, Chamber of Commerce, to Taft, December 19, 1907, NA, RG 94:1321681.
[40] New York Times, January 12, 1908.
[41] William E. Humphrey to Roosevelt, January 2, 1908, Roosevelt Papers; Humphrey to Metcalf, January 22, 1908, NA, RG 45: Subject File VN.

templated only minor Japanese raids against the Pacific Coast as long as the United States battle fleet was undefeated.[42]

But the condition of the nation's Pacific defenses worried the Joint Board. On February 19 it requested the President to urge upon the proper committees of Congress the rapid completion of defenses on the Pacific Coast, in the Pacific insular possessions, and at the Guantanamo naval base. "Should war occur before these projects are completed," the Joint Board warned, "the danger to the prestige, as well as to the real property, of the United States . . . would be very great and serious." If Pearl Harbor and the Philippines were lost, the American fleet would be unable to operate in Far Eastern waters.[43]

Roosevelt was eager to capitalize upon support from the Pacific Coast, and on February 21 he sent a long letter to Speaker Cannon and Vice President Fairbanks presenting urgent military and naval needs in the Pacific. The President asked particularly for the rapid completion of the defenses of Pearl Harbor, "the key to the Pacific," and Manila Bay. "It is impossible to foresee," Roosevelt wrote, "when the matter may become vital." [44] But Cannon, Hale, and Foss were unimpressed by the President's appeal or by Taft's public statement that war would find the United States unprepared. They agreed, Cannon later recalled, that the President had "said too much to assure us of peace, and not enough to indicate trouble." If there was an emergency calling for war preparations, Cannon informed Roosevelt, they wanted to know about it.[45] But Roosevelt, in a second letter to Cannon,

[42] Dewey to Taft, February 20, 1908, Joint Board, NA, RG 225.

[43] Dewey to Metcalf and Taft, February 19, 1908, Joint Board, NA, RG 225.

[44] Roosevelt to Joseph G. Cannon and Charles W. Fairbanks, February 21, 1908, *Letters*, VI, 950–952.

[45] *New York Times*, February 23, 1908; L. White Busbey, *Uncle Joe Cannon: The Story of a Pioneer American* (New York, 1927), pp. 224–226.

refused to put on paper all that he felt. "I am acting," he wrote, "with a view to the emergencies that there is a reasonable chance may arise within the next decade or two . . . not . . . with a view to an emergency of the next year or two." Congress should fortify Hawaii, establish a naval base at Pearl Harbor, and authorize four battleships.[46] Roosevelt's appeal was moderate and long-term. With the immigration negotiations with Japan largely concluded and with the future of Japanese-American relations more promising, the President justified his naval and military program in cautious terms.

As Roosevelt appealed to Congress for increased defense appropriations, his military and naval advisers argued that the battle fleet should be retained in the Pacific. In early February Chief of Staff Bell outlined four compelling reasons: (1) the seacoast defenses of the Pacific Coast could not within a reasonable time be made adequate to protect vital naval yards and cities from enemy raids; (2) in a war with Japan the American position in the Philippines and Hawaii would probably be impossible to maintain without a powerful Pacific fleet; (3) the absence of a fleet would probably make the retention of the Pearl Harbor naval base impossible, since only two or three hundred regular troops were stationed in the Hawaiian Islands; and (4) the United States army was too weak and poorly supplied to protect the Pacific Coast against strong raiding parties. The fleet should be kept in the Pacific, Bell concluded, "until conditions so change as to permit . . . its removal without danger to our insular and Pacific Coast possessions."[47] Roosevelt did not believe it would be possible to care permanently for the fleet on the Pacific Coast, but referred Bell's memorandum to the Joint Board. Following the guidance of the

[46] Roosevelt to Cannon, February 29, 1908, *Letters,* VI, 956.
[47] Memorandum by Bell for Taft, February 7, 1908, Roosevelt Papers.

General Board, the Joint Board insisted that normally the
fleet should be concentrated in the Atlantic, though it warned
of the danger of withdrawing the fleet "from the region of
threatening complications." [48] The President seemed impressed and ordered a report on how long the fleet could
be kept in first-class condition on the Pacific Coast. The
answer hardly surprised the well-informed Roosevelt. Naval
facilities were very limited, and the shortage of skilled labor
along with uncertain labor conditions on the coast made the
utilization of private docks risky. The maintenance of the
fleet there would be hazardous and would require large additional appropriations. [49]

Despite the obvious difficulties of retaining the fleet in
the Pacific, demands from the Pacific Coast to keep at least
a portion of it there grew. By early February commercial
organizations from many Washington cities insisted that a
squadron of six battleships be kept on the coast. [50] Senator
Samuel J. Piles, Republican of Washington, went beyond
this request and asked that the entire fleet be stationed in
the Pacific. More prominent politicians, such as Senator
Albert J. Beveridge, championed the Pacific Coast's cause, as
did William Howard Taft. [51] Taft believed "in the wisdom
of keeping the fleet in the Pacific Ocean for some time to
come," though he thought it might be impractical. Leonard
Wood wanted a powerful fleet in the Pacific until the defenses of Manila were completed, and afterwards a force at
least as strong as Japan's. Huntington Wilson, advocate of a

[48] Roosevelt to Tower, February 12, 1908, *Letters*, VI, 942; Dewey to
Taft, February 21, 1908, Roosevelt Papers, and William R. Braisted, "The
United States Navy's Dilemma in the Pacific, 1906–1909," *Pacific Historical
Review*, 26 (August, 1957), 235–244.

[49] Roosevelt to Metcalf, February 21, 1908, *Letters*, VI, 952; Newberry to
Roosevelt, February 28, 1908, Roosevelt Papers.

[50] See, for example, Seattle Commercial Club to Metcalf, February 10,
1908, NA, RG 80:25990.

[51] Samuel J. Piles to Metcalf, February 15, 1908, NA, RG 45: Area Nine
File; *Chicago Record Herald*, February 12, 1908, Roosevelt Scrapbooks.

stronger Far Eastern policy, thought "it is ridiculous for us not to keep in the Pacific, at least until the Canal is done, a fleet equal to that of Japan."[52]

From June, 1907, when the decision to dispatch the fleet was first made, the President had intended to keep it on the Pacific Coast about two months and then send it around the world. The pleas of naval, military, and political advisers did not shake his resolution. Their arguments were based upon short-term strategic considerations which had never greatly concerned Roosevelt. Even during the height of the Japanese-American tension, in the summer of 1907, he did not believe war was imminent, and by February, 1908, relations with Japan showed signs of improving. But Roosevelt was deeply concerned with the long-term strategic position of the United States in the Pacific and hoped to improve it by increasing the size of the American navy. The cruise had been originally intended as a means of stimulating popular support for larger naval appropriations. As the months passed it had acquired additional purposes — to display American power and preparedness to Japan and Europe, to make Japan realize the United States wanted a settlement of the immigration negotiations, and finally to symbolize the unity of the English-speaking peoples of the Pacific against Japanese encroachments. All these aims could be more fully achieved by sending the fleet around the world. An unofficial invitation from Australia had been received in early February, and both Roosevelt and Root were eager to accept it. If Roosevelt had really wanted to keep the fleet on the Pacific Coast, the maintenance problems could probably have been overcome. In fact, that would have been one way to force action from the Congress. But Roosevelt wished to send the fleet home via Australia, the Philippines, Japan, and Suez.

[52] Taft to Roosevelt, March 10, 1908, Roosevelt Papers; Wood to Roosevelt, January 30, 1908, Roosevelt Papers; memorandum by Huntington Wilson of conversation with Otto Franz, March 10, 1908, NA, RG 59:12611/1.

A visit to Japan could be made to symbolize the rapprochement already beginning, while retention of the fleet on the Pacific Coast would symbolize permanent suspicion and estrangement, and perhaps a stronger Far Eastern policy. And this, as we shall see, the President had no wish to suggest.

# X

# A HERITAGE OF STRENGTH

By early March, 1908, Roosevelt had brushed aside whatever doubts he may have had about sending the fleet across the Pacific, and by the middle of the month Secretary of the Navy Metcalf announced the fleet would return to the Atlantic Coast via Australia and the Philippines.[1] A world cruise seemed the surest way to bring all of the President's varied purposes to fruition and to establish the voyage of the Great White Fleet as perhaps the most spectacular accomplishment of Roosevelt's last years in office.

Developments in Australia had encouraged the President to make this decision. The Australian Prime Minister, Alfred Deakin, fully shared Roosevelt's view of the common interests of the United States and Australia in the Pacific. For years Deakin had tried to awaken his own people and the British government to Australia's defenseless position in the South Pacific. By 1907 Australians were responding to nationalist appeals for an adequate defense, but the British government still regarded their concerns as remote and was impatient with demands for an independent naval force. Nevertheless, in December, 1907, Deakin had proposed a far-reaching defense program to the Australian parliament, involving universal military service and an Australian squad-

[1] *New York Times*, March 14, 1908.

ron of the royal navy along with an independent Australian submarine and torpedo boat flotilla.[2]

A visit by the American fleet would encourage naval sentiment in Australia and symbolize the union of the two nations against Asiatic immigration. "We are . . . anxious," Deakin wrote Ambassador Reid in early 1908 "to have some opportunity of expressing our sympathy with our kinsmen in their timely demonstration of naval power in . . . our oceanic neighborhood." The *Melbourne Age* thought Deakin's message was an invitation to the American people "to admit the common trust of the two white races whose destinies are bound up in Pacific dominance." [3] Root was impressed with Deakin's letter. "The time will surely come," he wrote the President, "although probably after our day, when it will be important for the United States to have all ports friendly and all causes of sympathy alive in the Pacific." Roosevelt agreed and wrote in his *Autobiography* "that America should be ready to stand back of Australia in any serious emergency." [4]

Though the invitation and its acceptance pleased Australians and Americans, it did not please the British government. By extending an informal invitation to the United States, Deakin had left Britain with no choice but to endorse it. However, the British government was annoyed by the Prime Minister's irregular action, for it not only dramatized the common interests of Australia and the United States but also emphasized the conflict between Great Britain's obliga-

---

[2] Walter Murdoch, *Alfred Deakin: A Sketch* (London, 1923), pp. 229–233; for a discussion of Australian defense problems see Donald C. Gordon, *The Dominion Partnership in Imperial Defense, 1870–1914* (Baltimore, 1965), pp. 187–214.

[3] Deakin to Reid, January 7, 1908, enclosed in Carter to Root, February 10, 1908, NA, RG 59:8258/145; *Melbourne Age*, March 17, 1908, NA, RG 59:8258/360.

[4] Root to Roosevelt, February 21, 1908, NA, RG 59:8258/145; Roosevelt, *An Autobiography*, p. 553.

tions to the Anglo-Japanese Alliance and to its empire. The *English Review of Reviews* remarked that Deakin's act was the first outward sign of Australia's disposition to lean for support on the United States. It might, the magazine speculated, have no ultimate political significance; "on the other hand, the invitation to the American fleet may be a watershed of empire."[5]

After officially conveying the Australian request on March 2, 1908, Britain hoped to avoid a similar visit to any Canadian port. Such an event might arouse suspicion in Japan, precipitate an anti-Japanese demonstration in Vancouver, and encourage Canadian dependence on the United States. In order to avoid all of these eventualities, the British government informed both King and Laurier of its opposition to a visit by the fleet.[6] King agreed with the British position, but Laurier wavered in the face of strong pressure from civic and municipal leaders in Vancouver, who were eager for the fleet to stop at their city.[7] Japan's invitation to the American fleet averted a clash of imperial and Canadian interests and enabled the British government to propose a visit to the ports of British Columbia. But the United States declined the offer, because the Navy Department opposed any delay in the departure of the fleet from the Pacific Coast.[8]

The request of Japan, then of China, for the fleet to visit their shores ensured the success of the world cruise. The United States was quick to accept both invitations, and by the middle of March, after the completion of the fleet's trium-

[5] Donald C. Gordon, "Roosevelt's 'Smart Yankee Trick,'" *Pacific Historical Review*, 30 (November, 1961), 351–358; *English Review of Reviews*, 37 (March, 1908), 234.

[6] The British government's reaction and its correspondence with Canada is in PRO, FO 371/475.

[7] Alexander Bethune, Mayor of Vancouver, to Laurier, March 11, 1908, Laurier Papers.

[8] Bryce to Root, May 1, 1908, NA, RG 59:8258/353; Newberry to Root, March 28, 1908, NA, RG 59:8258/299.

phant cruise around South America, Roosevelt was pleased
with the impact of the voyage. Henry White wrote that
"nothing could have produced a greater impression of our
naval power — and indeed power in general — upon foreign
nations than this cruise." [9] The President agreed. He informed Admiral Evans that the voyage from Hampton Roads
to Magdalena Bay marked "the entrance of the United States
into the ranks of naval powers of the first class." [10] However,
Roosevelt confided to Whitelaw Reid that he had hoped
Japan would not invite the fleet since some "desperado"
might create an incident, and he cautioned Admiral Charles
S. Sperry (who replaced the ailing Evans as commander of
the fleet) to take "peculiar care" in Asiatic waters. [11] By early
April Roosevelt's doubts seemed to have passed, and they
were further quieted by assurances from Sperry that shore
leave could be granted at Yokohama. [12]

The proposed cruise to Chinese waters raised troublesome
problems in Peking, Tokyo, and Washington, for it became
entangled in the political relations of China, Japan, and the
United States. Chinese officials hoped to celebrate the visit
as marking a new era in China's foreign relations and planned
to have Admiral Sperry received by the Emperor. American
commercial interests in China hoped to attract a prominent
member of the American government during the fleet's stay
in order to reinforce the effect of Taft's Shanghai speech. [13]
In mid-April Rockhill warned Root that the fleet's visit might
be misinterpreted, since the United States was "supposed to

[9] Henry White to Roosevelt, March 20, 1908, Roosevelt Papers.
[10] Roosevelt to White, April 1, 1908, Roosevelt Papers; Roosevelt to Evans,
March 23, 1908, Letters, VI, 981.
[11] Roosevelt to Reid, March 20, 1908, Roosevelt Papers; Roosevelt to
Sperry, March 21, 1908, Letters, VI, 979.
[12] Roosevelt to Lee, April 8, 1908, Letters, VI, 995–996; Sperry to Roosevelt, April 7, 1908, Sperry Papers.
[13] Thomas F. Millard, America and the Far Eastern Question (New York,
1909), pp. 377–385; New York Times, April 30, May 2–3, 1908.

be championing [the] Chinese rights recovery policy, and [the] hope may be entertained of securing our active participation in upholding all Chinese pretensions." In late May Charles Denby, American Consul General at Shanghai, also cautioned that unless the United States intended to encourage a Chinese outbreak against Japan only three or four battleships should go to a Chinese port.[14]

After some initial indecision, Root heeded this advice and agreed that only one squadron should stop at Amoy.[15] He also instructed Ambassador Rockhill to combat any misinterpretation of the fleet's visit. "We hope the Chinese Government clearly realized," Root telegraphed, "[that] now as ever, we favor their legitimate aims, but that we see grave danger in any unduly captious attitude which could give just cause for serious offense in any quarter." [16] By carrying out Root's instructions, Rockhill disappointed China but pleased Japan. Japan was further reassured when Root in late May confided to Takahira that he felt the visit of the whole fleet to Japan and only part of it to China would convince the Chinese people of American sympathy for Japan.[17] Neither Roosevelt nor Root wanted the fleet's cruise in Far Eastern waters to symbolize a stronger American policy in China opposed to Japan's vital interests.

The arrival of the battle fleet at Magdalena Bay on March 12, 1908, and the subsequent announcement that it would go to Japan brought a new flurry of press comment. European naval critics were impressed by the efficient performance of the American ships, while the doubts expressed in the United States over the wisdom of the cruise were for-

---

[14] Rockhill to Root, April 18, 1908, NA, RG 59:8258/335; Denby to Root, April 18, 1908, NA, RG 59:8258/386.
[15] Takahira to Hayashi, April 23–24, 28, 1908, Telegram Series, JA.
[16] Root to Rockhill, April 28, 1908, NA, RG 59:8358/335.
[17] Rockhill to Root, May 4, 1908, NA, RG 59:8258/414; Takahira to Hayashi, May 29, 1908, Telegram Series, JA.

gotten in the national rejoicing over the navy's dramatic achievement.[18] Walter Wellman, Washington correspondent of the pro-Roosevelt *Chicago Record Herald*, thought the dispatch of the fleet to the Pacific and around the world was one of the "happiest strokes" of the Roosevelt administration. Representative George E. Foss, Republican of Illinois, believed everyone now recognized the President's original order was a good one.[19] Journalistic critics of the cruise, if not silent, admitted that the voyage had fostered international good will and found no risk in the proposed visit to Japan. However, one prominent writer on naval affairs, Park Benjamin, saw little cause for celebration. If there was a sound military reason for dispatching the fleet, he pointed out, it was "silly" to bring it back immediately from the Pacific Coast. Moreover, the fleet was unprepared for war and would return from its world "junketing expedition" as a less effective fighting force.[20] But the nation paid little attention to these criticisms. It was pleased, as Roosevelt realized, with the battle fleet's assertion of American power.

The widespread excitement on the Pacific Coast over the cruise was evident in Washington long before the battleships dropped anchors in San Diego Bay on April 14. Pacific Coast senators were inundated with requests for a visit from the fleet. The people of Humboldt, California, reported the Humboldt Chamber of Commerce, would go "wild with delight" if they could see the great white ships in their bay. The school pupils in San Luis Obispo, California, petitioned the Secretary of the Navy to have the fleet pass close to their city's shores, and one citizen of Seattle, Washington, thanked

---

[18] *New York Times,* March 13, 15, 18, and May 10, 1908; and *North American Review,* 187 (April, 1908), 633–634.

[19] *Chicago Record Herald,* March 19, 1908, Roosevelt Scrapbooks; *Congressional Record,* 60th Cong., 1st Sess., 4577.

[20] *Literary Digest,* 36 (March 28, 1908), 430–431; Park Benjamin, "Warships as Playthings," *Independent,* 64 (April 2, 1908), 737–740.

the President for recognizing the people of the west "as American citizens entitled to and worthy of the protection of Old Glory." [21] Chambers of commerce, too, were active in promoting the virtues of their individual cities, and many chambers wanted several battleship squadrons permanently stationed on the Pacific Coast.[22] But the outpouring of sentiment went much deeper than a mere desire for commercial development; the voyage of the fleet had touched the national feeling of the people of the Pacific Coast. Theodore Roosevelt, in the minds of many citizens there, had proved that he was president of the whole United States.

The arrival of the battle fleet at San Diego and later at Los Angeles brought a popular outburst such as the officers of the American navy had seldom if ever before witnessed. "Hearts Beat Proudly As Anchors Splash" headlined the *Los Angeles Times*, as extra trains poured people into San Diego and Los Angeles.[23] Prominent citizens, along with Pacific Coast newspapers, speculated upon the meaning of the fleet's arrival. "It marks an epoch," remarked David Starr Jordan, president of Stanford University, "if it does not create it, and the event it marks is in some degree the coming of age . . . of the Pacific States." Many papers emphasized the commercial importance of the Pacific Coast and its need for more adequate defenses. Admiral Evans thought that the nation's interests in the Pacific were greater than in the Atlantic, and Governor James Gillett predicted that the Pacific would be a battle ground of the future as nations strove for commercial and naval supremacy on it. So convinced of this was the *San Francisco Argonaut* that it could not believe the

[21] Humboldt, California, Chamber of Commerce to Metcalf, April 11, 1908, NA, RG 45: Subject File oo; Petition from school pupils of San Luis Obispo, California, March 19, 1908, NA, RG 24:6072/211.

[22] Frank W. Harned, Seattle, Washington, to Roosevelt, December 24, 1907, NA, RG 24:6072/201; Manufacturers' Association of Northwest to Metcalf, May 6, 1908, NA, RG 80:25990/4.

[23] Evans, *Admiral's Log*, p. 453; *Los Angeles Times*, April 6, 15, 1908.

fleet would ever leave the Pacific Coast to return to the Atlantic.[24]

The excitement in California over the battle fleet came at a propitious time, just as the House prepared to vote on the President's naval expansion program. Roosevelt badly needed whatever big-navy enthusiasm the fleet's arrival would generate, for from the very start of the session Congress had been cool to his naval program and to his other legislative proposals. While Roosevelt attempted to hold "the left center together," the majority of Republicans in both houses of Congress remained unresponsive to the mounting reform spirit across the country.[25] The financial panic of October and November, 1907, had led to a heated debate over its origins in which some businessmen charged that the President's attacks on business had undermined confidence. The President, however, continued to develop and press upon the Congress his program for a federal regulatory state. In his December, 1907, annual message Roosevelt urged, among other things, inheritance and income taxes, the national incorporation and regulation of interstate business, and the fixing of railway rates on the basis of physical evaluation. Stirred by the Congress's failure to act upon his recommendations, he sent an even stronger appeal to Congress in late January, 1908, repeating the proposals of his December message and adding one for the federal regulation of stock market gambling. More important was the inflammatory tone of his address, which denounced the "representatives of predatory wealth" and the "puppets" whom the corporations had purchased, along with those members of the judiciary who failed to stop the abuses of the "criminal rich" while unfairly repressing labor. The message brought

[24] John Francis Dyer, "The Great Naval Cruise," *World's Work*, 16 (June, 1908), 10752–10763; *Literary Digest*, 36 (April 25, 1908), 583–584.

[25] Roosevelt to Lee, December 26, 1907, *Letters*, VI, 875.

a storm of abuse from eastern conservatives and ended the President's friendship with the president of Columbia University, Nicholas Murray Butler. Among the Bryan Democrats and the handful of Republican progressives in Congress it received enthusiastic praise, as it did among the people in general. But the Congress remained hostile and conservative. Though Roosevelt sent numerous special messages throughout the session, Congress ignored most of them and concerned itself primarily with the problem of currency expansion.[26]

The President realized that the fulfillment of his four-battleship program would require a bitter and hard fight. But he gave no sign of backing down, for he believed it would be a "national folly" to fail to keep the navy at the highest point of efficiency as long as the possibility of a future conflict with Japan existed. Though Roosevelt did not anticipate war in the next two or three years, he wanted the United States to be prepared fully for some more distant emergency. Otherwise, the nation might lose the Philippines and Hawaii in a "bitterly humiliating and disastrous war."[27] Moreover, European developments made American naval expansion more imperative than ever. The failure of the Hague Conference had ended hopes in Great Britain for any large reduction in naval estimates, and the third dreadnought of Britain's 1907 program was laid down after the conference. The German Reichstag in February, 1908, passed an amendment to the naval law of 1900 which called for four capital ships per year until 1912. Although the British government actually decreased its naval estimates for 1908, Conservatives were critical, and uneasiness over the adequacy of the nation's naval program was growing. The Anglo-German

<hr/>

[26] Mowry, *Era of Theodore Roosevelt*, pp. 219–223; Harbaugh, *Power and Responsibility*, pp. 343–344; Pringle, *Roosevelt*, pp. 476–483.
[27] Roosevelt to Spring Rice, December 21, 1907, *Letters*, VI, 869–871.

naval rivalry was achieving a more prominent position in European politics.[28] To most Americans these events were remote, but to Roosevelt they were very real and affected the relative standing of the United States as a great power. Unless American naval expansion proceeded at a faster pace, the navy would drop to third place within a few years.

Conservative Republican leaders were less concerned about the future than the President. They were alarmed at the prospective deficit resulting from depressed economic conditions, and generally thought two ships would do. At least one party leader, James A. Tawney, the influential chairman of the House Appropriations Committee, planned to oppose even two battleships. By early February the Washington correspondent of the *New York Times* thought the odds were strongly against the administration getting four ships. In recognition of the need for Democratic support, Roosevelt called together the Democratic members of the House Committee on Naval Affairs to ask their aid.[29] Whatever Roosevelt told them, neither his efforts nor those of Richmond P. Hobson (elected to the Sixtieth Congress from Alabama) promised to alter the unfavorable situation in Congress. Cannon and Hale were unmoved by the President's letters in late February asking for four battleships and increased funds for fortifications. Chairman Foss of the House Committee on Naval Affairs favored four ships, but wished to report a program which could pass the House, and in late February the committee voted thirteen to five to recommend two battleships. Two Republicans joined three Democrats in supporting the President. Roosevelt clearly had lost the first round.[30]

Except on the Pacific Coast, the President had also failed

---

[28] Marder, *From the Dreadnought to Scapa Flow*, I, 134–139.

[29] *New York Times*, February 7, 11, 1908; *Baltimore Sun*, February 7, 1908, Roosevelt Scrapbooks.

[30] *The Navy*, 2 (February, 1908), 32, 34.

to rally strong public support behind his four-ship program. The press was divided, while eastern opponents of naval expansion were extremely vocal.[31] Impressive petitions signed by peace groups, clergymen, scholars, and university presidents were presented to Congress, and the *Nation* was certain the people were not with Roosevelt in his fight.[32] Even the *Outlook* thought Roosevelt's reasons for his change in policy were inadequate and denied any desire to enter into naval competition with European powers. Moreover, the *Outlook* was concerned over the effect a public debate on naval policy might have. A public discussion would involve American relations with Japan and might inflame the "passions and prejudices" of the people. This pro-Roosevelt journal speculated:

> There is a possible danger that the race feeling in America may manifest itself in such forms as will inflame the pride and passion of the Japanese to an uncontrollable degree. There is a possible danger that the popular passion in either or in both countries might be aroused to such a pitch that no Government could restrain it.
>
> It is believed by many that the Spanish Government would have relinquished its sovereignty over Cuba if it could have done so without peril of a revolution in Spain, and that the McKinley administration would have conceded a nominal sovereignty to Spain in Cuba if it could have done so without peril to its political prestige. Whether these contentions are correct or not, they illustrate the possible peril in a democratic community from a popular feeling for war too strong to be resisted by the wiser counsels of its leaders, however pacific their spirit.

The people should not settle the question of whether danger of war existed between the United States and Japan in the

---

[31] *Literary Digest*, 36 (February 22, 1908), 253–254.
[32] *Congressional Record*, 60th Cong., 1st Sess., 3822–3823, 2552, 2717, 2361, 4743–4744; *Nation*, 86 (April 23, 1908), 368.

next decade. They should leave this task, the *Outlook* concluded, to the administration and Congress.[33]

Nevertheless, administration spokesmen did attempt to arouse the public. Secretary of War Taft called for a navy commensurate with America's world position, and Admiral Dewey declared the nation needed two battle fleets. The President publicly wished that "all Americans would feel that American politics are world politics; that we are and will be concerned in all the great questions." [34] But as Roosevelt realized, this was a dream in 1908. The nation was moving inward, toward a confrontation with domestic problems, despite his attempt to make the people realize the responsibilities of world power.

The lack of a strong naval league, such as existed in Great Britain and Germany, also hampered the administration's efforts to secure naval expansion. The Navy League of the United States, founded in 1902, had neither money nor public support, and was limited by its commitment to influence public opinion rather than directly pressure the Congress. Its members numbered only 4,500 in 1907; the next year it failed to hold an annual convention.[35] Moreover, divisions of opinion existed within the ranks of big-navy advocates. Since the turn of the century several groups of reform-minded officers had grown up within the navy, discontented with the service's archaic promotion system, with the Navy Department's organization, and with defects in battleship design. In general Roosevelt had cooperated with these insurgents, and some reforms had been accomplished. But almost any change in the status quo met with the powerful opposition of Hale and Foss, who were closely tied to the department's bureaus and to more conservative naval officers.

[33] *Outlook*, 87 (December 14, 1907), 804–806.
[34] *Chicago Record Herald*, January 30, 1908, Roosevelt Scrapbooks; *New York Times*, March 15, 20, 24, 1908.
[35] Armin Rappaport, *The Navy League of the United States* (Detroit, 1962), pp. 1–15.

Roosevelt was aware of these difficulties and had chosen to forego pushing personnel legislation or departmental reorganization in order to concentrate on his naval expansion program. However, crusaders like William S. Sims and Albert L. Key felt that the various reform measures deserved priority over naval expansion and feared that with Roosevelt out of office their chances of achieving them would diminish greatly.[36] Sims, therefore, encouraged Henry Reuterdahl, a marine artist and the American editor of *Jane's Fighting Ships,* to publish an exposé of naval defects. The article, reflecting many of Sims' views, appeared in the January, 1908, issue of *McClure's Magazine* under the title, "The Needs of Our Navy." Coming just as the nation focused its attention on the departing battle fleet, Reuterdahl's contentions created a sensation. Though most of the nation's press suspended judgment on the accuracy of his charges, both editorial writers and members of Congress demanded an investigation.[37]

In late February the Senate Committee on Naval Affairs began an investigation which dragged on inconclusively until the middle of March. Hale had intended from the start to whitewash the bureau system, but having discovered during the hearings that the criticism was well founded, his committee suddenly went into executive session and adjourned without making a report. The naval insurgents had succeeded in creating a broader public awareness of the need

[36] Morison, *Sims,* pp. 176–185.

[37] Henry Reuterdahl, "The Needs of Our Navy," *McClure's Magazine,* 30 (January, 1908), 251–263; *Literary Digest,* 36 (January 4, 1908), 1–3; service unity was also impaired by the resignation of Admiral Willard Brownson, Chief of the Bureau of Navigation, in late December, 1907. Brownson objected to Roosevelt's appointment of a medical officer as commander of the hospital ship *Relief.* The dispute involved both bureau jurisdiction and line and staff prerogatives. Brownson's resignation angered Roosevelt, for it emphasized service conflicts and damaged confidence in the navy. But the President's intemperate abuse of Brownson only made matters worse. For an analysis of the incident, see notes in *Letters,* VI, 876, 891.

for reform, but at the same time they had annoyed the President and publicized bitter dissensions within the service at a time when unity was badly needed. With doubt created about the efficiency of the Navy Department and the preparedness of the fleet for war, some members of Congress were reluctant to expand the navy until changes were made.[38]

The President was impressed by the arguments of the naval reformers. He realized the organization of the Navy Department and the navy's promotion system were defective; he agreed that the American dreadnoughts under construction were inferior to their Japanese equivalents. But he was unwilling, despite strong arguments from Key, to take any corrective steps in March or April of 1908. Removing older men in important departmental positions and replacing them with younger ones would, Roosevelt predicted, "cause a perfect explosion in the Congress, among the people, *and in the navy.*" [39] With his drive for four battleships coming to a climax in April, the last thing Roosevelt wanted was a heated controversy over naval reforms. Instead, the President continued his campaign for naval expansion. In late March he again asked Cannon for four battleships and a base at Pearl Harbor, and reminded the Speaker of the trouble he was having resisting the demand for a tariff commission. With Cannon giving no sign of yielding, the situation in Congress remained bleak.[40]

Congress's refusal to be pushed into substantially larger defense appropriations was made clear by its treatment of the War Department's request for over $38,000,000 for

[38] Morison, *Sims*, pp. 185–198; for example, see the comment of Senator Teller, *Congressional Record*, 60th Cong., 1st Sess., 2197; *New York Times*, December 27, 1907.

[39] Note in *Letters*, VI, 980; Roosevelt to Key, April 10, 1908, *Letters*, VI, 999–1001.

[40] Roosevelt to Cannon, March 23, 1908, *Letters*, VI, 980–981; *New York Times*, March 28, 1908.

coastal and insular fortifications. The House Subcommittee on Fortifications reported only $8,200,000, and met little opposition on the floor. Chairman Walter I. Smith of Iowa did not fear war with Japan and thought that with "a great national deficit" an increase of $3,000,000 over 1907 was sufficient.[41] Taft was able to intervene with Senator Perkins of California, chairman of the Senate subcommittee, to get over $3,000,000 restored, but the final bill was far short of the department's urgent needs. The single compensation was that it heavily favored Pacific Coast and insular fortifications.[42]

The Congress proved more responsive to the President's plea for a naval base at Pearl Harbor. On April 6 the House approved a $900,000 appropriation with but one dissenting vote, and the Senate endorsed the measure without debate later in the month. Many in Congress regarded Pearl Harbor as the "key to the Pacific" and demonstrated an eagerness to develop it which they had never shown for Subig Bay.[43]

Discussion in the House on naval appropriations began on April 10 with Foss's report of the Committee on Naval Affairs. The committee recommended two dreadnoughts and other construction which would cost $30,000,000, far below the department's request for nearly $70,000,000. The debate was more intense than usual, but lacked the heat of the forthcoming Senate struggle. Pacific Coast representatives praised the cruise of the fleet and demanded a strong force permanently stationed in the Pacific. Richmond P. Hobson, Democrat of Alabama, predicted the United States would slip in naval rank to fourth or fifth place if only two battle-

[41] *Congressional Record*, 60th Cong., 1st Sess., 3718; memorandum for Taft by General Arthur Murray, Chief of Artillery, March 27, 1908, Roosevelt Papers.

[42] Taft to George C. Perkins, March 30, 1908, Taft Papers; *Congressional Record*, 60th Cong., 1st Sess., 4472.

[43] *Congressional Record*, 60th Cong., 1st Sess., 4443–4447, 5019; *Literary Digest*, 36 (May 9, 1908), 667.

ships were authorized, and asked for six. Roosevelt's brother-in-law, Nicholas Longworth, Republican of Ohio, urged Republicans to stand by the President, but Chairman Tawney warned that the President's program would entail a $150,-000,000 deficit. As the debate drew to a close on April 14, Roosevelt sent a special message explaining in more detail the need for naval expansion. The President claimed that the failure of the Hague Conference and the development of the dreadnought made the nation's naval program inadequate. To provide but one or two battleships per year, Roosevelt said, meant that the United States "shall go backward in naval rank and relative power among the great nations." It was a temperate and thoughtful message, but most congressmen saw little or no connection between world developments and American policy. A program of two ships a year, promised by Foss, seemed adequate, and on April 15 Hobson's amendment for four ships was defeated, 83 to 199, while Tawney's amendment for one ship was also defeated 65 to 205. Foss had shrewdly sensed the temper of the House.[44]

In a House consisting of 224 Republicans and 167 Democrats, Roosevelt's program won only 83 votes. The Pacific Coast delegation stood solidly for four ships, and the measure drew considerable support from New England and New York representatives, but it was not a strongly partisan vote. Naval expansion had, for example, appealed to southern Democrats, while it had been opposed by the Republican leadership of the House.[45] Roosevelt was disappointed with the one-sided outcome. "Yesterday," he wrote Hobson on April 16, "the House seemed to possess an infinite capacity

[44] *Congressional Record*, 6oth Cong., 1st Sess., 4574–4577, 4596–4600, 4606–4611, 4741, 4802–4803, 4782–4785, 4806; Roosevelt had angered many House Republicans by threatening to veto the public buildings and grounds bill unless he got four battleships. Hobson claimed Roosevelt made the threat under provocation (*Los Angeles Times*, April 11, 1908).

[45] *Los Angeles Times*, April 16, 1908; Sprouts, *Rise of American Naval Power*, p. 267.

to go wrong, except, praise Heaven! in beating the scandalously unpatriotic proposal to cut down the increase of the navy to one battleship." [46]

By the end of the House debate the impact of the battle fleet's cruise was beginning to be reflected in the nation's press. The *New York Times* believed the people favored a policy of naval expansion, and a poll by the *New York Telegram* of publishers and editors found 80 percent for four ships. The *Literary Digest*, too, reported a heavy majority of the nation's press endorsing the President's program and thought that all of the press would do so if the Treasury did not face a deficit.[47] Support of Roosevelt's policy cut across party lines. Some hostile papers, such as the *New York Sun*, wanted four ships, while some pro-Roosevelt papers, such as the *Boston Transcript*, opposed the large increase. Outside the Pacific Coast, few signs existed of a powerful demand among the people for naval expansion.[48]

Before the Senate debate began on April 21, Roosevelt realized that the upper house would not restore two battleships. He wrote Kermit that he had made "a hard fight to get Congress to give me four battleships, but they wouldn't do it. Most of them mean well enough, but do not know much, and the leaders are narrow-minded and selfish. . . . I cannot give in public my reasons for being apprehensive about Japan, for of course to do so might bring on grave trouble; but I said enough to put Congress thoroly on its guard. . . . I do not believe there will be war with Japan, but I do believe that there is enough chance of war to make it eminently wise to insure against it by building such a navy as to forbid Japan's hoping for success. I happen to know that the Japanese military party is inclined for war with us

[46] Roosevelt to Hobson, April 16, 1908, *Letters*, VI, 1008–1009.
[47] *New York Times*, April 16, 1908; *Literary Digest*, 36 (May 2, 1908), 631–632.
[48] *Literary Digest*, 36 (April 25, 1908), 579–580.

and is not only confident of success, but confident that they could land a large expeditionary force in California and conquer all of the United States west of the Rockies. I fully believe that they would in the end pay dearly for this, but meantime we would have been set back at least a generation by the loss of life, the humiliation, and the material damage." [49]

The President wisely expected little from the Senate's conservative Republican leadership. As he had moved to the left after his re-election in November, 1904, conservative Republicans such as Nelson W. Aldrich of Rhode Island, John C. Spooner of Wisconsin, Orville H. Platt of New York, and Eugene Hale of Maine had continued to defend the status quo tenaciously. An open break had been averted, and on some issues Roosevelt was able to work with the Republican leadership until the end of his second term; but by the spring of 1908 the tension between the President and the Senate oligarchy was great. Most of Roosevelt's reform proposals of December and January had been ignored, as had his many special messages. The Senate had not even heard Roosevelt's battleship message of April 14, because of the turmoil following a speech by Joseph B. Foraker of Ohio on the Brownsville affair. While the clerk skimmed over Roosevelt's address, many conservative Republicans were congratulating the President's bitter enemy. [50]

By the spring of 1908, however, the Senate oligarchy was no longer so firmly in control. Platt had died in 1905. Spooner, challenged by Robert M. La Follette in Wisconsin, had left the Senate. William B. Allison was in poor health and becoming less conservative in response to progressive pressures in Iowa. Of the old leaders only Aldrich remained,

[49] Roosevelt to Kermit Roosevelt, April 19, 1908, *Letters*, VI, 1012–1013.
[50] Pringle, *Theodore Roosevelt*, pp. 476–483; Mowry, *Era of Theodore Roosevelt*, pp. 211–212, 220, 225.

aided increasingly by Hale. As the oligarchy disintegrated from within, it had to deal after 1906 with an increasing number of progressive, independent-minded senators. Some, such as La Follette, Jonathan Bourne, Jr. of Oregon, and William E. Borah of Idaho, were newcomers; others, such as Jonathan Dolliver of Iowa and Albert J. Beveridge of Indiana were former conservatives.[51] Once an eloquent defender of conservatism, Beveridge had declared his progressivism in the autumn of 1906; since then he had been a thorn in the side of the Republican leaders, particularly through his advocacy of a child labor law and a tariff commission. In late 1907 Hale had threatened to keep Beveridge off the Senate Finance Committee if he persisted in demanding a tariff commission, but Beveridge had done so, further irritating Aldrich and the senator from Maine. Moreover, Beveridge had become floor manager of Roosevelt's naval program in the Senate, after some of the younger Republican senators had asked him to do so.[52] Beveridge's decision meant that the contest in the Senate would involve a fight with the Republican leaders and would have ramifications far beyond the immediate issue of naval expansion.

Although Beveridge realized that the four battleship proposal had no chance, he was determined to shake the Senate's leadership. Along with the President, he applied considerable pressure on wavering senators.[53] *The Navy* thought the Congress had not shown so much interest in naval affairs since the opening of the Spanish-American War, and the Washington correspondent of the *New York Times* described the

[51] Nathaniel W. Stephenson, *Nelson W. Aldrich: A Leader in American Politics* (New York, 1930), pp. 265–266, 268, 284, 309, 320; Robert M. La Follette, *Autobiography* (Madison, 1913), p. 183.

[52] Claude G. Bowers, *Beveridge and the Progressive Era* (Boston, 1932), pp. 226, *passim*, 270, 277; Beveridge to Frederick A. Joss, April 28, 1908, Beveridge Papers.

[53] Memorandum for the President of telephone call from Beveridge, April 20, 1908, Roosevelt Papers; *Los Angeles Times*, April 22, 1908.

Senate debate as the hottest since the Hepburn bill.[54] From the start, Hale showed a willingness to compromise on a program of two battleships per year, but Senator Samuel H. Piles, Republican of Washington, introduced and vigorously supported an amendment for four ships. The people of the Pacific Coast, Piles argued, demanded four because of the uncertainty of future relations with Japan. Beveridge, too, stressed the uncertainties of the future and the insistence of the American people on large naval increases. "What the Executive may have in his possession," the great Indiana orator proclaimed, "no man knows"; and he went on to claim that if "the probability of conflict with any specific power" could be discussed, few would cast their vote against Roosevelt's naval program. Beveridge and Piles also emphasized the relative decline of American naval power. In dreadnought strength, and therefore in actual fighting strength, Beveridge warned, the United States stood fourth or fifth, not second. Hale and Aldrich scoffed at the probability of any foreign complications in the future; they insisted that the United States was and would remain second in fleet strength. Aldrich also attacked with biting sarcasm the intimation of Beveridge and Piles that they spoke with the authority of the President and with a knowledge of certain hidden facts which they could not reveal.[55]

But the Senate's leadership was on the defensive. Aldrich, who normally exercised his influence behind the scenes, was forced to engage in open and prolonged debate with Beveridge. The *New York Times* correspondent described him, at one point, as "white with anger." Toward the close of the debate the outcome seemed less certain than at the begin-

[54] *The Navy*, 2 (May, 1908), 3; *New York Times*, April 28, 1908.
[55] Bowers, *Beveridge*, pp. 277–282, gives a superb if one-sided account of the Senate debate; *Congressional Record*, 60th Cong., 1st Sess., 5012, 5161–5163, 5165–5175, 5221–5224, 5158–5159, 5212–5218, 5222–5224, 5288–5289, 5290.

ning. Under pressure from the President, Henry Cabot Lodge had unenthusiastically committed himself to four ships.[56] Worried that others might join Lodge, Hale and Aldrich asked older senators to stand together and suppress the insurrection. On April 27, the final day of debate, Allison took the floor for the first time in the session and attempted to minimize the conflict. He would be willing, Allison said, to provide for two ships every year, and he thought most senators would agree. Hale quickly did so. He promised a moderate program of two dreadnoughts per year which would give the United States "a very great navy, and keep us in the second place in the world." The Senate then defeated the Piles amendment twenty-three to fifty, with nineteen members not voting. The great naval debate had ended in a compromise.[57]

One big-navy advocate, Edward E. Higgins, president of *Success Magazine,* was dissatisfied with the results and urged the President to veto the naval appropriation bill. Higgins believed a veto message would bring "a flame of patriotism from all parts of the country," and claimed Senators Bourne and Beveridge approved of this course.[58] But Roosevelt had little inclination to follow Higgins' radical advice. To Ambassador Bryce he spoke "gleefully" of the success of his efforts for the navy and then wrote Kermit that the Congress had "really done well" in foreign matters and in regard to the army and navy. On the very day the Senate voted, Roosevelt admitted to Henry White that he had not supposed Congress would stand for four battleships. "But I knew," he added, "I would not get thru two and have those two hurried up unless I made a violent fight for four." And pledging the Congress to a steady policy of two ships per year was "a

[56] *New York Times,* April 28, 1908; Roosevelt to Lodge, April 22, 1908, *Letters,* VI, 1014.

[57] *Congressional Record,* 60th Cong., 1st Sess., 5218–5220, 5281, 5291.

[58] Edward E. Higgins to Roosevelt, April 24, 1908, Roosevelt Papers.

great gain." [59] Moreover, construction would be rapid since Roosevelt had forced the Senate and House to appropriate immediately money for the two ships authorized.

The President had good reason to be satisfied. With skill and persistence he had persuaded a reluctant Congress to adopt once again a policy of naval expansion. As Roosevelt had planned, the cruise of the battle fleet created a timely interest in the navy and solidified popular support for naval expansion on the Pacific Coast. The almost solid vote Pacific Coast senators and congressmen gave Roosevelt's program reflected the enthusiasm there. The President had been careful not to use sensational methods which might have created another war scare with Japan and interfered with his aim of a Japanese-American rapprochement. He wanted to leave to his successor both a heritage of naval strength and a heritage of friendship with Japan.

Beveridge, too, was pleased with the results of the Senate struggle. On the morning after the battle he wrote:

> We have just had the greatest fight and greatest moral victory ever seen in the Senate. . . . This morning . . . it is we who stood behind the President and voted for a greater navy who are happy, and it is the men who are against the President and voted against a greater navy that are unhappy. We were right and they were wrong, we have the people back of us and they have the people against them, and they know it. Aldrich, Hale, and that crowd did everything in God's world that could be done or ever has been done to defeat us. The House organization, with Cannon at its head, did the same thing. Promises and pledges, threats of all kinds, personal appeals . . . were made to Senators in order to get them to line up against the President's recommendations.
>
> The plain truth about it is that it was not a battleship fight at all but a fight against Theodore Roosevelt.[60]

[59] Bryce to Grey, April 30, 1908, Roosevelt Memorial Association Microfilm; Roosevelt to Kermit Roosevelt, May 30, 1908, *Letters*, VI, 1044; Roosevelt to Henry White, April 27, 1908, *Letters*, VI, 1017–1018.

[60] Beveridge to Joss, April 28, 1908, Beveridge Papers.

Beveridge claimed it was the first time any senators had seriously opposed a program of Aldrich and Hale, and that the young, energetic senators who had fought the "leaders" would "hang together till hell freezes over." Certainly in Beveridge's own mind the impact of the debate lingered on, for in the autumn of 1908 he refused to campaign for Eugene Hale in Maine.[61]

The Senate struggle was a serious revolt against the Republican leadership, for nineteen out of sixty-one Republicans voted against Aldrich. Though the *Saturday Evening Post* was exaggerating when it reported that the Senate oligarchy was "tottery and wobbly at the knees" after the debate, the attacks by Beveridge on the Senate leadership were telling.[62] The naval battle of 1907, rather than the Payne-Aldrich tariff debate of 1909, marked the first organized challenge to Aldrich's rule. But the naval debate should not be interpreted as a contest between progressives and conservatives, such as the struggle over the Payne-Aldrich tariff.[63] None of the progressive group which opposed the Aldrich rates in 1909, with the exception of Beveridge, prominently figured in the naval debate. Moses E. Clapp of Minnesota voted against four battleships, as did Joseph M. Dixon of Montana, and neither Dolliver nor La Follette bothered to vote at all. Bourne of

[61] Beveridge to Charles R. Lane, April 30, to C. B. Landis, April 28, to Senator William P. Frye, August 12, 1908, Beveridge Papers; Beveridge believed the fight for four battleships was popular throughout the country. The Pacific Coast, according to Senator Frank P. Flint, unanimously approved of Roosevelt's program, and Flint thought Perkins was nearly defeated for re-election because of his vote against four ships (Beveridge to Flint, August 12, 1908, Flint to Beveridge, September 7, 1908, Beveridge Papers).

[62] *Saturday Evening Post*, 180 (May 23, 1908), 18–19.

[63] As William E. Leuchtenburg does in his "Progressivism and Imperialism: The Progressive Movement and American Foreign Policy, 1898–1916," *Mississippi Valley Historical Review*, 39 (December, 1952), 483–504. A far more convincing explanation of the attitudes of progressives toward foreign policy is in John Braeman, "Seven Progressives," *Business History Review*, 35 (Winter 1961), 581–592.

Oregon and Borah of Idaho voted with Beveridge but did not join him in the floor debate. Two of the younger senators most active in supporting Roosevelt's program — Flint of California and Piles of Washington — were conservatives. Flint was tied to California's Southern Pacific machine and regular Republican organization; Piles opposed Roosevelt's conservation policies and in 1909 became a chief supporter of the Western Conservation League, an organization dedicated to freeing natural resources from the grip of eastern socialists.[64] Senator Charles W. Fulton of Oregon was anti-Roosevelt, conservative, and associated with the state's regular Republican organization, but he too voted for four ships.[65] So did the conservative Republican Reed Smoot of Utah.

The fact that Roosevelt's naval expansion program received conservative votes, particularly from the Pacific Coast, is a useful reminder of the support conservatives had consistently given Roosevelt's foreign and naval policies in the past. Many of the conservatives who opposed four ships — certainly Aldrich and Hale — had not become anti-navy. Hale, for example, had three colliers placed in the 1908 naval appropriations bill because of his alarm over the fleet's deficiency in auxiliary vessels. Conservatives fought Roosevelt's request for four ships because of a desire for economy, because of reaction against his strong use of executive power, and because of a growing estrangement from his domestic political goals.[66] To men who had little grasp of America's position in world affairs, the difference between two and four ships seemed small when balanced against their strong desire to give the President a telling setback.

[64] Mowry, *California Progressives*, p. 16; Mowry, *Era of Theodore Roosevelt*, pp. 251–252.

[65] Albert H. Pike, Jr., "Jonathan Bourne, Jr., Progressive" (unpublished Ph.D. dissertation, University of Oregon, 1957), p. 87.

[66] Bryce to Grey, April 30, 1908, Roosevelt Memorial Association Microfilm.

The American press regarded the outcome of the naval battle as a victory for neither side. Some big-navy papers were disappointed by a further delay in attaining a two ocean navy, but many pro-Roosevelt journals thought the President had got as many battleships as he had expected. What the President really wanted, the *Review of Reviews* argued, was a definite notice to the world that the United States navy would be maintained at a point of high efficiency. The promise of two ships per year more than demonstrated this fact.[67]

Roosevelt had, in fact, done well, but most of the nation's press failed to realize that he had not done well enough to maintain the relative rank of the United States. The expanded German naval program of 1908 meant that Germany would within several years replace the United States as the world's second naval power.[68]

[67] *Current Literature,* 34 (June, 1908), 597–599; *Review of Reviews,* 37 (June, 1908), 650.

[68] Brassey, *The Naval Annual,* 1908, pp. 48, 55–56; Brassey, *The Naval Annual,* 1909, pp. 44, 51, 50.

# XI

# RECONCILIATION WITH JAPAN

By the late spring of 1908 considerable optimism existed in Washington over the future of Japanese-American relations. "Everything between us and Japan," Elihu Root confided to Ambassador Reid, "is moving very smoothly now." [1] The two nations had recently concluded an arbitration treaty, treaties for the reciprocal protection of trade marks, copyrights and patents in China and Korea, and, most important, a detailed Gentlemen's Agreement which was gradually becoming more effective. The President had also secured a modest increase in American naval strength. All of these developments helped insure a peaceful future and made it more likely that the cruise of the battle fleet would aid the rapprochement between the United States and Japan.

Unresolved problems, however, still troubled the two governments. Before departing for Oyster Bay in the middle of June, the President informed Ambassador Takahira of the American public's increasing friendliness toward Japan and remarked that only the immigration question could upset that trend. But he was displeased that Japanese immigration had not decreased more rapidly, and he left Takahira with the impression that some explanation was needed. To Root the President expressed much stronger dissatisfaction with the

[1] Root to Reid, May 22, 1908, Root Papers.

results of Japan's restriction. Japan could expect nothing but an exclusion law, Roosevelt warned, unless the figures began to show a "totally different complexion." [2]

A week after Roosevelt's conversation with Takahira, Foreign Minister Hayashi attempted to reassure the annoyed President. The Japanese Foreign Office had brought under its direct control the issuance of all passports, and Hayashi was certain the regulations would become more effective. Washington remained officially dissatisfied, however, and Acting Secretary of State Robert Bacon told Takahira he hoped the issue could be settled before the opening of Congress in December. The Japanese Ambassador was eager for a rapid adjustment, too, for he thought the pressure on Roosevelt for exclusion legislation could be relieved only if the immigration of Japanese laborers was completely stopped. With presidential elections not far off, Takahira regarded political considerations as crucial to the administration and urged Hayashi to take immediate action. [3]

Takahira's fears were probably exaggerated. By early July the downward trend in Japanese immigration, interrupted in April and May, was once again evident. While 717 Japanese arrived in the continental United States in December, 1907, only 446 came in June, 1908. [4] The President was impressed with the fact that more Japanese were leaving than entering the country. He agreed with Root's opinion that too much must not be expected of the new Japanese system of regulation. "Time and patience and persistency will doubtless be necessary," Root counseled, "but I am sure that the subject

---

[2] Takahira to Hayashi, June 13, 1908, Telegram Series, JA; Roosevelt to Root, June 18, 1908, Roosevelt Papers.

[3] Hayashi to Takahira, June 18, 1908, NA, RG 59:2542/643; Takahira to Hayashi, July 8, 1908, Telegram Series, JA.

[4] "Report of the Commissioner-General of Immigration, July 1, 1908," in *Reports of the Department of Commerce and Labor, 1908* (Washington, D.C., 1909), pp. 100, 186.

is being dealt with in the right spirit and in the right way." [5]

While the immigration of Japanese laborers to American shores was no longer an acute problem, Roosevelt was still conscious of a strong undercurrent of popular suspicion of Japan. This was particularly evident on the Pacific Coast; it largely explained the frenzied welcome which the battle fleet received at San Francisco in early May. The new commander, Admiral Charles S. Sperry, had never before seen men listen so intently to his discussion of the needs of the navy. Richmond P. Hobson was on hand to announce that the United States regained control of the Pacific. The fleet must be kept in the Pacific, Hobson argued, and be joined by those battleships still in the Atlantic.[6] The *San Francisco Argonaut* also saw the Pacific as the battleground of the future and thought the cruise expressed the nation's intention "to have a finger or possibly a whole hand in the Pacific pie." No longer could Japan and Europe doubt the role the United States would play in "the rising world of the Pacific Ocean." [7]

Outside the Pacific Coast, however, the nation seemed far less disturbed over Japanese-American relations. This calmness was apparent at the Democratic National Convention in July, 1908. Temporary Chairman Theodore Bell of California predicted a "mighty commercial struggle" in the Pacific and called for naval strength in the Pacific and the exclusion of all Asiatics. The convention responded to his plea by adopting a resolution which, in effect, endorsed an Asiatic exclusion law. But the convention responded in quite a different way to a fervent speech by Hobson on the danger of war with Japan and the need for huge defense preparations. Hobson's remarks brought uproarious laughter and loud

[5] Roosevelt to Takahira, July 8, 1908, Roosevelt Papers; Root to Roosevelt, August 1, 1908, Roosevelt Papers.

[6] *New York Times*, May 7, 1908; Sperry to C. S. Sperry, Jr., May 28, 1908, Sperry Papers; *San Francisco Examiner*, May 7, 1908, Hobson Papers.

[7] *Literary Digest*, 36 (May 23, 1908), 747–748.

hoots. Goaded by the unfriendly reception, the hero of the *Merrimac* decided "to state the cold facts." He confided that President Roosevelt had told him not so long ago that "there exists the greatest possibility of a war with Japan." An uproar followed, punctuated by cries of "rot" and "you're crazy" from the floor and galleries; and it was only with difficulty that Hobson managed to conclude his speech.[8] Rejected by his party, Hobson was also soon repudiated by the President, who vehemently denied the statement attributed to him.[9] The Democratic convention provided convincing evidence that the nation was in no mood for war with Japan.

Roosevelt himself misjudged the temper of the nation's press. In a speech before a naval conference at Newport, Rhode Island, on July 22, he demanded a "hard-hitting" navy and reminded his fellow countrymen that immigration caused many points of friction with other nations. If America had to defend its right to supervise and restrict immigration, he said, it could only do so with a powerful navy.[10] While most Republican papers agreed with the President on the need for

[8] *New York Times,* July 8–10, 1908; Hobson to Grizelda Hobson, July 9, 1908, Hobson Papers.

[9] Roosevelt to Hobson, July 9, 1908, *Letters,* VI, 1116–1117. The incident abruptly ended the collaboration between the President and Hobson, which had reached its height during the battleship fight in April, 1908. Roosevelt considered Hobson a "cad" and "blackguard" and refused ever again to converse privately with him. Hobson, however, stuck to his story and expressed his "scorn and loathing" for Roosevelt and his "crafty evasion." Years later Hobson claimed that Congressman James Watson of Indiana, who was present during the conversation, verified his version. Wherever the truth may lie, Roosevelt had, prior to July, 1908, encouraged Hobson's anti-Japanese campaign. On June 19, 1908, for example, the President of the Army War College, W. W. Wotherspoon, forwarded to Hobson at the request of Chief of Staff Bell confidential information on the alleged war preparations of Japanese residents on the Pacific Coast. Hobson was allowed to use the material but not to reveal its source. Roosevelt to Root, August 8, 1908, to Hobson, July 24, 1908, *Letters,* VI, 1163–1164, 1142–1143; Hobson to Roosevelt, July 21, August 1, 9, 1908, Hobson Papers; note of August 7, 1928, Hobson Papers; W. W. Wotherspoon to Hobson, June 19, 1908, Hobson Papers.

[10] *New York Times,* July 23, 1908.

naval expansion, few defended the timeliness of his statement, and Democratic and independent papers strongly denounced his outburst. The *New York Evening Post* called the
speech "vicious," particularly since it came when the "anti-
Japanese craze" gave signs of dying out. And the *Springfield
Republican* complained that "the fever and fret of his
[Roosevelt's] intense nature wear upon the nerves of those
who still have a vital faith in the teachings of the New
Testament." [11]

The criticism of the President did not extend to his most
spectacular project, the cruise of the battle fleet. By late July
few papers were still hostile to the voyage. The dominant
tone of newspaper comment, reported the *Literary Digest*,
was one of "quiet confidence" in the American navy and of
"comfortable pride" in its dramatic display of power.[12] The
fleet's visit to New Zealand and various Australian ports
strengthened this consensus of the nation's press. The re-
ceptions in both nations surpassed even those on the Pacific
Coast and were widely interpreted as demonstrating the
determination of the three nations to remain white man's
country. Some papers, such as the *New York Sun,* went
further and saw in the massive welcomes a recognition of
the United States as an ally in the struggle between the
white and yellow races for mastery of the Pacific. In Australia, according to the *Melbourne Age,* the pressure for self-
defense was growing stronger as the nation realized its
"perilous position south of the awakening Asiatic peoples." [13]
Prime Minister Deakin told Robert Patchin, correspondent
of the *New York Herald,* that the fleet's visit insured the
passage of his compulsory military training bill. As the great
fleet departed from Australian shores, Admiral Sperry re-

[11] *Literary Digest,* 37 (August 1, 1908), 137–139.
[12] *Literary Digest,* 37 (July 25, 1908), 103–104.
[13] *Literary Digest,* 37 (August 22, 1908), 239, 242; *Current Literature,*
45 (October, 1908), 369–373.

flected on the "monumental success" of the visit and on the intensity of the "Yellow Peril scare" in Australia. "The cruise is . . . no . . . menace to Japan," Sperry concluded, "but it establishes a curious sort of protectorate — a new Monroe Doctrine." [14]

The visit to New Zealand and Australia encouraged the tendency both in the United States and in Europe to view the voyage of the battle fleet as an assertion of American power in the Pacific. To politicians and editorial writers who felt the nation's destiny lay in that ocean, the sixteen battleships seemed the harbinger of a more vigorous Far Eastern policy. In the middle of August the Washington correspondent of the *New York Times* predicted the administration would respond to a rapidly forming national demand for a firm check on Japan's ambitions in China. Its most powerful members allegedly felt an acute need for establishing the nation's Far Eastern policy on a firmer basis.[15] Whatever the origins of this dispatch, it had little relation to the policy actually being pursued by Roosevelt in the summer of 1908. The President, it is true, had done nothing to dispel the many misconceptions of the purposes of the fleet's cruise; in fact, some of his statements had implied that the fleet did symbolize a tougher policy toward Japan. But Roosevelt and Root did not intend to become deeply involved in controversies over China and Manchuria, nor had they since the end of the Russo-Japanese War. In fact, both still hoped for an agreement with Japan similar to the one proposed by Ambassador Aoki in late October, 1907.

The development of Roosevelt's Far Eastern policy in the summer and autumn of 1908 can best be understood in relation to American policy toward Manchuria. The slow restora-

[14] Robert H. Patchin to Rockhill, September 19, 1908, Rockhill Papers; Sperry to Edith Sperry, August 16, September 9, 16, 1908, Sperry Papers.
[15] See, for example, *World's Work*, 16 (September, 1908), 10631–10633; *New York Times*, August 16, 1908.

tion of normal trade conditions in Manchuria after the Russo-Japanese War created concern in Washington and led to sporadic diplomatic correspondence with Japan. Despite the pledges by the Japanese government to observe the Open Door, it was not until the summer of 1907 that customs houses opened at Dairen and Antung. In northern Manchuria the customs question was not settled until November. By August Rockhill believed that for the time being the United States could merely watch developments in Manchuria, and Roosevelt and Root were content to follow his advice.[16]

Some American diplomats, however, were increasingly disturbed over Japan's policy in Manchuria. Both Willard Straight, American Consul General at Mukden, and F. M. Huntington Wilson wanted to counter Japanese predominance there with an "expanded concept of the Open Door." Equality of commercial opportunity in Manchuria, which Japan seemed willing to grant, was not enough; America must also vigorously support the territorial and administrative integrity of China in Manchuria and obtain equality of investment opportunity.[17] The introduction of American capital, Straight thought, would create an American interest in Manchuria which would aid progressive Chinese officials in their efforts to resist Japanese domination. In the autumn of 1907 Straight attempted to interest Edward H. Harriman in a plan for the construction of a railway from Hsinmintun to Fakumen, but the American financier rejected the offer because of the panic of October, 1907; in November Tang Shao-yi, governor of Fengtien province, contracted with British capitalists for the construction of the line.[18]

[16] The diplomatic correspondence is in Foreign Relations, 1906, I, 170–227, and NA, RG 59:511.

[17] Raymond A. Esthus, "The Changing Concept of the Open Door, 1899–1910," Mississippi Valley Historical Review, 46 (December, 1959), 440–442.

[18] Willard Straight to Bacon, September 28, 1907, NA, RG 59:2321/13; Vevier, United States and China, pp. 46–51.

Straight was dejected because American capital would not participate in this blow at Japan's special position in southern Manchuria. He had, however, other plans, which he outlined to William Howard Taft on a journey from Vladivostok to Harbin in November, 1907. Straight strongly attacked Japan's policy in southern Manchuria and enthusiastically described the prospects for American investment there. More particularly, he advocated a plan proposed by Tang Shao-yi for using the remitted portion of the American share of the Boxer indemnity as security for a Manchurian loan by American capitalists. Though Taft gave Straight's scheme only slight encouragement, he did say that China was turning to America as its only disinterested friend. He hoped "we might do something," and Straight, who had assured Taft that "the fruit is ripe and it is ours to pluck," felt that his words had made some impact on the Secretary of War. "If they [the President and Secretary of State] accept the advice which I think Mr. Taft will give," Straight concluded, "[they will] . . . regard Manchuria as a fair field and not as one that must be approached . . . with special regard for the sensibilities of the Japanese." [19] Taft was, in fact, impressed by the suspicions of American diplomats and merchants in the Far East over Japan's policy in Manchuria, and even before talking to Straight, he warned Root that a strong protest in support of the Open Door might be needed.[20] Once back in Washington, however, the Secretary of War did nothing to further the plans of the ambitious Consul General or to stiffen the administration's Far Eastern policy.

Neither Straight's financial projects nor Taft's warning

[19] For Straight's conversation with Taft, see Vevier, *United States and China*, pp. 61–63; Herbert Croly, *Willard Straight* (New York, 1924), pp. 250–251; Straight, memorandum on Manchurian Affairs, December 2, 1907, NA, RG 59:2413/97.

[20] Taft to Root, October 10, 1907, Mischler's Diaries, Taft Papers.

affected that policy. Root rejected Straight's plan for using the indemnity remission as loan security and ordered him to stay out of the negotiations. Moreover, the project for the Hsinmintun-Fakumen Railway failed when Japan protested in late 1907 that the construction of such a line, parallel to the South Manchuria Railway, was a violation of secret protocols to the Sino-Japanese Treaty of 1905. Straight felt that Japan's attitude toward this project was not consistent with its repeated declarations on the Open Door.[21] Assistant Secretaries of State William Phillips and Huntington Wilson were also disturbed over Japan's aggressive policy in southern Manchuria. Phillips was convinced that Japan was violating the principles of the Open Door and the integrity of China. "The United States ought to decide," he argued, "whether it is going to carry out Mr. Hay's policy in regard to the Far East. It is a subject of vast importance to our trade interests and one which ought not to be shelved to await developments."[22]

Parts of the American press echoed the charges made against Japan in the lower echelons of the State Department. Thomas F. Millard published a stream of accusations against Japanese policy on the Asiatic mainland, and some important papers, such as the *New York Times*, believed Japan intended to dominate Eastern Asia. In February, 1908, the *Times* Washington correspondent reported that large American commercial interests were urging the government to stop Japan's discriminatory practices in Manchuria. Throughout February, March and April, 1908, rumors of an impending diplomatic protest filled the nation's press.[23]

[21] Vevier, *United States and China*, pp. 64, 51–52; Straight to Bacon, February 12, 1908, NA, RG 59:6625/41.
[22] William Phillips to Huntington Wilson, February 14, 1908, NA, RG 59:2321/19; Huntington Wilson to Root, March 6, 1908, NA, RG 59:551/92.
[23] Thomas F. Millard, "The 'Open Door' in Manchuria," *Scribner's Magazine,* 41 (April, 1907), 497–504; *New York Times,* November 26, 1907, January 26, February 18, 20, April 2, 1908; *Chicago Record Herald,* February 25, 1908, Roosevelt Scrapbooks.

Japanese newspapers also discussed the apparent intention of the American government to take a stronger stand in Manchuria. The *Japan Advertiser* thought the United States was about to realize its stake in the Pacific, while the *Yorozu Choho* interpreted Roosevelt's naval program as an indication of a more active Far Eastern policy. The Anglo-Japanese Alliance, this yellow sheet predicted, would now have to be turned against American aggrandizement. The organ of Count Katsura, the *Kokumin Shimbun*, was surprised at the alleged determination of the United States to raise the Manchurian question, for the Japanese government had made many concessions in the immigration dispute in order to enjoy greater freedom of action in Manchuria.[24]

Root gave no indication, publicly or privately, that the administration was about to do anything in Manchuria. Though American trade had not returned to its prewar levels, Consul Roger S. Greene at Dalny found no cause for alarm. Nor did the American Asiatic Association, which continued to explain the decline in trade as a result of natural dislocations.[25] On March 1, 1908, Root discussed with Takahira the complaints of China against Japan's practices in Manchuria. After receiving assurances from the Japanese Ambassador that Japan would strictly observe the Open Door, Root summarized the situation: "Japan has control of railways, telegraphs, etc. in South Manchuria with a force of officials and men of her own nationality for their management and these officials and men are naturally treating their nationals with more facilities than foreigners can obtain and the latter are dissatisfied with, and make complaints against Japanese who are in a more advantageous position than others as a result of occupancy, but such a state of things is only natural

[24] *Japan Advertiser,* February 28, 1908, NA, RG 59:12611/10; *Yorozu Choho,* quoted in *Japan Times,* April 24, 1908, NA, RG 59:12611/9; *Kokumin Shimbun,* February 27, 1908, NA, RG 59:511/96.
[25] Roger S. Greene to Bacon, January 29, 1908, NA, RG 59:511/90; *Journal of the American Asiatic Association,* 8 (July, 1908), 162.

to occur where one nation has special interest and influence. The condition of affairs in the Panama Canal Zone is another example." Takahira concluded that Root did not place much importance on press reports as long as the principle of the Open Door was maintained.[26]

Other moves by Root had confirmed this impression of the Japanese Ambassador. By December, 1907, the State Department was reasonably certain that the Russo-Japanese Agreement of July 30, 1907, contained secret clauses dividing Manchuria into spheres of interest. As early as October, 1907, Huntington Wilson urged the Secretary of State to ask Japan and Russia if such clauses existed and then to indicate a refusal to recognize such spheres. Root did nothing until March, 1908, when he instructed Ambassador John W. Riddle in St. Petersburg to question Foreign Minister Alexander Izvolski about the secret clauses. Izvolski denied their existence and Root dropped the matter.[27] About the same time as Root's inquiry, Huntington Wilson completed the draft of an information series circular on the Open Door policy. He included a heated attack on Japan's misbehavior in Manchuria, which Root deleted from the draft. The circular, as finally sent, was an innocuous history of that policy.[28] Finally, in early April, 1908, the State Department asked George Marvin, formerly Straight's assistant at Mukden, to cease his activities as a champion of China's case against Japan.[29] Washington did not want trouble stirred up in the Far East just as relations with Japan were improving.

Most of the nation's press shared the administration's reluctance to become involved in disputes over Manchuria. Even newspapers critical of Japan's actions there, such as the *New York Times,* did not believe the United States could

[26] Takahira to Hayashi, February 28, 1908, Telegram Series, JA.
[27] For the correspondence, see NA, RG 59:3919.
[28] "Notes on the policy of the 'Open Door,'" in NA, RG 59:551/99.
[29] Vevier, *United States and China*, p. 68.

ever aid China directly. The *New York Journal of Commerce and Commercial Bulletin* thought everyone had understood since the issuance of the Open Door Notes that the United States would never go to war to uphold them.[30] But Thomas Millard was astounded that many American politicians and newspapermen assumed that "Japan's aspirations to dominate China . . . [were] entirely legitimate."[31] Few Americans advocated either the effective enforcement or the complete abandonment of the Open Door doctrine. The tactful exercise of diplomatic pressure seemed a popular middle course.

In one Manchurian dispute, beginning in the spring of 1908, the administration demonstrated just how far it would go. Consul Fred D. Fisher at Harbin had refused to recognize Russia's attempt to create a municipal administration based upon the concession for the construction of the Chinese Eastern Railway. In early April, in an interview with the Russian ambassador, Baron Roman Rosen, Root supported Fisher, arguing that the authority for such an administration could only be derived from the treaties between China and the powers. At Harbin the United States and other powers had few interests, but the dispute was important because of the precedent it might set for Japan in southern Manchuria. There American interests would be affected by a Japanese attempt to exercise similar powers within its railway zone. Root regarded the principle at stake as one "of paramount importance to the future of Manchuria," as did many other American diplomats, and he vigorously sought to strengthen the American position in the ensuing months by securing the assistance of Germany and Great Britain. The German government quickly promised to cooperate, but Foreign Secretary Grey was reluctant to join a dispute which did not

[30] *New York Times*, April 18, 1908; *New York Journal of Commerce and Commercial Bulletin*, October 11, 1907, Roosevelt Scrapbooks.
[31] *New York Times*, April 26, 1908.

directly involve British interests. Not until early June did he caution the Japanese ambassador against a similar claim by his government.[32] Root had several conferences with Takahira along the same line in the spring and summer of 1908.[33] But while pressing the American contention throughout the remainder of the Roosevelt administration, the Secretary of State carefully avoided a serious controversy with Japan and Russia. The "true policy" of the United States was a "quiet, firm" maintenance of its position; there was no cause for "undue excitement."[34] In December he informed Rosen that a municipality based on the powers' treaty rights would differ only in principle from one based upon the railway concession. But Root's attempt to minimize the issue proved unavailing, and it remained unsettled when he left office.

Root's position in the Harbin controversy encouraged advocates of a stronger Far Eastern policy within the State Department, as did his decision in July, 1908, to recall Willard Straight. Harriman had asked Root to do so, for the panic of 1907 was over and he wanted to consult with Straight about investment opportunities in Manchuria. Straight's recall coincided with the decision of the Chinese government to send Tang Shao-yi on a mission to the United States, ostensibly to thank the American government for the remission of a portion of the Boxer indemnity. Washington knew, however, that Tang's real purposes were to raise a large loan for Manchurian development and to reach some kind of agreement for checking Japanese encroachments. Straight had urged Tang to seek a loan in the United States with the indemnity remission as security, and before leaving Mukden he had actually signed a memorandum with the

[32] Esthus, "Changing Concept of the Open Door," 445–448, has a detailed discussion of the Harbin controversy. The correspondence is in NA, RG 59:4002.

[33] Takahira to Hayashi, April 5, 11, 1908, Telegram Series, JA.

[34] Root to Adee, June 19, 1908, NA, RG 59:4002/110.

governor outlining its terms. The project was opposed by W. W. Rockhill, who wanted the returned indemnity funds used for the education of Chinese students in the United States. With Root supporting Rockhill's position, the prospect for successful loan negotiations seemed poor.[35]

Tang's proposal for an American-German-Chinese entente had even less chance of success. Months before, during the winter of 1907–1908, Roosevelt had let William II believe that he eventually might conclude an agreement. But by early August, 1908, tension with Japan had largely passed, and Roosevelt no longer bothered to feign interest. The President revealed his attitude by his reaction to an interview William II gave to William Bayard Hale of the *New York Times* in July, 1908. For nearly two hours the Emperor talked to this unknown reporter in language which, if made public, would have created an international explosion similar to that created by the *Daily Telegraph* interview a few months later. The Emperor denounced England as "a traitor to the white man's cause" and predicted war between the United States and Japan within ten years. The solution to the eastern question, William II claimed, was about to be made by Germany and the United States, for he had agreed with "Mr. Roosevelt to divide the East against itself by becoming the recognized friends of China." Within a few months a high Chinese official would visit the United States and Germany and the terms would be made known. Hale learned from the German Foreign Office that this Chinese official was none other than Tang Shao-yi. The editors of the *Times* had no intention of publishing the indiscreet interview, but thinking the President should know of its contents, they sent Oscar King Davis to Oyster Bay with copies of Hale's letters. Roosevelt's reaction was explosive:

[35] Vevier, *United States and China*, pp. 68–73.

This is the funniest thing I have ever known. That Jack of an
Emperor talks just as if what he happens to want is already
an accomplished fact. He has been at me for over a year to
make this kind of an agreement about China, but every time
I have replied, "that means a treaty, to which the Senate must
consent." . . . This is the first time I have ever heard the
name of Tang-Shao-yi. For at least nine months he — that
Jack — has been telling me that a distinguished Chinese official
was "on his way" to this country and Germany to settle affairs,
but he has never come. I do not know whether this is the
man or not, or whether he is really on his way or not. But
the policy [of the Open Door], as I have always told the
Emperor, is ours. It has been our policy for seven or eight
years, ever since Hay first enunciated it.[36]

No war would come with Japan, Roosevelt concluded, as
long as the nation kept its navy prepared. The Emperor was
indulging "in red dreams of glory." [37]

Roosevelt and Root did not seem worried about relations
with Japan or events in Manchuria during the late summer
of 1908. They ignored a warning from W. W. Rockhill that
Japan's intention to monopolize southern Manchuria railways
created a "very serious danger" to American interests and
policy there. In early September Root wrote Whitelaw Reid
that he was certain both the government and the leaders of
opinion in Japan and the United States wanted peace. The
forces which a year and a half ago threatened to "bring the
two nations into conflict at some time in the future . . .
[had] been very materially checked." [38] News from J. C.
O'Laughlin confirmed the optimism of the Secretary of State.
O'Laughlin, who had been appointed secretary to the American commissioners to the Tokyo Exposition of 1912, was in

[36] Oscar King Davis, *Released for Publication: Some Inside Political History of Theodore Roosevelt and His Times, 1898–1918* (Boston, 1925), pp.
82–89.
[37] Roosevelt to Lee, October 17, 1908, *Letters*, VI, 1293–1294.
[38] Rockhill to Root, July 6, 1908, NA, RG 59:5767/32; Root to Reid,
September 3, 1908, in Jessup, *Root*, II, 34.

San Francisco, about to depart for Japan. The President's friend believed the administration's immigration policy had succeeded both from a national and sectional point of view. The people of the Pacific Coast realized the wisdom of the Gentlemen's Agreement and understood the potential danger of the situation. Because of this, O'Laughlin informed the Secretary of State, Democrats could not effectively attack the arrangement with Japan, and he predicted the administration's immigration policy would not hurt Pacific Coast Republicans in the November elections. A few weeks later O'Laughlin visited Honolulu and reported to Roosevelt that the Japanese population in the Hawaiian Islands no longer presented any danger. But this was a recent development, brought about by firm diplomacy and by the cruise of the fleet to the Pacific.[39]

By late September the President was "delighted with the way that things are going in the fleet." Its efficiency was constantly improving and the prospects for a successful visit to Japan seemed excellent.[40] Inwardly Roosevelt must have been excited over the culmination of his bold project. A warm welcome would seal America's friendship with Japan and confirm beyond all doubt the success of the world cruise. But before the ships reached Yokohama, some nervousness existed over the outcome of this visit. Alfred Thayer Mahan feared the Japanese people might get out of hand and cause an unpleasant incident, while Admiral Sperry found some members of his staff certain "a row with Japan was imminent." Sperry himself did not expect trouble, but had taken careful precautions to avoid it by writing a letter to Henry W. Denison describing the needs of his men on shore leave.[41]

[39] O'Laughlin to Root, September 5, 1908, Root Papers; O'Laughlin to Roosevelt, September 30, 1908, Roosevelt Papers.

[40] Roosevelt to Sims, September 29, 1908, Roosevelt Papers.

[41] Mahan to B. F. Clark, September 11, 1908, Mahan Papers; Sperry to C. S. Sperry, Jr., January 6, 1909, and to Henry W. Denison, June 19, 1908, Sperry Papers.

When the fleet arrived on October 18, 1908, it received an enthusiastic greeting which soon dispelled all doubts. In Yokohama and Tokyo the Americans were wildly feted and met by crowds of Japanese school children singing the "Star-Spangled Banner" in English.[42] Sperry found the arrangements made for his sailors on shore leave "marvelously perfect" and judged the whole visit to be "successful beyond hope." He was, however, surprised at the "nervous tension" in Japanese government circles, but this soon passed and Denison reported the Emperor and cabinet ministers pleased with the course of events.[43]

Ambassadors O'Brien and MacDonald agreed with Sperry's estimate of the visit. MacDonald felt it had the effect the Japanese government wanted and "put an end to all nonsensical war talk." [44] The president of the *Outlook,* Lawrence Abbott, praised the voyage for performing "one of the greatest achievements of recent times in [the] promotion of international peace." Abbott's reaction was typical of the feeling throughout the American press, where Japan's welcome silenced even the sharpest critics of the President's project. The *Literary Digest* now summed up the cruise as a "gigantic frolic," and the *New York Journal of Commerce and Commercial Bulletin* thought the spectacle at Yokohama indicated "the depth of the conviction that with the destiny of the countries of Eastern Asia the future of the United States must be closely identified." Most papers, however, simply rejoiced over the dissipation of all remnants of the war scare with Japan.[45]

[42] *New York Times,* October 18–24, 1908; Franklin Matthews, *Back to Hampton Roads,* pp. 183–208.

[43] Sperry to C. S. Sperry, Jr., October 30, 1908, Sperry Papers; Sperry to Roosevelt, October 28, 1908, Sperry Papers.

[44] O'Brien to Root, October 25, 1908, NA, RG 59:8258/575; MacDonald to Grey, October 26, 1908, *British Documents,* VIII, 459–460.

[45] Lawrence Abbott to Roosevelt, October 23, 1908, Roosevelt Papers; *Literary Digest,* 37 (October 31, 1908), 614–616.

The Japanese press was also enthusiastic over the results of the visit. In the face of these expressions of good will, the *Jiji Shimpo* claimed, "wild rumors will disappear like dewdrops after the sunrise." The *Nichi Nichi Shimbun* spoke of a "new era" in Japanese-American relations, and the *Kokumin Shimbun* prophesied an alliance between the two nations. The visit of the American fleet to Yokohama would serve the same purpose as had the visit of the Russian fleet to Toulon in 1893.[46]

From Yokohama eight battleships journeyed to Amoy, where they received an apathetic reception. The coldness of the welcome reflected both the Chinese government's humiliation over the failure of the entire fleet to visit an important port and its waning hopes for a combination with Germany and the United States against Japan.[47] The results of the fleet's cruise in Far Eastern waters suggested that a Japanese-American agreement was far more likely.

Prince Saionji no longer led the Japanese government which greeted the fleet. His cabinet's position had been weakened by continued friction with the *genro* over financial matters and by its failure to repress the growing socialist agitation. Alarmed by popular unrest, Yamagata worked behind the scenes for Saionji's downfall and in early July finally succeeded. Yamagata's protégé, Prince Taro Katsura, once again took up the reins of government. As Washington realized, the change was a matter of internal politics and would not basically affect Japanese foreign policy. Saionji and Katsura consulted on foreign and domestic policy, as they had in the past, and the *Seiyukai* supported the new cabinet in the Diet.[48]

[46] *Jiji Shimpo*, October 22, 1908, *Nichi Nichi Shimbun*, October 29, 1908, *Kokumin Shimbun*, October 29, 1908, all in NA, RG 59:8258/575–579.

[47] *New York Times*, July 27, October 31, November 1, 5, 1908; Hart, *The Great White Fleet*, pp. 240–249.

[48] For the background of the cabinet change, see Bailey, "Saionji," 133, 155–158; Hackett, "Yamagata," 368–382.

Katsura took office, according to the *Paris Temps*, determined to remove the suspicions of Japan prevalent among the American people. In late September, several weeks before the arrival of the fleet, Foreign Minister Jutaro Komura revealed to Ambassador Takahira the ministry's plan to ensure permanent good relations. Japan intended, for trade and political reasons, to conclude an entente with the United States, which would "wipe away the uneasiness of the American public and leave no room for the anti-Japanese movement to agitate against Japan." [49]

John C. O'Laughlin, who arrived in Tokyo in early October, soon learned of the intentions of the new ministry from Viscount Aoki, who explained that Katsura was eager to give some striking indication of friendly relations and planned to make an overwhelming demonstration when the fleet arrived. The Prime Minister also wanted something more tangible and thus had revived Aoki's proposed agreement of a year ago, which, according to Aoki, he regretted had not been adopted at that time. O'Laughlin was jubilant, for he thought such an agreement would be widely regarded as a vindication of the Far Eastern policy pursued by the Roosevelt administration. [50]

Foreign Minister Komura assured the President's unofficial envoy that Japanese emigration to the United States would be totally shut off or he would thoroughly investigate. But Japan would not tolerate an insult to its dignity and would resent an exclusion law. In fact, Komura warned that upon the expiration of the treaty of 1894, Japan would insist upon the elimination of the present clause giving the United States the right to regulate Japanese immigration. Otherwise no treaty would be signed. O'Laughlin predicted to Roose-

---

[49] *Literary Digest*, 37 (August 22, 1908), 241–242; Kamikawa, *Japan-American Diplomatic Relations*, p. 269.

[50] O'Laughlin to Roosevelt, October 11, 1908, Roosevelt Papers.

velt that 1911 and 1912 would be the critical years in Japanese-American relations. He urged the elimination of all mistrust between the two nations and the continuance of a strong American naval program. The latter was essential because in three years American naval power would have a great impact upon Japanese policy. Finally, O'Laughlin reported that Komura admitted Japan's intention ultimately to annex Korea and concluded that the Japanese government would not commit obvious violations of the integrity of China and the Open Door.[51]

Two days after the arrival of the fleet, on October 20, O'Laughlin accepted an invitation from Katsura to discuss the reasons for suspicion of Japan in the United States. In a conversation which lasted over two hours, the Prime Minister claimed Japan had never intended to make war on the United States and that during the tension of the past few years no mention was ever made in the councils of the *genro* of military preparations against the United States. Katsura added that he had been very successful in restraining the Japanese press. Japan's interests demanded the integrity of China and the Open Door, and he hoped the United States would keep the Philippines and maintain a direct interest in the Far East. In turn, O'Laughlin denied reports that the United States was preparing for war and explained that the cruise of the fleet did not menace Japan. It aimed at improving naval efficiency and was motivated by the administration's desire to arouse patriotism on the Pacific Coast. Moreover, Secretary Metcalf, who had senatorial aspirations, was pleased by the fleet's stay in San Francisco Bay. O'Laughlin praised Japan's cooperation in helping to make the immigration agreement work admirably, and asked if Japan would permit the United States to retain the right to regulate immigration in a new treaty, if naturalization was

[51] *Ibid.*

conceded. Katsura, unlike Komura, answered "yes." O'Laughlin closed the discussion by mentioning the great interest Roosevelt had taken in Aoki's agreement and by emphasizing the President's desire for some such proof of friendly relations.[52]

The reassuring conversations between O'Laughlin and the Japanese ministers probably strengthened the cabinet's intention to seek an agreement with the United States, and on October 25 a draft was sent to Takahira. Japan had long been watching for an appropriate time to propose an entente, Komura cabled, and now felt that the warm welcome given the fleet created the right atmosphere for negotiations.[53] From Tokyo's point of view, the obstacles which had prevented an agreement a year earlier were now removed. With the immigration dispute settled, and Roosevelt's friendship toward Japan firmly established, Katsura and Komura reasoned that an agreement would clear the air and help cement friendly relations by reassuring both the American people and government of the peaceful and limited aims of Japan in the Far East.[54]

Though the primary reason for the Japanese move was a

[52] O'Laughlin to Roosevelt, October 20, 1908, Roosevelt Papers.

[53] Kamikawa, *Japan-American Diplomatic Relations,* p. 271.

[54] Aoki claimed responsibility for Japan's decision to seek an agreement with the United States. The former ambassador explained to O'Laughlin that he had shown his reports of October and November, 1907, to Yamagata and Katsura, only to discover that Hayashi had suppressed them. According to Hayashi's *Secret Memoirs,* however, the cabinet was fully consulted and rejected Aoki's proposition, as did Ito and Katsura. Hayashi's version is more plausible than Aoki's, given the dependence of the Saionji cabinet on the *genro* and considering the whole structure of the Japanese government. Curiously, however, Hayashi was unable to understand why Katsura changed his mind, and could only suggest that perhaps Katsura thought an agreement with the United States would indicate a renewal of energy in Japan's foreign policy. If Hayashi's explanation in November, 1907, was valid (that the agreement could not be concluded because of the unsettled immigration question), then nothing any longer stood in the way of a Japanese-American understanding in the autumn of 1908. (O'Laughlin to Roosevelt, October 11, 1908, Roosevelt Papers; Hayashi, *Secret Memoirs,* pp. 240–242.)

desire to end tension with the United States, the mission of Tang Shao-yi added a compelling secondary motive. Aware of Tang's aims, the Japanese government had warned him against seeking an alliance with the United States and Germany. Moreover, Japan knew of Germany's sympathy for Tang's anti-Japanese schemes and of William II's persistent offers of military aid to Roosevelt.[55] If any possible doubt of the Emperor's anti-Japanese mania remained, the *Daily Telegraph* interview of October 28 surely dispelled it. Katsura and Komura realized that Tang's mission had little chance of success, and they would no doubt have sought an agreement even without the threat of an American-German-Chinese entente. But they may have speeded negotiations in order to present Tang with a fait accompli when he arrived in Washington.[56]

On October 26, 1908, Takahira began negotiations by suggesting an agreement similar to that proposed by Aoki a year before. The only significant departure from Aoki's draft and from the traditional declarations of the powers on China was the omission of the phrase "territorial integrity." Root at first took no notice of this deficiency and concentrated on the form of the agreement. A formal declaration, Root explained, would require the consent of the Senate, where objections were certain to be raised. He preferred, therefore, an informal exchange of notes. Komura quickly agreed, though he did not want Japan's initiative to be apparent.[57]

Since Takahira and Root decided on October 22 to ex-

---

[55] MacDonald to Grey, November 27, 1908, *British Documents*, VIII, 461; Vevier, *United States and China*, p. 75, and Edward H. Zabriskie, *American-Russian Rivalry in the Far East* (Philadelphia, 1946), p. 142, suggest Japan sought an agreement with the United States primarily to block Tang's mission.

[56] Takahira to Komura, September 6, 1908, MT 1.2.3.5, JA.

[57] Draft handed to the President by Takahira on October 26, 1908, NA, RG 59:16533/1; Kamikawa, *Japan-American Diplomatic Relations*, pp. 271–272.

clude Manchuria from their deliberations, there was little danger of a serious disagreement. The only dispute of any significance came over a guarantee of the territorial integrity of China. On November 7 Root urged the insertion of such a phrase, since it restated traditional American policy. Two days later he went further and asked for a pledge to maintain both "the territorial integrity and administrative entity of China." "Without some such clause," Root claimed, "both countries might be regarded as having abandoned that position, which, of course, neither of us wishes to do." [58] A long memorandum by Willard Straight apparently convinced Root that the "administrative entity" of China ought to be affirmed. Straight felt that any agreement, whatever its contents, would isolate Germany and China and array the United States "morally" on the side of Japan. Japan, through accords with Great Britain, France, and Russia, had gained recognition of a special sphere of influence in southern Manchuria acquired at China's expense and had no intention of observing its "solemn international obligations." But if an agreement must be signed, Straight argued, it should affirm both the "territorial integrity and administrative entity" of China. Otherwise it would be interpreted as a "severe blow to American prestige in the Orient . . . [and as a] sign of weakness and surrender." [59]

Japan was willing to guarantee the territorial integrity of China, though Komura preferred the phrase "independence and territorial integrity." But Japan could not, Komura instructed Takahira, agree to maintain the "administrative entity" of China. Such a pledge would "conflict with the administrative rights of Japan in the leased territory in Manchuria and in the land along the South Manchurian

[58] Takahira to Komura, October 25, 1908, Telegram Series, JA; Kamikawa, *Japan-American Diplomatic Relations,* pp. 272–273; Root to Takahira, November 11, 1908, NA, RG 59:16533/4.

[59] Memorandum by Straight, November 11, 1908, NA, RG 59:16533/6.

Railway," and might lead to some future misunderstanding. Takahira informed Root that Japan would accept a clause on the territorial integrity of China, though it was not necessary and might offend the Chinese government. He may have been more frank in explaining Japan's objections to the phrase "administrative entity." [60] For a few days Takahira feared serious complications, such as the State Department's introduction of the Harbin dispute into the negotiations. But Root, if he ever seriously considered such a plan, soon disgarded it and accepted a compromise which affirmed "the independence and integrity of China and the principle of equal opportunity for the commerce and industry of all nations in that Empire." [61] Despite minor imperfections in the final form of the agreement, Takahira urged its acceptance. He was convinced Root had seen Roosevelt "very often and taken much pains [sic] before coming to this decision" and feared that modifications by Japan would bring further delay. Komura agreed and on November 30, 1908, Root and Takahira exchanged the notes which future scholars, one historian complains, "have pored over as if they were a Biblical text." [62]

In the years since the Root-Takahira Agreement took final shape, historians have tended to advance two interpretations. A. Whitney Griswold, in his *The Far Eastern Policy of the United States*, argues that the President's fear of Japan and consequently his uneasiness over the safety of the Philippines grew so intense during the Russo-Japanese War that he first traded Korea for a guarantee of the Philippines in the Taft-Katsura conversation of July, 1905, and finally, in the Root-Takahira Agreement of No-

[60] Kamikawa, *Japan-American Diplomatic Relations*, pp. 273–274; Takahira to Root, November 14, 1908, NA, RG 59: 16533/7.
[61] Takahira to Komura, November 15, 17, 19, 1908, Telegram Series, JA.
[62] Takahira to Komura, November 21, 1908, and Komura to Takahira, November 24, 1908, Telegram Series, JA; Leopold, *Elihu Root*, p. 62.

vember, 1908, he went even further and gave Japan a "free hand" in Manchuria in return for a second guarantee of the Philippines and a promise of cooperation in immigration restriction. We now know that Griswold read far too much into the exchange of views between Taft and Katsura.[63] Many scholars, however, still accept his interpretation of the Root-Takahira Agreement, while others contend that it was nothing more than an attempt to clear the air and restore Japanese-American friendship. The exchange of notes, according to this latter group, was meant as a symbol of cordial relations, not as a means of a covert withdrawal from the Orient.[64] Actually, the President hoped to accomplish both an easing of tension with Japan and a more thorough understanding of the vital interests of each nation in the Far East. The first goal was the obvious intent of each government; the second becomes clear only through an examination of the correspondence of Roosevelt's special agent in Japan, John Callan O'Laughlin.

O'Laughlin's letters relating his interviews with Aoki, Komura, and Katsura arrived in Washington after the negotiations between Root and Takahira had begun. The President's reaction was guarded. "There are things I cannot put down in writing," he told O'Laughlin, "which I shall tell you of in full when I see you." His policy remained one of strengthening the navy and securing the naturalization of the Japanese. As he wrote several days later, a pow-

[63] A. Whitney Griswold, The Far Eastern Policy of the United States (New York, 1938), pp. 122–132; Raymond A. Esthus, "The Taft-Katsura Agreement—Reality or Myth?" Journal of Modern History, 32 (March, 1959), 46–51.

[64] Griswold's influence can be seen in Harbaugh, Power and Responsibility, p. 301; and in Charles W. Toth's "Elihu Root," Norman Graebner (ed.), An Uncertain Tradition: American Secretaries of State in the Twentieth Century (New York, 1961), pp. 50–51; the agreement is viewed simply as a symbol of cordial relations in Leopold, Elihu Root, p. 62, and in Esthus, Theodore Roosevelt and Japan, pp. 284–286. Esthus' account of the Root-Takahira negotiations differs greatly from my own.

erful fleet would be the most "potent factor" in keeping the peace with Japan.[65]

In late November more information arrived from O'Laughlin which further clarified Japan's policy in Manchuria. Japan, Komura frankly explained on October 21, still upheld the policy of the Open Door and integrity of China, but did not regard Mongolia and Manchuria as part of China. Japanese interests were slight in Mongolia and defined in an agreement with Russia. Southern Manchuria, however, was Japan's outer line of defense, protecting the home islands against a renewal of war by some future Russian government. Japan considered that region not as a sphere of influence but as an outpost and sphere of interest. The Open Door there remained in full force and American trade would be treated the same as Japanese trade, but the Foreign Minister excluded Manchuria from previous pledges to observe the integrity of China. O'Laughlin thought Japan was keeping its pledge to give equal treatment to foreign trade in Manchuria, for American businessmen who had recently been there assured him of this.[66] He was convinced that Russia and Japan fully understood each other and that Japan would not be driven from Manchuria except by force. Japan would constantly attempt to strengthen its position in the southern half of that enormous area. O'Laughlin concluded that Japan, not China, was America's vital problem in the Far East.[67]

Japan did not, however, want trouble with the United Japan could dominate the Pacific if only they would cooperate States. In fact, Komura suggested that the United States and

---

[65] Roosevelt to O'Laughlin, November 13, 1908, *Letters*, VI, 1342; Roosevelt to Lee, October 17, 1908, *Letters*, VI, 1292–1294.

[66] Memorandum by O'Laughlin of conversation with Count Komura, October 21, 1908, in NA, RG 59:12611/22 and also in Roosevelt Papers; and O'Laughlin to Root, November 18, 1908, NA, RG 59:12611/22.

[67] O'Laughlin to Roosevelt, November 20, 1908, Roosevelt Papers.

erate. O'Laughlin was certain the cruise of the fleet had
made the Japanese realize as never before the strength of the
United States and the nation's intention to retain its Pacific
possessions and its position as a great Pacific power. It
had brought good results by increasing Japan's desire for
friendship with the United States.[68] If O'Laughlin's predic-
tion of Japan's Manchurian policy was correct, a strong
friendship would be needed to weather what might be a
stormy future.

O'Laughlin's conversations with Katsura and Komura,
along with the record of American Far Eastern policy from
1906 to 1909, give context to the Root-Takahira Agreement.
Both governments primarily hoped to ensure friendly relations by reducing the tension generated since the autumn
of 1906. Thus the terms of the agreement were not so important as the impression created by them. In order to quiet
popular suspicions in the United States over Japan's intentions toward the Philippines, the notes included a pledge
to respect each nation's territorial possessions in the Pacific.
Neither before nor after 1906 did Roosevelt share these
fears. Japanese leaders were eager to secure an explicit recognition of their nation's predominance in southern Manchuria. But Ambassador Takahira found Root unwilling to
go this far and he had to settle for the Roosevelt administration's tacit acquiescence to Japan's position in that vital
region. Certainly such an acceptance of Japan's sphere had
been implicit in Roosevelt's Far Eastern policy since the
end of the Russo-Japanese War. But events since the autumn
of 1906 had created considerable uneasiness in Tokyo over
American aims and a clarification of each nation's policy
was needed. From the American point of view, such a
clarification involved a summation of rather than a deviation
from past policy. Roosevelt and Root, following in John
Hay's tradition, were mainly concerned with preserving

[68] *Ibid.*

equal commercial opportunity in Manchuria. They accepted both the Japanese and Russian spheres of influence, with their necessary infringements of China's territorial and administrative integrity and of the principle of equal investment opportunity. While willing to make some effort to preserve these concepts, Roosevelt and Root were cautious and reluctant to push very far. As long as American businessmen could sell their goods, the demand for an extension of the Open Door would probably be small.[69]

Raymond A. Esthus has suggested that Roosevelt favored a "free hand" for Japan in Manchuria, but that Root, who actually dealt with Manchurian affairs from 1906 to 1909, followed a middle-of-the-road policy, accepting Japan's sphere while attempting to keep the extension of Japanese rights within bounds. It is unlikely, however, that any divergence existed between the Manchurian policies of Root and Roosevelt from 1906 to 1909, or that Roosevelt's failure to discuss Manchurian developments in his letters justifies the belief that Root was doing more than executing the President's policy. Root became secretary of state after Roosevelt's views on Far Eastern affairs were largely developed, and he took little initiative on matters involving that region.[70] The detailed negotiations over Harbin and

[69] Charles Vevier, "The Open Door: An Idea in Action, 1906–1913," *Pacific Historical Review*, 24 (February, 1955), 50, and Esthus, "Changing Concept of the Open Door," 437, 451–453, point out Hay's limited conception of the Open Door policy and the way in which Roosevelt and Root largely followed it; Roosevelt reaffirmed his acceptance of Japan's sphere of influence in Manchuria during a conversation with Takahira in early September, 1908. (Takahira to Komura, September 6, 1908, Telegram Series, JA.)

[70] Esthus, *Theodore Roosevelt and Japan*, pp. 300–308; Jessup, *Root*, II, 3–4. Later statements by Root revealed his acceptance of Roosevelt's Manchurian policy. At the Washington Conference he informed the Japanese delegation that the United States desired no changes in Japan's status in Manchuria. When Japan invaded that province in 1931, Root reminded Secretary of State Henry L. Stimson of Japanese rights there. (Sadao Asada, "Japan's 'Special Interests' and the Washington Conference, 1921–1922," *American Historical Review*, 67 (October, 1961), pp. 62–70; Leopold, *Elihu Root*, p. 172.)

other Manchurian problems were handled by Root within the framework of well-understood policy. The President probably consulted occasionally with Root orally over these matters, but he had little inclination at the time or later to write about his Manchurian or Far Eastern policy. The Root-Takahira Agreement, for example, is not even mentioned in his letters of the period. Roosevelt preferred to talk and write about events which could be dramatized, such as the cruise of the battle fleet and the Gentlemen's Agreement with Japan.

Nevertheless, the President wished to see his understanding with Japan maintained and in early 1909 explained its broad outlines to Philander C. Knox, soon to become Taft's secretary of state. Roosevelt believed that the American people, particularly on the Pacific Coast, demanded the Japanese be kept out, and he felt this demand must be heeded so long as the Japanese were treated courteously. The Gentlemen's Agreement with Japan was finally working and should be maintained in the future if trouble was to be averted. The American navy should remain prepared so that Japan would never consider an appeal to force; and finally, Roosevelt informed Knox that Japan's wisest statesmen realized war with the United States would hinder Japan's pursuit of its vital interests "in China and on the Asiatic mainland." [71] Implicitly Roosevelt suggested that Japan would continue to restrict immigration if largely left alone to develop its special interests in southern Manchuria. Thus friction could be avoided and the vital interests of each nation fulfilled.

The Japanese government was also aware of this connection, for it was probably not a coincidence that Komura's explanation of Japan's Manchurian policy was coupled with

[71] Roosevelt to Philander C. Knox, February 8, 1909, *Letters*, VI, 1510–1514.

an avowal of the government's determination to restrict emigration. Two years later, in December, 1910, Roosevelt made his policy more explicit in letters to William Howard Taft: "Our vital interest is to keep the Japanese out of our country, and at the same time to preserve the good will of Japan. The vital interest of the Japanese . . . is in Manchuria and Korea. It is therefore peculiarly our interest not to take any steps as regards Manchuria which will give the Japanese cause to feel, with or without reason, that we are hostile to them, or a menace — in however slight a degree — to their interests." The immigration problem, in short, must be considered within the framework of the nation's entire Japanese policy.[72]

This passage was not quite an accurate statement of the Manchurian policy Roosevelt had himself pursued from 1906 to 1909. In the same letter to Taft in 1910 Roosevelt explained that "as regards Manchuria, if the Japanese choose to follow a course of conduct to which we are adverse, we cannot stop it unless we are prepared to go to war, and a successful war about Manchuria would require a fleet as good as that of England, plus an army as good as that of Germany. The 'open-door' policy in China was an excellent thing, and will I hope be a good thing in the future, so far as it can be maintained by general diplomatic agreement; but as has been proved by the whole history of Manchuria, alike under Russia and under Japan, the 'open-door' policy, as a matter of fact, completely disappears as soon as a powerful nation determines to disregard it. . . . Our interests in Manchuria are really unimportant, and not such that the American people would be content to run the slightest risk of collision about them." [73]

[72] Roosevelt to Taft, December 22, 1910, December 8, 1910, Letters, VII, 189–192, 180–181.
[73] Roosevelt to Taft, December 22, 1910, Letters, VII, 189–192.

From 1906 to 1909 Roosevelt and Root did not give Japan a "free hand" in Manchuria. They were at times willing to use diplomatic pressure to preserve the Open Door and to a lesser extent the territorial and administrative integrity of China. The commitment of the American people to these principles, as they realized, was paradoxical. Most Americans, while believing in the policy of John Hay, did not want to employ force to sustain it, and were content to have moral and diplomatic measures used. To avoid political criticisms the administration had to go this far but no further and hope that Japan would not pursue a ruthlessly aggressive Manchurian policy. Such a course would expose the basic ineffectuality of America's efforts to preserve the Open Door. Fortunately the chances for Japanese restraint were good, since the tension between Japan and Russia was still great and continuing and since Japan could not be certain of what the United States would do if its Manchurian interests were badly injured.[74] But it was imperative, from the American point of view, to avoid offending Japan and to encourage a relationship which would foster a mutual respect for each nation's vital interests.

The Root-Takahira Agreement satisfied all the complex necessities of the administration's Far Eastern policy. It affirmed the Open Door in a way that pleased the general public and helped to remove suspicions of Japan. The very vagueness and ambiguity of the notes prevented an attack by advocates of a strong Far Eastern policy. The administration, however, was wary of too much scrutiny of its terms, either by the public or by the Senate. This attitude was reflected by Roosevelt's silence in his letters and shaped the very form of the exchange. Ambassador Bryce was surprised that Root was willing to stretch the powers of the executive so far, but neither Root nor Roosevelt seemed

[74] Zabriskie, *American-Russian Rivalry in the Far East,* pp. 148–149.

to have any qualms about doing so. In Root's draft of the message transmitting the exchange of notes to the Senate, Roosevelt crossed out the phrase "for any expression of views which that body [the Senate] may see fit to make." "Why invite the expression of views," the President asked, "with which we may not agree?" [75] He shrewdly avoided exposing fully to public view the nature of the settlement finally reached with Japan.

The reaction to the exchange of letters between Root and Takahira was all that the President could have hoped for. Arthur Lee voiced the general sentiment when he wrote that it was a "real knock-out for the mischief-mongers on both sides of the Atlantic." Roosevelt agreed and boasted that his policy of "constant friendliness and courtesy toward Japan, *coupled with sending the fleet around the world,* has borne good results." [76] American diplomats were generally enthusiastic over the effects of the agreement, as were the governments of the major European powers. Foreign Secretary Grey thought it was "very good news," for the notes seemed to have in view the same object as the Anglo-Japanese Alliance. [77] Even Admiral Tirpitz and Chancellor Bülow claimed the agreement coincided with Germany's Far Eastern policy. [78]

In the United States the agreement seemed to satisfy the most diverse political elements. One prominent peace advocate, Representative Richard Bartholdt of Missouri,

[75] Bryce to Grey, December 1, 1908, *British Documents,* VIII, 464; Jessup, *Root,* II, 43.

[76] Lee to Roosevelt, December 1, 1908, Roosevelt Papers; Roosevelt to Lee, December 20, 1908, *Letters,* VI, 1432–1433. Roosevelt seemed to think that the voyage of the fleet greatly influenced Japan's desire for an agreement (Roosevelt to Reid, December 4, 1908, *Letters,* VI, 1410).

[77] See, for example, Lloyd C. Griscom to Huntington Wilson, December 9, 1908, Huntington Wilson Papers; Grey to Bryce, November 23, 1908, *British Documents,* VIII, 460–461.

[78] David J. Hill to Root, November 23, 1908, NA, RG 59:16533/10; *New York Times,* December 8, 1908.

thought the exchange would "go down in history as one of the greatest achievements of the present administration." Thomas F. Millard, failing to find much meaning in the text of the notes, concluded the administration actually intended to assert its fundamental interest in China.[79] Most of the American press thought the Root-Takahira exchange would reduce tension with Japan and accepted the State Department's explanation that it was intended to demonstrate to the world the friendship between the two nations. "It is a patriotic service of the highest order," remarked the *New York Evening Post*, "and ought to end once and for all the silly talk of war with Japan." A few papers, such as the *New York Press*, felt the agreement was an entangling alliance and demanded its submission to the Senate. But the general reaction indicated that the Root-Takahira Agreement fulfilled the main purpose intended by Roosevelt and Root.[80]

Much of the Japanese press was indifferent or hostile because the agreement ignored immigration and the question of discrimination against Japanese residents in the United States. However, the *Japan Times* thought the Gentlemen's Agreement was working well and that negotiations should not be reopened. "The long and short of it is," warned the *Times*, "that we must choose between voluntary restriction on the one hand and exclusion on the other."[81] Count Okuma gave his approval, and important papers such as the *Mainichi Dempo* and *Nichi Nichi Shimbun* recognized the usefulness of ending all causes for misunderstanding, particularly among the American people. The most extravagant claims were made by the *Kokumin Shimbun*, which

[79] *Congressional Record*, 60th Cong., 2d Sess., 1303; *New York Times*, January 10, 1909.

[80] *Literary Digest*, 37 (December 5, 1908), 832.

[81] *Japan Weekly Mail*, December 5, 1908; *Literary Digest*, 37 (February 6, 1909), 205–206.

argued that the Root-Takahira Agreement was "tantamount to an offensive and defensive alliance" and nearly the equivalent in significance of the Anglo-Japanese Alliance.[82] Whatever the faults of the agreement, Japanese newspapers welcomed the renewed friendship between the two nations.

However, Ambassador Rex at Peking was displeased at this unexpected blow to his hopes for an American-German-Chinese entente. He thought the United States and Japan had reached an agreement because neither was prepared for war and reported that the Chinese government distrusted the understanding. W. W. Rockhill learned of Chinese suspicion when he informed Foreign Minister Yuan Shih-K'ai of the exchange of notes. Yuan was surprised and irritated and asked why Washington had not awaited the arrival of Tang Shao-yi. The Foreign Minister intimated that Japan had sought an agreement in order to forestall a similar attempt by China's special envoy.[83] Willard Straight, deep in plans for an American loan to China, agreed with this interpretation of Japan's motives. A year later he wrote that the Root-Takahira Agreement, "like the Korean withdrawal, was a terrible diplomatic blunder to be laid to the door of T. R." Straight's collaborator for a stronger Far Eastern policy, F. M. Huntington Wilson, was away from the State Department from August to early November and could not remember being consulted during Root's negotiations with Takahira. Though he left no record of his impression at the time, he thought in 1945 that it represented "the old policy of unreality and fine words." [84]

As they gathered in Washington, some senators also ex-

[82] Japan Times, December 5, 1908, Kokumin Shimbun, December 1, 1908, NA, RG 59:16533/52.
[83] Rex to Bülow, December 15, 1908, Grosse Politik, XXV (1), 97–98; Rockhill to Root, December 3, 1908, NA, RG 59:16533/46.
[84] Croly, Straight, pp. 275–276; Huntington Wilson, Memoirs, pp. 163, 169–170.

pressed disapproval. Shelby M. Cullom, chairman of the Foreign Relations Committee, assured Root that the Senate would not cause any trouble, but Walter Wellman, Washington correspondent of the *Chicago Record Herald,* expected violent attacks by Democrats, who believed the administration must consult the Senate on such matters.[85] Root's appearance before the Foreign Relations Committee in February, 1909, when he explained the nature of the exchange, quieted senatorial critics.[86]

The exchange of letters between Root and Takahira ended the hopes of Tang Shao-yi that China might reach an accord with the United States. Root delayed the final signing of the notes until Tang arrived in Washington on November 30 and had a chance to look at the text.[87] But this delay of a few hours was small consolation to the discouraged Chinese envoy, who soon learned that neither Roosevelt nor Root had any intention of placing the United States on China's side in its struggles with Japan. Tang was informed, the *New York Times* authoritatively announced, "that the American people would not support any administration in a war arising out of the question whether Chinese or Japanese . . . should control Manchuria." Roosevelt gave the same explanation to George Marvin, a protégé of Willard Straight's, who had prepared the way for Tang in Washington, adding that he had "never bluffed in his life" and did not intend to do so over Manchuria.[88] In late December Roosevelt informed Sternburg's successor, Count Johann H. A. von Bernstorff, that he had been unable to enter into a joint guarantee of China's integrity with Ger-

[85] *New York Times,* December 1, 7–8, 1908; *Los Angeles Times,* December 10, 1908.

[86] *Washington Post,* February 7, 1909, Roosevelt Scrapbooks.

[87] Croly, *Straight,* p. 276; Jessup, *Root,* II, 40.

[88] *New York Times,* December 30, 1908; Vevier, *United States and China,* p. 75.

many because it might have driven China into a policy hostile to Japan. A Sino-Japanese war, Roosevelt said, would have "found China totally unarmed, in which case neither Germany nor America were prepared to defend her against Japan. We could not send our fleet into the Pacific, and America could not fight for China, because her public opinion would not have permitted it. If there had to be an American-Japanese war, it could only be for purely American interests. . . . [I] explained this idea quite frankly to . . . Tang Shao-yi . . . for complete frankness was the right policy. Lies had short legs. 'One is always found out.' " [89]

Tang's second project, a loan for Manchurian development, showed some promise of success. With the State Department's permission, Straight approached Harriman and his bankers, Kuhn, Loeb and Company, who were interested in the loan proposal as well as in a Manchurian railways project. On December 9 Root finally saw Tang and approved of a large foreign loan to promote reforms in Manchuria. Root even agreed that a portion of the remitted indemnity funds could serve as security, if the interest was used to finance the education of Chinese students in the United States. And he instructed Straight to render unofficial aid to Tang in his negotiations with American financiers. [90] By late December the prospects for a substantial loan seemed bright.

In early January, however, Tang Shao-yi was recalled before the completion of the financial negotiations. The death of the Empress Dowager in November, 1908, had undermined the position of his patron, Yuan Shih-K'ai, who was removed in late December, 1908. Disappointed by the turn of events, Willard Straight argued that the conclusion

[89] *Grosse Politik*, XXV (1), 97.
[90] See Vevier, *United States and China*, pp. 77–83, for the financial negotiations. The relevant documents are in NA, RG 59:2413.

of the Root-Takahira Agreement had damaged the prestige
of Yuan while strengthening that of the pro-Japanese faction at Peking.[91] The fall of Yuan and the failure of the loan
negotiations also probably disturbed Root. The President,
however, did not show any signs of concern. "The Chinese
are so helpless to carry out any fixed policy," he wrote William II, "whether home or foreign, that it is difficult to
have any but the most cautious dealings with them." [92]
Roosevelt had, in short, realistically chosen to support Japan
over China in Manchuria.

[91] John G. Reid, *The Manchu Abdication and the Powers, 1908–1912*
(Berkeley, 1935), 13–23; memorandum regarding the present situation in
China, by Straight, January 7, 1909, NA, RG 59:1518/271.
[92] Roosevelt to William II, January 2, 1909, in Joseph Bucklin Bishop,
*Theodore Roosevelt and His Time Shown in His Own Letters* (2 vols.;
New York, 1920), II, 287.

# XII

# THE FINAL CRISIS

The signing of the Root-Takahira Agreement and the favorable reaction to it seemed to indicate that the last months of Roosevelt's presidency would witness no new strains on Japanese-American relations. Japan was keeping its word; immigration to the American mainland dropped from 329 in July, 1908, to 199 in December.[1] With the Gentlemen's Agreement working so well, the administration did not expect any trouble from the California legislature, which convened in January, 1909. The regular Republican organization quickly organized both houses and efficiently re-elected Senator George C. Perkins, the servant of the Southern Pacific machine.

As was soon apparent, however, the spread of Japanese settlers into rural areas and the growth of the progressive impulse had given anti-oriental feeling a broader base in California society. Moreover, the influx of Republican progressives into the legislature had weakened the ability of the regular Republican organization to contain the anti-Japanese movement.[2] All of these changes were reflected

[1] "Report of the Commissioner-General of Immigration, July 1, 1909," in *Reports of the Department of Commerce and Labor, 1909* (Washington, D.C., 1910), p. 196.
[2] Daniels, *The Politics of Prejudice*, pp. 45–47; Mowry, *California Progressives*, pp. 80–81.

in the strong support for four bills introduced in the Assembly by Alexander M. Drew, a member of the Lincoln-Roosevelt League from Fresno, and by Grove L. Johnson, a conservative Republican and the father of Hiram Johnson. Several of these bills had been introduced in the 1907 session of the legislature and one, Drew's alien land proposal, had actually passed the Assembly. But it had gone no further after the Assembly complied with the request of Roosevelt and Gillett to defer action on all anti-Japanese legislation for the remainder of the session. Johnson believed that in the intervening two years hostility to Japan had grown so rapidly that the proposals would pass. At any rate, he vowed to make a fight and to force the legislature to go on record, even if Washington again objected.[3]

California politicians advised the President that the bills had a chance of becoming law, and on January 16, the day after a committee had reported favorably Drew's alien land measure, Roosevelt wired Gillett asking him to hold up progress on the bills until receiving his letter. "Passage of the proposed legislation," Roosevelt warned, "would be of incalculable damage to . . . California as well as to [the] whole Union." [4] In the letter which followed, Roosevelt argued that discriminatory acts would produce great irritation in Japan and might upset the immigration agreement, "throwing open the whole situation again." Japan was restricting its emigration so effectively, Roosevelt contended, that in the six months ending October 30, 1908, more Japanese had left than entered the United States. Three days after writing Gillett, the President made a national issue out of the threatened action of the California legislature by releasing his letter to the press. And speaking before a Meth-

[3] *Los Angeles Times*, January 7, 14, 1909.
[4] *New York Times*, January 20, 1909; Roosevelt to Gillett, telegram, January 16, 1909, *Letters*, VI, 1477.

odist meeting in Washington on the same day, January 19, he demanded a "square deal" for Japan.[5]

The President's open intervention gained impressive support from many California politicians. Governor James N. Gillett, Speaker Philip A. Stanton, and Lieutenant Governor Warren R. Porter, all opposed any anti-Japanese legislation and cooperated with the administration. A conference with legislative leaders convinced Gillett no action was imminent, and he decided not to send a special message. Reports from Sacramento indicated the California Senate would block any discriminatory measures approved by the Assembly.[6] In Washington, Senator Frank P. Flint endorsed Roosevelt's vigorous action, and even Representative Julius Kahn admitted that Roosevelt and Root knew best what effect the laws would have in Japan. Most Californians in Congress went along with the administration, but they warned the President that anti-Japanese agitation in the state was widespread. They also doubted that the nation's Japanese population was actually decreasing.[7] Secretary of Commerce and Labor Straus defended his department's statistics, and Roosevelt advised the Californians to wait a few years in order to give Japan's policy of voluntary exclusion a fair trial. According to one report, he hoped the California legislature could be "jollied along" until the acute stage of the crisis had passed.[8]

By January 23, 1909, the situation had cleared rapidly. Roosevelt believed that, by rejecting the "Buchanan view" of the presidency, he had controlled the agitation in Cali-

[5] Roosevelt to Gillett, letter, January 16, 1909, *Letters*, VI, 1477–1478; *Washington Post*, January 19, 20, 1909, Roosevelt Scrapbooks.

[6] *Los Angeles Times*, January 20, 22, 1909.

[7] *Washington Post*, January 20, 1909, *Chicago Record Herald*, January 22, 1909, Roosevelt Scrapbooks.

[8] *Washington Post*, January 22, 1909, Roosevelt Scrapbooks.

fornia.[9] Senator Flint agreed with Roosevelt's estimate of the situation. California business groups were protesting against the anti-Japanese measures and the entire southern California delegation in the Assembly was solidly behind Governor Gillett.[10] But other signs were less encouraging. Representative Hayes demanded that the legislature be left alone to solve the Japanese problem, while Johnson and Drew remained determined to push their measures. The *Los Angeles Times* reported half the members of the Assembly ready to support them.[11]

In appealing to California Roosevelt genuinely feared that the legislature might pass measures which would seriously damage Japanese-American relations. By publicizing the issue, he hoped to arouse the nation and intensify the pressure on Pacific Coast legislators. The well-informed Walter Wellman thought the President was willing to give Californians a "little fright" in order to impress them with the responsibility they bore and in order to arouse Pacific Coast businessmen and conservative leaders to action.[12] Roosevelt may also have hoped to give a boost to his naval program, which the House began debating on January 19. Once again, he asked for a large building program, including four battleships; once again the House Committee on Naval Affairs reported only two.[13] Though chances for securing a two-ship program were good, some uncertainty existed because of deteriorating relations between the President and Congress. Roosevelt's annual message was another radical document which offended many conservatives, and he compounded his difficulties by getting into a needless contro-

---

[9] Roosevelt to Kermit Roosevelt, January 23, 1909, *Letters*, VI, 1480–1481.

[10] *New York Times*, January 23, 1909; *Los Angeles Times*, January 25, 1909.

[11] *Brooklyn Eagle*, January 23, 1909, Roosevelt Scrapbooks; *Los Angeles Times*, January 24, 26, 1909.

[12] *Los Angeles Times*, January 22, 1909.

[13] *New York Times*, December 9, 1908, January 12, 1909.

versy with the Congress over Secret Service funds. His contention that congressmen wished to limit the activities of the Secret Service because they feared investigation of themselves outraged both houses, and in early January the House formally rebuked the President by a lopsided vote.[14]

Roosevelt's defiant stand only strengthened the congressional opponents of naval expansion, who were aided by the protests of educational and religious leaders.[15] Roosevelt knew of this opposition and carefully avoided inflaming service conflicts while the House considered the naval bill. Not until it had approved two ships, did he appoint a commission which seriously considered naval reorganization. Moreover, the day before the House voted on the increase of the navy, the War Department released a General Staff report on the immediate need for fortifications at San Pedro Harbor.[16] To the congressional enemies of naval expansion this was only one more example of the annual Japanese war-scare "cooked up" by the President. Whatever the effect of Roosevelt's moves, the House on January 22 rejected Tawney's annual amendment for only one battleship, 158 to 108, and then went on to approve the two-ship program of Foss's committee. "It really looks," Roosevelt wrote Kermit, "as if I shall get the two battleships on which I had my heart set." [17] Though Senator Hale was reportedly "sulking" because the administration had asked for four rather

[14] Mowry, *Era of Theodore Roosevelt*, pp. 223–224; Harbaugh, *Power and Responsibility*, pp. 365–366.

[15] *Washington Post*, January 22, 1909, Roosevelt Scrapbooks; see, for example, Pennsylvania Peace Society to Roosevelt, December 31, 1908, NA, RG 80:3809/220.

[16] Note in *Letters*, VI, 1456; *Los Angeles Times*, January 22, 1909.

[17] *Congressional Record*, 60th Cong., 2d Sess., 1314–1315; in 1909 the House defeated the amendment for one battleship by 50 votes; in 1908 by 140. Growing opposition to naval expansion was also indicated by the failure of any representative in 1909 to introduce an amendment for four ships; Roosevelt to Kermit Roosevelt, January 23, 1909, *Letters*, VI, 1480–1481.

than two ships, prospects in the Senate looked good. Two days after the House vote, Aldrich assured Roosevelt that the Senate leaders would accept the House program.[18]

With his naval program well along the road to success, Roosevelt turned again to his difficulties with the California legislature. On January 26, in response to a message from Governor Gillett, he wrote a long letter embodying his views and those of Root on the most important of the anti-Japanese bills. At the same time Root and Roosevelt each telegraphed Gillett that the only measure to which they did not object was an alien land law treating all aliens alike and specifically reserving their treaty rights.[19] Upon receiving these telegrams, Gillett sent a powerful special message to the legislature, arguing that the immigration arrangement with Japan was working well and that any discriminatory action would only make the task of the federal government more difficult. A year ago in Washington, Gillett revealed, he had been shown the diplomatic correspondence leading up to the Gentlemen's Agreement, and since then the State Department had assured him that Japan was keeping its word. Foreign Minister Komura, moreover, had told the United States government that the Katsura ministry would be embarrassed by the passage of discriminatory legislation. Gillett urged that no bills be approved and that a census be taken to determine whether the Japanese population in California was increasing or decreasing.[20] While refusing to

[18] *New York Times,* January 6, 1909; *Washington Star,* January 24, 1909, Roosevelt Scrapbooks.

[19] Roosevelt to Gillett, January 26, 1909, letter, to Gillett, January 26, 1909, telegram, *Letters,* VI, 1483–1486; it is surprising the President and Secretary of State did not also object to an alien land law, since orientals, unlike other aliens, could not avoid its provisions by becoming citizens.

[20] *Los Angeles Times,* January 27, 1909. Where Gillett obtained the information about the alleged statement of Komura is a mystery, since this writer has seen no evidence indicating that Komura either privately or officially communicated such views to the American government. Perhaps Gillett was referring to similar statements by Hayashi which Root may have shown him a year earlier.

drop the pending anti-Japanese measures, the Assembly did agree to postpone action on them until the President's letter arrived. Assemblyman Drew even consented to amend his proposal so that it applied to all aliens and not just to Japanese residents.[21]

On January 21 Gillett made public Roosevelt's letter, which consisted mainly of a long memorandum by Root on several of the proposed bills. Drew's measure, as Root had already telegraphed, was acceptable if it applied to all aliens and reserved their treaty rights. But the Secretary of State strongly objected to Grove Johnson's proposal to compel school boards to establish separate schools for Japanese as well as Chinese children. Japan had originally entered into an informal immigration agreement with the United States only after the San Francisco Board of Education had ceased to segregate Japanese children. Passage of the Johnson bill would immediately terminate the Gentlemen's Agreement, and the substitution of an exclusion act would be less efficient and would create "ill-feeling and resentment" in Japan. Thus the enactment of the school segregation bill, Root warned, would be a "violation of patriotic duty . . . certain to plunge the entire Union into the doubtful conditions of enmity to a great and hitherto most friendly power which is our neighbor upon the Pacific." [22] Root's memorandum, reported the Los Angeles Times, made a deep impression on the legislators. Drew and Johnson, however, remained determined to bring their measures to a vote. "The President's letter has no more effect on me," Johnson irreverently remarked, "than water on a duck's back." [23]

[21] Los Angeles Times, January 28, 1909.
[22] Roosevelt to Gillett, January 26, 1909, Letters, VI, 1483–1486; the Johnson bill would not, any more than the original code section, have compelled a board of education to segregate all orientals. However, once a board did so Japanese would have to be included. No longer, for example, could the San Francisco Board of Education only have segregated Chinese students.
[23] Los Angeles Times, February 2, 1909.

As the President's struggle with the California legislature neared a showdown, new and unexpected complications suddenly arose. On February 1 a resolution was introduced into the Nevada Assembly censuring Roosevelt for his attempt to "coerce and intimidate" California and urging the California legislature to disregard his advice. The next day, after removing the personal attacks on the President, the Assembly passed the resolution. At the same time an alien land bill was introduced.[24] At first Roosevelt decided to ignore this untimely outbreak, but the possibility of similar action by the Idaho legislature and of race riots in the West soon weakened his resolve. On February 3 he called in Senators Francis G. Newlands and George S. Nixon of Nevada and William E. Borah of Idaho and asked them to restrain their respective legislatures. The senators agreed to cooperate and by February 4 the situation in Nevada was well in hand.[25]

Information received in Washington indicated that moderate elements also were in control at Sacramento. Fremont Older, reform-minded editor of the *San Francisco Bulletin*, informed Roosevelt that most Californians favored the administration's immigration policy and opposed discriminatory legislation.[26] Concrete evidence of Older's contention came on February 3, when the California Assembly, after a heated debate, defeated Drew's alien land bill, 48 to 28. In answer to Drew's charges that the state was being overrun with Japanese, opponents of the measure argued it would drive out a billion dollars of foreign capital and endanger friendly relations with Japan. The intensive efforts of the regular Republican organization, led by Gillett and Stanton, reversed the anti-Japanese trend in the Assembly and pro-

[24] *Los Angeles Times,* February 2, 3, 1909.
[25] *Washington Post,* February 4, 1909, Roosevelt Scrapbooks; *Los Angeles Times,* February 5, 1909.
[26] *Washington Post,* February 3, 1909, Roosevelt Scrapbooks.

duced a final vote in which only a few Republicans joined the Democratic minority in support of Drew's bill. The majority of assemblymen from the coast and mountain counties and from southern California cooperated with the Republican machine, while those from San Francisco, the bay counties, and the Sacramento and San Joaquin valleys remained strongly anti-Japanese.[27]

The next day, however, the Assembly shifted in the opposite direction and approved Grove Johnson's school segregation bill, 46 to 28. His two other anti-Japanese measures, prohibiting aliens from becoming members of corporations and providing for the segregation of Japanese living areas, were both defeated. But as the alarmed President telegraphed Gillett, "the most offensive bill of all" had passed.[28] The President's appeal brought immediate results. On February 5 the Governor again sent a strong special message to the legislature, arguing that the public did not demand such legislation and warning that Japan would be offended. Speaker Stanton reinforced Gillett's plea for a reconsideration of the Johnson bill. He took the floor to inform the Assembly that it faced a "grave crisis" and confided to his colleagues: "I would that I could tell you what I know, but my lips are sealed. But I can tell you that we are treading on dangerous ground. I can feel it slipping from underneath my feet. This matter . . . should be postponed. Within a few days I believe that further information will be given you." The reporter of the Los Angeles Times compared the powerful Speaker to "an experienced cowboy among a herd of frightened steers. He simply rounded up the whole bunch and they went with docility into the corral." The anti-Jap-

[27] Los Angeles Times, February 4, 1909, and San Francisco Chronicle, January 25, 1909.

[28] Los Angeles Times, February 5, 1909; Roosevelt to Gillett, telegram, February 4, 1909, Letters, VI, 1502. See also Meyer, Diary, February 5, 1909, in Howe, Meyer, p. 416.

anese stampede was checked and the Assembly unanimously agreed to postpone further action until February 10.[29]

The day after Stanton's dramatic speech the President thought he would succeed in "holding the lid down." At Gillett's request he wired the Speaker a brief résumé of the administration's policy, which was soon made public.[30] Roosevelt's Japanese policy had actually not changed much over two years. He felt the demand for Japanese exclusion on the Pacific Coast was too strong to be disregarded, and so he was determined to "face the facts" and heed it. Hopefully this could be done with a "minimum of friction and the maximum of courtesy" by persuading Japan to restrict voluntarily its own emigration and by preventing anti-Japanese legislation or incidents on the Pacific Coast. What he most feared was that the nation would "amble along with insane complacency, committed to a policy which shall combine insult and helplessness, and which could only end in disaster." Thus a strong navy was an essential corollary to the administration's immigration policy, as was a respect for Japan's vital interests in Manchuria.[31]

Gillett's desire for a more detailed statement of the administration's position, along with ominous press reports from Sacramento, convinced the President to send a much longer telegram to Stanton. This message, which Roosevelt regarded as aimed just as much at Japan as at California, was simply a restatement of well-known policy. Roosevelt reaffirmed the intention of the federal government to meet the wishes of California in restricting Japanese immigration. He claimed it was already doing so through the Gen-

[29] *Los Angeles Times,* February 5, 6, 1909.

[30] Roosevelt to Theodore Roosevelt, Jr., February 6, 1909, *Letters,* VI, 1506; Roosevelt to Philip A. Stanton, February 6, 1909, telegram, *Letters,* VI, 1505–1506.

[31] Roosevelt to William Kent, February 4, 1909, to Lee, February 7, 1909, to Knox, February 8, 1909, *Letters,* VI, 1503–1504, 1507–1508, 1510–1514.

tlemen's Agreement, which was working well and would end all cause for future friction. Anti-Japanese legislation, Roosevelt warned, would only imperil the arrangement; in effect he promised to support exclusion legislation if within the next year or two the Gentlemen's Agreement failed to curtail effectively Japanese immigration.[32]

By February 8 the President's policy had lost considerable support among the California congressional delegation. Some of its members resented what they viewed as the President's attempt to intimated them with an artificial war scare. The Californians were also offended by Roosevelt's intemperate abuse of Senator Perkins, who openly sympathized with the California legislature.[33] Roosevelt had turned his full wrath upon the "feebly malicious angleworm" and "milk-faced grub" who favored a policy of insult and naval weakness.[34] Senator Flint took the floor of the Senate to defend Perkins against Roosevelt's attacks and went on to predict that the legislature would ultimately enact anti-Japanese legislation unless convinced of a decrease in Japanese immigration. California did not think, Flint concluded, that the present arrangement worked. Representative Hayes went further than Flint and claimed hundreds of Japanese crossed the Rio Grande illegally every day. And the majority of the California congressional delegation, wrote Walter Wellman, thought the anti-Japanese legislation before the legislature truly represented public opinion in the state.[35]

The discontent among the Californians did not develop

[32] Roosevelt to Chester H. Rowell, February 11, 1909, Roosevelt Papers; Roosevelt to Stanton, February 8, 1909, telegram, *Letters*, VI, 1509–1510.
[33] *Chicago Record Herald,* February 9, 1909, Roosevelt Scrapbooks; *New York Times,* February 9, 1909.
[34] Roosevelt to Theodore Roosevelt, Jr., February 6, 1909, *Letters*, VI, 1506.
[35] *Washington Post,* February 9, 1909, Roosevelt Scrapbooks; *Congressional Record,* 60th Cong., 2d Sess., 3144–3145; *Chicago Record Herald,* February 9, 1909, Roosevelt Scrapbooks.

into a full-fledged revolt, partly because of the widespread popular support given the President's Japanese policy. Most editorial writers approved of Roosevelt's course and agreed with his belief that nothing in Congress was half so important as the Japanese-California question. Even on the Pacific Coast the majority of papers were against legislation at the present time. The *San Francisco Argonaut* believed Japanese immigration was effectively checked and saw no reason for "reopening the wound that is healing healthily." The *San Francisco Chronicle* thought legislation would only decrease the possibility of eventually getting an exclusion law.[36] And two of the strongest commercial organizations on the Pacific Coast, the Los Angeles and San Francisco Chambers of Commerce, deplored measures which would offend Japan. The attitude of the American press was encouraged by Foreign Minister Komura's expression of faith in the American government and by his statement that Japan would confine its emigration to the Far East.[37] Some papers consistently hostile to the President, such as the *New York Sun* and *New York World,* blamed him for encouraging jingo outbreaks, while the *Nation* deplored his "slap-dash methods" and dangerous overstatement.[38] But in the final crisis with Japan Roosevelt carried the nation with him.

The day before the California Assembly again took up the Johnson school segregation bill, the President's policy seemed likely to fail. A poll of the Assembly indicated that Speaker Stanton barely lacked the majority needed to bring about reconsideration. Scenting victory, Grove Johnson refused to

---

[36] *Literary Digest,* 37 (January 30, 1909), 159–160 (February 6, 1909), 200–201 (February 13, 1909), 239–240.

[37] *Los Angeles Times,* January 25, 1909; *Japan Weekly Mail,* February 6, 1909.

[38] *Current Literature,* 46 (March, 1909), 251–261; *Nation,* 88 (February 11, 1909), 127.

withdraw his bill in a stormy meeting with Gillett and Stanton. But overnight the Speaker picked up the necessary votes. On February 10 the Assembly voted to reconsider Johnson's bill, 43 to 34 and then defeated it, 41 to 37. Even Senator Perkins had finally advised his supporters to cooperate with the Governor.[39] Roosevelt's impression that he had finally won was confirmed by Governor Gillett, who wrote on February 17 that the crisis was over and that its settlement pleased the people of California. Had it not been for the President's intervention, Gillett thought, the anti-Japanese bills would have passed the Assembly and possibly the Senate.[40] The relief felt by the President and Governor was shared by the nation's press, which acclaimed the defeat of the anti-Japanese agitators in California.[41]

Thomas A. Bailey has accused Roosevelt of overstating the seriousness of this final crisis with Japan. He points out that the President placed much more importance on the crisis than did the Japanese press, which reacted very mildly to the outbreak in California. By early February, when Japanese papers showed signs of becoming aroused, the school bill had lost and the anti-Japanese agitation had subsided.[42] But the calm reaction of the Japanese press and government was not an accurate measure of the importance of the President's dispute with the California legislature. The government restrained the press through official and unofficial channels. Moreover, the reaction of

[39] *Los Angeles Times,* February 10, 11, 1909; *Washington Post,* February 11, 1909, Roosevelt Scrapbooks.

[40] Roosevelt to Theodore Roosevelt, Jr., February 13, 1909, *Letters,* VI, 1520–1521; Gillett to Roosevelt, February 17, 1909, Roosevelt Papers.

[41] *Literary Digest,* 37 (February 20, 1909), 279–281.

[42] Bailey, *Theodore Roosevelt and the Japanese-American Crises,* pp. 306–307, 311–313. *Letters,* VI, notes, 1342, 1477, follows Bailey's interpretation; State Department files do not contain clippings from Japanese papers since the legislation never became a diplomatic incident. Japanese press reaction, or the lack of it, must be determined from the *Japan Weekly Mail* of January 16, 23, 30, February 6, 13, 27, 1909.

Japanese newspapers was largely irrelevant, since Roosevelt worried less about the immediate effects of the legislation than about its long-term impact. All of the bills would irritate Japan, but the school bill was clearly the most offensive. Its passage might again bring about the segregation of Japanese pupils in the San Francisco schools and endanger the Gentlemen's Agreement. Though renewed segregation would probably not have caused Japan to cease effective emigration restriction, the United States would be under a heavy obligation to right the situation and would no longer be able to insist upon tighter restriction. And when the treaty of 1894 came up for renegotiation in 1911 or 1912, the position of the American government would be considerably weaker. Finally, the failure of the administration to repress anti-Japanese measures might affect Japan's Manchurian policy. With the American government failing to protect Japanese interests on the Pacific Coast, the Japanese government might be less willing to protect American interests in Manchuria. The President, of course, did not know precisely what effect school segregation legislation would have, and he exaggerated in claiming it would destroy the Gentlemen's Agreement. But Root made the same claims that Roosevelt did. Both knew any anti-Japanese legislation would make a policy respectful of American interests more difficult for any Japanese ministry to pursue and in that sense would imperil the future friendship between the two nations.

Thus the President publicly intervened to head off the mounting anti-Japanese movement both in California and in other western states. His strong words were an essentially accurate description of the situation, which the nation's press also viewed as extremely serious. The complex understanding which Roosevelt and Root had striven to erect between the two nations for over two years was threatened, and the President's deep concern led him to take decisive action. His success enabled him to bequeath to Taft a restored friendship with Japan.

As the anti-Japanese feeling in the California legislature ebbed, the United States Senate took up the naval appropriations bill for 1909. Confident the upper house would give him two ships, Roosevelt was no longer reluctant to stir up a naval reorganization controversy. In late January he appointed a commission to investigate the Navy Department.[43] Though few papers strongly supported a four- rather than a two-ship program, the nation's press largely agreed that the bureau system was obsolete and needed drastic modification. Dissatisfaction was further aroused by George Kibbe Turner's article in the February, 1909, issue of *McClure's Magazine* entitled, "Our Navy on the Land: The Greatest Waste of National Funds in the History of the United States." Turner claimed forty million dollars per year were wasted because of the political and bureaucratic management of the navy.[44]

Senator Hale, whom Turner labeled "the Owner of the Navy," smarted under these attacks and attempted to defend the administration of the navy yards. The real trouble with the naval budget, Hale argued, when he introduced the naval appropriations bill in the Senate on February 15, was the size of battleships, which he would gladly reduce. His committee, however, had reported the House program of two 26,000-ton ships because they felt a smaller program would not carry the Senate at a time when "the whole country is convulsed with a fury and a fever in favor of the navy,

---

[43] Roosevelt to George K. Turner, February 10, 1909, *Letters*, VI, 1515; Morison, *Sims*, p. 225.

[44] *Literary Digest*, 37 (December 12, 1908), 875–876; George K. Turner, "Our Navy on the Land: The Greatest Waste of National Funds in the History of the United States," *McClure's Magazine*, 32 (February, 1909), 397–410.

and the exploits of the navy in navigating the globe." Hale's feeling proved largely correct. The Senate at first reduced the size of the two authorized battleships to 21,000 tons, but after a strong appeal by Senator Lodge, reversed itself and approved the House program.[45] It was a victory for the President, who was pleased with the navy's growth in the last eight years. "It is not nearly as much as we should have accomplished," he remarked, "but it marks a very great advance indeed." [46]

One of Roosevelt's most cherished naval doctrines was threatened, however, by an amendment introduced by Senator Fulton of Oregon. Passed on February 16, it urged that one-half the navy, at the discretion of the President, be kept on the Pacific Coast. The amendment reflected the widespread feeling among senators and congressmen — particularly those from the West Coast — that a larger naval force was needed on the Pacific.[47] But Roosevelt was in no mood to repeat the mistake made by Russia in its war with Japan and succeeded in getting the amendment dropped by the conference committee. He agreed that naval facilities on the Pacific Coast were inadequate, but he insisted on keeping the fleet in the Atlantic until the nation had a real two-ocean navy.[48] Alfred Thayer Mahan was alarmed by the prospect of a popular outcry for a division of the fleet and urged Roosevelt to warn the incoming President never to divide the battle fleet between the two oceans. Roosevelt immediately did so. "When I sent the fleet around the world," he wrote Taft, "there was a wild clamor that some of it should be sent to the Pacific, and an equally mad

[45] *Congressional Record*, 60th Cong., 2d Sess., 2378–2380, 2458, 2545–2549; *The Navy*, 3 (February, 1909), 4.

[46] Roosevelt to Turner, February 10, 1909, *Letters*, VI, 1515.

[47] *Congressional Record*, 60th Cong., 2d Sess., 2455–2456; *Los Angeles Times*, January 23, 1909.

[48] Roosevelt to Foss, February 18, 1909, *Letters*, VI, 1524–1526.

clamor that some of it should be left in the Atlantic. I disregarded both." [49] On this issue, at least, Taft was to follow Roosevelt's advice despite a continuing demand from the Pacific Coast for more naval protection.

Theodore Roosevelt had during his years as President done much to strengthen the navy, but by 1909 America's naval supremacy over Japan was less than in 1901, and the President had failed to maintain the position of the United States vis-à-vis the European naval powers. Both Mahan and the General Board realized that a two-ship program would not keep the United States navy in second place as long as the naval race between Germany and Great Britain continued. [50] With England in the midst of the greatest naval scare of its history, there seemed no chance early in 1909 that European naval competition would diminish. Mahan felt Germany wanted territorial acquisitions in the Western Hemisphere and wondered how the nation could expect to enforce the Monroe Doctrine if its navy was inferior to Germany's. [51] But few others, outside naval and military circles, pondered the same question. Only small, technical periodicals, such as the *Scientific American* and *The Navy*, saw clearly the relative decline in American naval power. The American people, *The Navy* complained, failed to realize the nation could not remain the world's second naval power with only moderate annual appropriations. [52]

The triumphant return of the battle fleet on February 22

[49] Mahan to Roosevelt, March 2, 1909, Roosevelt Papers; Roosevelt to Taft, March 3, 1909, *Letters*, VI, 1543.

[50] Mahan to Charles W. Stewart, March 19, 1909, Mahan Papers; Dewey to the Secretary of the Navy, April 21, 1909, No. 420–422, General Board Papers.

[51] Marder, *From the Dreadnought to Scapa Flow*, I, 150–153; Mahan to Stewart, March 19, 1909, Mahan Papers.

[52] *Scientific American*, 100 (March 6, 1909), 182; *The Navy*, 3 (March, 1909), 5–6.

helped to obscure the weakening of the nation's naval position. The day was bleak and overcast, marred by a misting rain, but the *New York Times* correspondent found that the "gloomy splendor" provided the proper setting for "the one supreme, magnificent moment" in Roosevelt's career.[53] The President himself was in a joyous mood. "The hearts of all who saw you," he announced to the officers and men of the fleet, "thrilled with pride as the hulls of the mighty warships lifted above the horizon." And he confided to Taft that popular feeling, at first "nearly a unit against" the cruise, was now "nearly a unit in favor of what I did." [54] Though exaggerating the strength of the original opposition, Roosevelt correctly sensed the almost universal approval in February, 1909, of the fleet's accomplishments. Critics of the operation, such as the *New York Sun* and the *Nation,* now joined in the chorus of praise by the nation's press.[55] *The Navy* and the *Scientific American* felt the voyage had greatly increased foreign respect for the American navy. The cruise of the battle fleet, claimed the *Review of Reviews,* was "convincing evidence that the United States had entered the rank of world-powers." [56] Lawrence F. Abbott, who accompanied Roosevelt during his visit to European capitals in 1910, noticed the eagerness of German naval officers to meet the man who had sent the fleet around the world. Abbott was certain that "the dramatic and complete success of this unprecedented adventure did more to convince the European nations of the possibilities of efficiency in a self-governing democracy than untold volumes of blue books and state

[53] *New York Times,* February 23, 1909.
[54] Roosevelt, *An Autobiography,* p. 557; Roosevelt to Taft, March 3, 1909, *Letters,* VI, 1543.
[55] *Literary Digest,* 37 (February 27, 1909), 326–327, (March 6, 1909), 366–367; *Nation,* 88 (February 25, 1909), 181.
[56] *The Navy,* 3 (March, 1909), 5–6; *Scientific American,* 100 (February 20, 1909), 146; *Review of Reviews,* 37 (January, 1909), 97–99.

papers." [57] As Abbott's views suggest, it was the impression the fleet made on other nations that struck most Americans as its major accomplishment. It seemed a fitting climax to Roosevelt's presidency and to the period which witnessed America's rise to world power.

[57] Lawrence F. Abbott, *Impressions of Theodore Roosevelt* (New York, 1919), pp. 112–113.

# XIII

## ROOSEVELT'S LEGACY

The Far Eastern policy pursued by Theodore Roosevelt during his last three years in office differed only in clarity and completeness from his earlier policy. Roosevelt had entered the presidency convinced that the American people would not support extensive involvement in the Orient, and he had never attempted to alter this limitation. In fact, throughout his presidency Roosevelt's actions suggested that he placed a low value on American interests in China and Manchuria. Though irritated by Russian aggression in Manchuria, Roosevelt never forcefully challenged it and instead viewed Japan as the nation best fitted to limit Russian expansion and to exercise a benevolent influence on China. With the outbreak of the Russo-Japanese War, Roosevelt favored Japan and eventually undertook a limited diplomatic initiative in the Far East to end the war on terms which, while advantageous to Japan, also left a residue of Russian power in the Orient. He was, however, less interested in maintaining this balanced antagonism than in establishing a close understanding with Japan. Thus he not only befriended that nation in the peace negotiations, but also quickly recognized Japanese hegemony over Korea, approved the renewal and extension of the Anglo-Japanese Alliance, and endorsed the important conversation between William Howard Taft and Prime Minister Taro Katsura in

July, 1905. His hope was that Japan would exercise its power on the mainland of Asia responsibly and wisely and that it would preserve equality of commercial opportunity in its Manchurian sphere of influence. Roosevelt cared little about the preservation of China's territorial and administrative integrity; he regarded friendship with Japan as far more important.

Japan's spectacular emergence as the dominant power in the Far East, along with the Japanese-American crisis in immigration, threatened to destroy this understanding between the two nations. Previously there had been no direct clash of vital interests; now there was the immigration question and the widespread feeling among the American people that a conflict over the control of the Pacific was inevitable. Mainly concerned with the growing reform movement in the United States, Roosevelt reluctantly gave considerable attention to the crisis with Japan and developed a policy which balanced conflicting foreign and domestic interests. He was angered by the San Francisco school segregation order and disturbed by the impact it had on Japanese-American relations. At the same time, however, he wanted to satisfy the demands of California politicians and labor leaders, who, as he soon learned, were primarily concerned with the immigration of Japanese laborers to the Pacific Coast. Hoping to placate the Californians — short of exclusion legislation — while retaining good relations with Japan, Roosevelt devised a solution which would trade the termination of school segregation in the San Francisco public schools for a treaty of reciprocal exclusion with Japan.

During negotiations with Japan in the winter of 1906–1907, Roosevelt found, however, that the Japanese government would sign a treaty of reciprocal exclusion only if major concessions were made. Therefore he dropped this plan and achieved a temporary solution in the Gentlemen's

Agreement of February, 1907. This accord was the prelude rather than the final solution to Japanese-American difficulties, for the task of curtailing Japanese immigration proved complex and tedious. Moreover, the administration had only a marginal influence over events in California, where some politicians exploited popular fears of Japan.

By the late spring of 1907 the President realized the long-term nature of Japanese-American tension and the difficulty of controlling its causes. Aside from the immigration question, there was widespread suspicion in the United States over Japan's Asiatic policy. And in Japan, the sensational press and the opponents of the Saionji ministry encouraged the people to resent the treatment of their compatriots in California. In 1905 Roosevelt had called a halt to the expansion of the American navy; now he decided that the possibility of a future conflict with Japan made an increase again imperative. Fully aware of the strong opposition to naval appropriations in the Congress, Roosevelt resolved to send the battle fleet around the world, primarily to stimulate big-navy sentiment in Congress but also to strengthen his damaged political position on the Pacific Coast. At that time and later many journalists and politicians regarded the cruise as a demonstration aimed at Japan and at those European powers which underestimated the naval strength of the United States. Though Roosevelt later came to regard these aims as legitimate objects of the cruise, his original motives were much more restricted.

While the President displayed considerable imagination in creating popular support for his naval program, he was slow and hesitant in coming to grips with the immigration question. Most of the information he received indicated that the Japanese government would not agree to a treaty of reciprocal exclusion without substantial concessions. Yet throughout the summer of 1907 the immigration negotia-

tions remained suspended, while the administration pondered various measures which might break the deadlock. By
early August Roosevelt decided to concede naturalization
for a treaty of reciprocal exclusion, but the concession came
too late. For mounting tension during this dangerous hiatus
made the Japanese government unwilling to conclude an
immigration restriction treaty with the United States. Taft's
mission to Japan finally convinced Roosevelt and Root that
a treaty was impossible and that an administrative solution
would have to do.

As soon as Taft's conversations in Tokyo in October, 1907,
clarified the situation, Roosevelt and Root moved quickly.
Both realized time was running out and that if immigration
did not soon diminish, growing suspicion between the two
governments or another outbreak in California might end
all hope for a settlement. Shrewdly exaggerating the dangers
of exclusion legislation, Roosevelt and Root in the winter of
1907–1908 persuaded the Japanese government of the need
for effective restriction and secured an accord on a number
of administrative regulations. These made the Gentlemen's
Agreement of February, 1907, complete.

But relations between the two governments had deteriorated so far by January, 1908, that Roosevelt, while hoping
for the best, prepared for the worst. In 1905 he had been
troubled by the failure of Japanese statesmen to moderate
the ambitions of the Japanese people; now it seemed that
they were again reluctant to oppose public opinion by limit-
ing immigration effectively and promptly. This reluctance
puzzled and annoyed Roosevelt and eroded his confidence
in the Japanese government. With the public in each nation
aroused, Roosevelt feared an unexpected incident might
precipitate war. Or, even if no incident occurred, American
exclusion legislation might bring an upheaval in Japan. These
possibilities did not seem remote to a man who remembered

how mass hysteria had pushed the nation into war in 1898. Undoubtedly Roosevelt exaggerated the influence of public opinion in Japan and partly misunderstood the nature of the Japanese government. Nevertheless, he attempted to guard against these alleged dangers in a number of ways.[1] He continued negotiating with Japan for an effective immigration agreement. At the same time he sought diplomatic support from Canada and Great Britain in an attempt to create a common front against Asiatic immigration. Neither nation could afford to reject completely Roosevelt's overture, yet neither shared most of the President's fears. The result was an exchange of views which, while it had no impact on Japan, brought a fuller awareness in Ottawa and London of Roosevelt's position and laid the groundwork for future collaboration.

Aside from these diplomatic efforts, Roosevelt also strove to strengthen the nation's military and naval might in the Pacific. In April, 1908, in one of the most bitter legislative battles of his career, he partly succeeded in achieving the naval program he thought the nation needed. Roosevelt did not think war was likely either in the immediate or more distant future; but, believing that wars were brought about more by the people than by their leaders, he sought to prepare the nation for such an eventuality.

Even before the great naval debate of April, 1908, relations between the United States and Japan improved. The immigration agreement became progressively more effective; no new outbreaks occurred in San Francisco; and many of the suspicions harbored by Roosevelt and Root over Japan's integrity and purposes passed away. Both worked to avoid controversies with Japan over Manchuria and China; both desired a rapprochement before they left office.

[1] For an interesting discussion of an American "generation of ninety-eight," see Ernest R. May, *Imperial Democracy: The Emergence of America as a Great Power* (New York, 1961), p. 269.

Government leaders in Japan also wanted an easing of tension between the two nations. From the beginning of the crisis the Saionji ministry attempted to settle the school and immigration difficulties as quietly as possible, but was reluctant to agree to any immigration restriction treaty which might arouse resentment in Japan. The government deferred so much to Japanese public opinion because it seriously misjudged the vigor of the anti-Japanese agitation in the United States and the urgency of Theodore Roosevelt's political predicament. Thus Japan restricted emigration slowly and rejected in November, 1907, an effort by Ambassador Aoki and President Roosevelt to conclude an understanding. Like the Roosevelt administration, the Saionji ministry remained preoccupied with domestic considerations until the end of 1907, when it finally realized the need for substantial concessions in the immigration dispute. The Japanese-American crisis of 1906–1909 was, in one sense, a race between broadening perspectives and deteriorating relations. Because statesmen finally rose above their own immediate domestic concerns, they liquidated the immigration question by the spring of 1908 and made possible a general statement of friendship. The visit of the battle fleet to Yokohama in October, 1908, followed first by conversations between John C. O'Laughlin and Katsura and Komura and then by the Root-Takahira Agreement, cleared the air and assured a more peaceful future. The energy with which Roosevelt intervened in the final crisis with California indicated his determination to leave Taft a heritage of friendship with Japan.

These three years of crisis between the United States and Japan left a deep impact on the policies of the American government. In the realm of strategic thinking American military and naval planners finally realized the consequences for America's Pacific defenses of Japan's rise to power in Asia. Despite the navy's insistence upon developing a great naval base at Subig Bay, the Joint Board decided in late January, 1908, to locate the main Far Eastern naval base behind the defenses of Manila Bay. But as the lag between planning and actual developments in the far Pacific closed, it became apparent to the army's general staff that American forces in the Philippines would be in a desperate situation should war with Japan break out. Because American troops would probably retreat to Corregidor Island, any naval base which was not located there would soon fall to the enemy. The obvious implication was that no major base should be located west of Hawaii.

Led by Admiral George Dewey, the General Board, however, tenaciously refused to relinquish the hope for a great base at Subig Bay. After the Joint Board's choice of Manila over Subig Bay in early 1908, the naval members avoided convening the Joint Board and thus made the location of the base within Manila Bay impossible. Admiral Dewey thought the navy should attempt to defend Subig Bay with its own resources. The army also spurned cooperation and pursued an independent course. In early August, 1908, Chief of Staff Bell issued orders for the concentration of all forces at Manila in case of war and for their withdrawal to Corregidor should the lines around Manila fail to hold. Both Bell and the Secretary of War seemed willing to ignore the Joint Board's decision that all forces in the Philippines should be used to defend the temporary naval base at Subig Bay until a site at Manila Bay was chosen and developed. Considering the navy's refusal to implement the decision of late January, 1908, in good faith, they had little choice if the army's point of view was to be sustained.[2]

The General Board made a final assault on the army's posi-

[2] W. L. Rodgers to Stephen B. Luce, November 12, 1908, Luce Papers; memorandum by Bell for Adjutant General, August 4, 1908, NA, RG 165, Report No. 2990, August 3, 1908.

tion in late February, 1909, when it advocated the establishment of a separate Pacific fleet more powerful than any probable enemy in the Pacific. The existence of such a fleet, the General Board pointed out, would probably prevent a land attack on Subig Bay and relieve the army of the task of defending the Philippine naval base. Then the choice between the two sites could be made solely on the basis of natural advantages. The General Board's special pleading conflicted with the advice the President gave Taft and ignored the declining relative naval position of the United States. It was a disturbing example of the way in which interservice rivalries could affect strategic planning.[3]

By February, 1909, however, the whole controversy had acquired an air of unreality. In 1909 as in 1908, the Congress appropriated $900,000 for the development of Pearl Harbor, and there was little chance, whatever the naval and military planners decided, that it would ever appropriate enough money for the creation of a major base beyond the Hawaiian Islands. In early November the Joint Board finally confirmed what had been apparent for some time — that Pearl Harbor would be the nation's chief Pacific outpost. A small repair and docking station would be maintained at Subig Bay, which the army was not committed to defend against land attack. Actually, the location of the Far Eastern naval base was still not completely settled, and Subig Bay remained a subject of contention between the two services for many years.[4]

The events which altered strategic planning for the Pacific also deeply influenced the Roosevelt administration's Far

[3] Dewey to Secretary of the Navy, October 19, 1908, No. 404, General Board Papers; Dewey to Secretary of the Navy, February 24, 1909, No. 420–421, General Board Papers; see also William R. Braisted, "The United States Navy's Dilemma in the Pacific, 1906–1909," *Pacific Historical Review,* 26 (August, 1957), 235–244.

[4] Dewey to Secretary of the Navy, November 8, 1909, Joint Board, NA, RG 225; Braisted, *United States Navy in the Pacific,* pp. 236–239.

Eastern policy. The crisis with Japan strengthened Roosevelt's belief that any deep involvement in the Far East would be unwise. Despite mounting pressure from an activist group within the State Department, Roosevelt avoided serious conflicts over Manchuria and sought to remove tension with Japan through an accord which would demonstrate to the whole world the friendship between the two nations. In November, 1907, he failed to achieve an understanding when the Japanese government refused to support Ambassador Aoki's overture; but a year later the Root-Takahira exchange of notes fulfilled his purposes. This public declaration was supplemented by private conversations between John Callan O'Laughlin and Katsura and Komura which further clarified the relations of the two governments. Japan agreed to exclude its laborers from the mainland of the United States and to respect the Open Door for commerce in Manchuria, while Roosevelt tacitly acquiesced in Japan's sphere of influence in southern Manchuria and to the violations of China's territorial and administrative integrity which it involved. The Root-Takahira Agreement was the natural culmination of the Far Eastern policy pursued by Roosevelt since 1901. It was not the result of disillusionment over his ability to shape events in the Far East, but rather an expression of his desire for a complete accommodation with Japan.

Many factors influenced Roosevelt in his refusal to follow a more active Far Eastern policy. The American public did not seem willing to support any vigorous steps to preserve the integrity of China and Manchuria, and Roosevelt was not inclined to create this popular base for a strong policy because of the pull of more pressing foreign and domestic problems. Moreover, the nation's stake in China did not strike Roosevelt as very large. Unwilling to adopt what he termed a policy of bluff or to attempt to rally the American people behind a confrontation with Japan over China and

Manchuria, Roosevelt sought an accommodation with that nation. He was careful to conceal from the American people, however, the nature of this accommodation and the extent to which the United States recognized Japan's sphere in southern Manchuria. Thus Roosevelt's desire to avoid criticism of America's lack of commitment in the Far East helped perpetuate popular misunderstanding of the position of the United States in that region. More important, he was unable to convince William Howard Taft and Philander C. Knox of the political and military limitations upon American involvement in the Orient. They took advice from those in the State Department who wanted to oppose Japan's expansion on the Asiatic mainland and attempted to weaken Japan's hold on southern Manchuria. Understandably they failed. Taft's reversal of Roosevelt's policy, along with many other developments, soon led to the destruction of the rapprochement Roosevelt had achieved with Japan and to the steady deterioration in the relations between the two nations.

Theodore Roosevelt can hardly be blamed for the ultimate failure of his policy toward Japan. By the close of his presidency it was a largely successful policy based upon political realities at home and in the Far East and upon a firm belief that friendship with Japan was essential to preserve American interests in the Pacific. His assumptions about Japan did not bear up with the passage of time. They were, nonetheless, reasonable ones for a statesman operating within the atmosphere of the early twentieth century. Remembering both the context of his era and his actual accomplishments, Roosevelt's diplomacy during the Japanese-American crisis of 1906–1909 was shrewd, skillful, and responsible.

# SELECTED BIBLIOGRAPHY

# PRIMARY SOURCES

## 1. Manuscript Collections and Government Archives

*United States*

Library of Congress
  Albert J. Beveridge MSS.
  George Dewey MSS.
  James R. Garfield MSS.
  Albert Gleaves MSS.
  Richmond P. Hobson MSS.
  George Kennan MSS.
  Philander C. Knox MSS.
  Stephen B. Luce MSS.
  Alfred Thayer Mahan MSS.
  John Callan O'Laughlin MSS.
  Horace Porter MSS.
  Whitelaw Reid MSS.
  Theodore Roosevelt MSS.
  Elihu Root MSS.
  Charles S. Sperry MSS.
  Benjamin F. Tracy MSS.
  James Harrison Wilson MSS.
  Leonard Wood MSS.
Harvard University Library
  W. Cameron Forbes MSS.
  William W. Rockhill MSS.
Massachusetts Historical Society
  Henry Cabot Lodge MSS.
  George von Lengerke Meyer MSS.
National Archives
  Department of the Interior
    RG 350: Bureau of Insular Affairs.
  Department of the Navy
    RG 24: Bureau of Navigation.
    RG 38: Office of Naval Intelligence.

RG 45: Office of Naval Records and Library.
RG 80: General Records of the Department of the Navy.
Department of State
RG 59: General Records of the Department of State.
Department of War
RG 94: Office of the Adjutant General.
RG 107: Office of the Secretary of War.
RG 165: Office of the Chief of Staff.
RG 225: Joint Army and Navy Board.
Department of the Navy, Division of Naval History
William S. Sims MSS.
General Board Papers.
Ursinus College Library
Francis M. Huntington Wilson MSS.

*Great Britain*

Bodleian Library
Herbert H. Asquith MSS.
James Bryce MSS.
British Museum
Henry Campbell-Bannerman MSS.
Foreign Office Library
Cecil Spring Rice MSS.
Public Record Office
Foreign Office
F.O. 371: General political correspondence.
F.O. 405: Confidential print, China.
F.O. 410: Confidential print, Japan.
F.O. 412: Confidential print, miscellaneous.
F.O. 414: Confidential print, North America.
F.O. 420: Confidential print, South and Central America.
F.O. 534: Confidential print, Pacific Islands.
Cabinet Office
Cab. 2: Minutes of the Committee of Imperial Defense.
Cab. 4: Miscellaneous memoranda.
Cab. 5: Memoranda on colonial defense.
Cab. 7: Minutes of the Colonial Defense Committee.
Cab. 17: Correspondence and miscellaneous papers of the Committee of Imperial Defense.
Colonial Office
C.O. 42: Original correspondence, Canada.
C.O. 532: Original correspondence, Dominions.
C.O. 880: Confidential print, North America.
C.O. 881: Confidential print, Australia.

C.O. 886: Confidential print, Dominions.
War Office
W.O. 33: Reports and miscellaneous papers.
W.O. 106: Papers of Directorate of Military Operations and Intelligence.
Admiralty
Adm. 1: General Papers.
Adm. 116/1231 B and C: Anglo-Japanese Agreement, 1902–1917.
Roosevelt Memorial Association
Dispatches from the British Ambassador in Washington (microfilm).

*Canada*

Public Archives of Canada
Robert Laird Borden MSS.
Albert Henry George Grey MSS.
William Lyon Mackenzie King MSS.
Wilfrid Laurier MSS.
Rodolphe Lemieux MSS.
RG 7: Governor General's Office.

*Japan*

Archives of the Japanese Ministry of Foreign Affairs (microfilm),
Library of Congress.

2. Government Reports and Printed Records

*Annual Reports of the Department of Commerce and Labor.*
*Annual Reports of the Navy Department.*
*Annual Reports of the War Department.*
Commission de Publication des Documents aux Origines de la Guerre
1914, Ministère des Affaires Étrangères, *Documents diplomatiques français, 1871–1914.* 3rd Series, 41 vols. Paris, 1929–1959.
*Congressional Record.*
Gooch, G. P., and Harold W. V. Temperley (eds.). *British Documents on the Origins of the World War, 1898–1914.* 11 vols. London, 1926–1936.
*Journal of the California Assembly.*
*Journal of the California Senate.*
Lepsius, Johannes, Albrecht Bartholdy, and Friederich Thimme (eds.). *Die grosse Politik der europäischen Kabinette, 1871–1914: Sammlung der diplomatischen Akten des Auswärtigen Amtes.* 40 vols. Berlin, 1922–27.
Metcalf, Victor H. "Japanese in the City of San Francisco, California,"

*Senate Document No. 147.* 59th Cong., 2d Sess. Washington, D.C., 1906.

*Papers Relating to the Foreign Relations of the United States.* Washington, D.C., 1861–.

Pulsifer, Pitman. *Navy Yearbook. Compilation of Annual Naval Appropriation Laws from 1883 to 1908.* Washington, D.C., 1908.

### 3. MEMOIRS, LETTERS, AND CONTEMPORARY ACCOUNTS

Abbott, Lawrence F. *Impressions of Theodore Roosevelt.* New York, 1919.

Aubert, Louis. *Americains et Japonais.* Paris, 1908.

Begbie, Harold. *Albert, Fourth Earl Grey: A Last Word.* London, 1917.

Borden, Henry (ed.). *Robert Laird Borden: His Memoirs.* 2 vols. Toronto, 1938.

Brassey, Thomas A., and John Leyland (eds.). *The Naval Annual.* Portsmouth, Eng., 1886–.

Davis, Oscar King. *Released for Publication: Some Inside Political History of Theodore Roosevelt and His Times, 1898–1918.* Boston, 1925.

Dyer, Henry. *Japan in World Politics: A Study in International Dynamics.* London, 1909.

Evans, Robley D. *An Admiral's Log.* New York, 1910.

Gérard, A. *Ma mission au Japon, 1907–1914.* Paris, 1919.

Gompers, Samuel. *Seventy Years of Life and Labor: An Autobiography.* 2 vols. New York, 1925.

Grey, Sir Edward. *Twenty-Five Years, 1892–1916.* 2 vols. New York, 1925.

Gwynn, Stephen (ed.). *The Letters and Friendships of Sir Cecil Spring Rice.* 2 vols. Boston, 1929.

Hichborn, Franklin. *Story of the Session of the California Legislature of 1909.* San Francisco, 1909.

———. *"The System" as Uncovered by the San Francisco Graft Prosecution.* San Francisco, 1915.

Huntington Wilson, Francis M. *Memoirs of an Ex-Diplomat.* Boston, 1945.

Johnson, Herbert B. *Discrimination Against the Japanese in California.* Berkeley, 1907.

Jordan, David Starr. *The Days of a Man: Being Memories of a Naturalist, Teacher and Minor Prophet of Democracy.* 2 vols. Yonkers-on-Hudson, N.Y., 1922.

Jusserand, Jules J. *What Me Befell: The Reminiscences of J. J. Jusserand.* Boston, 1933.

La Follette, Robert M. *Autobiography.* Madison, 1913.

Latané, John H. *America as a World Power, 1897–1907*. New York, 1907.

Matthews, Franklin. *With the Battle Fleet*. New York, 1909.

————. *Back to Hampton Roads*. New York, 1909.

Millard, Thomas F. *America and the Far Eastern Question*. New York, 1909.

Morison, Elting E. (ed.). *The Letters of Theodore Roosevelt*. 8 vols. Cambridge, Mass., 1951–1954.

Oxford and Asquith, Herbert Henry, Earl of. *Memoirs and Reflections, 1852–1927*. 2 vols. London, 1928.

Pooley, A. M. (ed.). *The Secret Memoirs of Count Tadasu Hayashi*. New York, 1915.

Pope, Maurice (ed.). *Public Servant: The Memoirs of Sir Joseph Pope*. Toronto, 1960.

Roosevelt, Theodore. *An Autobiography*. New York, 1913.

————. *The Strenuous Life: Essays and Addresses*. New York, 1900.

Smalley, George W. *Anglo-American Memoirs*. 2 vols. London, 1910–1912.

Stoddard, Henry L. *It Costs to Be President*. New York, 1938.

Straus, Oscar S. *Under Four Administrations: From Cleveland to Taft*. Boston, 1922.

Tardieu, André. *Notes sur les États-Unis, la société — la politique — la diplomatie*. Paris, 1908.

Tirpitz, Alfred von. *My Memoirs*. 2 vols. London, 1919.

## SECONDARY SOURCES

### 1. Books and Articles

Akagi, Roy H. *Japan's Foreign Relations, 1542–1936*. Tokyo, 1936.

Albion, Robert G. "The Administration of the Navy, 1798–1945," *Public Administration Review*, 5 (Autumn 1945), 293–302.

Anderson, Thornton. *Brooks Adams: Constructive Conservative*. Ithaca, 1951.

Bailey, Thomas A. "California, Japan and the Alien Land Legislation of 1913," *Pacific Historical Review*, 1 (March, 1932), 36–59.

————. *Theodore Roosevelt and the Japanese-American Crises*. Stanford, 1934.

————. "The Root–Takahira Agreement of 1908," *Pacific Historical Review*, 9 (March, 1940), 19–35.

————. "The World Cruise of the American Battleship Fleet, 1907–1909," *Pacific Historical Review*, 1 (December, 1932), 389–423.

Beale, Howard K. *Theodore Roosevelt and the Rise of America to World Power*. Baltimore, 1956.

Bean, Walton. *Boss Ruef's San Francisco: The Story of the Union Labor Party, Big Business, and the Graft Prosecution.* Los Angeles, 1952.

Bemis, Samuel Flagg (ed.). *The American Secretaries of State and Their Diplomacy.* 10 vols. New York, 1927–1929.

Bishop, Joseph Bucklin. *Theodore Roosevelt and His Time Shown in His Own Letters.* 2 vols. New York, 1920.

Blum, John Morton. *The Republican Roosevelt.* Cambridge, Mass., 1954.

Bolles, Blair. *Tyrant from Illinois: Uncle Joe Cannon's Experiment With Personal Power.* New York, 1951.

Bowers, Claude G. *Beveridge and the Progressive Era.* Boston, 1932.

Braeman, John. "Seven Progressives," *Business History Review,* 35 (Winter 1961), 581–592.

Braisted, William Reynolds. "The Philippine Naval Base Problem, 1898–1909," *Mississippi Valley Historical Review,* 41 (June 1954), 21–40.

————. *The United States Navy in the Pacific, 1897–1909.* Austin, 1958.

————. "The United States Navy's Dilemma in the Pacific, 1906–1909," *Pacific Historical Review,* 26 (August, 1957), 235–244.

Buell, Raymond L. "The Development of the Anti-Japanese Agitation in the United States," *Political Science Quarterly,* 37 (December, 1922), 605–638.

Busbey, L. White. *Uncle Joe Cannon: The Story of a Pioneer American.* New York, 1927.

Callahan, James M. *American Foreign Policy in Canadian Relations.* New York, 1937.

Campbell, Charles S., Jr. *Special Business Interests and the Open Door Policy.* New Haven, 1951.

Ch'en, Jerome. *Yuan Shih-K'ai, 1859–1916.* Stanford, 1961.

Clinard, Outten Jones. *Japan's Influence on American Naval Power, 1897–1917.* Berkeley, 1947.

Clyde, Paul Hibbert. *International Rivalries in Manchuria, 1689–1922.* Columbus, 1926.

Cortissoz, Royal. *The Life of Whitelaw Reid.* 2 vols. New York, 1921.

Croly, Herbert. *Willard Straight.* New York, 1924.

Cummings, Captain Damon E. *Admiral Richard Wainwright and the United States Fleet.* Washington, D.C., 1962.

Dafoe, John W. *Laurier: A Study in Canadian Politics.* Revised ed. Toronto, 1963.

Daniels, Roger. *The Politics of Prejudice: The Anti-Japanese Movement in California and the Struggle for Japanese Exclusion.* Berkeley, 1962.

Dawson, R. MacGregor. *William Lyon Mackenzie King: A Political Biography, 1874–1923.* Toronto, 1958.

Dennett, Tyler. *Americans in Eastern Asia.* New York, 1922.

———. *John Hay: From Poetry to Politics.* New York, 1933.

———. *Roosevelt and the Russo-Japanese War.* New York, 1925.

Dugdale, Blanche E. C. *Arthur James Balfour.* 2 vols. New York, 1937.

Dulles, Foster Rhea. *Forty Years of American-Japanese Relations.* New York, 1937.

Edwards, E. E. "The Far Eastern Agreements of 1907," *Journal of Modern History,* 26 (December, 1954), 340–355.

Esthus, Raymond A. "The Changing Concept of the Open Door, 1899–1910," *Mississippi Valley Historical Review.* 46 (December, 1959), 435–454.

———. "The Taft-Katsura Agreement — Reality or Myth?" *Journal of Modern History,* 32 (March, 1959), 46–51.

———. *Theodore Roosevelt and Japan.* Seattle, 1966.

Fairbank, John K., Edwin O. Reischauer, and Albert M. Craig. *East Asia, The Modern Transformation.* Boston, 1965.

Falk, Edwin A. *Fighting Bob Evans.* New York, 1931.

Fisher, Herbert A. L. *James Bryce.* 2 vols. New York, 1927.

Garraty, John A. *Henry Cabot Lodge: A Biography.* New York, 1953.

Gelber, Lionel M. *The Rise of Anglo-American Friendship, 1898–1906.* London, 1938.

Gordon, Donald C. "Roosevelt's 'Smart Yankee Trick,'" *Pacific Historical Review,* 30 (November, 1961), 351–358.

———. *The Dominion Partnership in Imperial Defense, 1870–1914.* Baltimore, 1965.

Graebner, Norman A. (ed.). *An Uncertain Tradition: American Secretaries of State in the Twentieth Century.* New York, 1961.

Greene, Fred. "The Military View of American National Policy, 1904–1940," *American Historical Review,* 66 (January, 1961), 354–377.

Grenville, John A. S., and George Berkeley Young. *Politics, Strategy, and American Diplomacy: Studies in Foreign Policy, 1873–1917.* New Haven, 1966.

Griswold, A. Whitney. *The Far Eastern Policy of the United States.* New York, 1938.

Hagedorn, Hermann. *Leonard Wood: A Biography.* 2 vols. New York, 1931.

——— (ed.). *The Works of Theodore Roosevelt.* National Ed. 20 vols. New York, 1926.

Hall, Luella J. "The Abortive German-American-Chinese Entente of 1907–1908," *Journal of Modern History,* 1 (June, 1929), 219–235.

Harbaugh, William H. *Power and Responsibility: The Life and Times of Theodore Roosevelt.* New York, 1961.

Hart, Robert A. *The Great White Fleet: Its Voyage Around the World, 1907–1909.* Boston, 1965.

Harvey, Rowland Hill. *Samuel Gompers: Champion of the Toiling Masses.* Stanford, 1935.

Hays, Samuel H. *Conservation and the Gospel of Efficiency: The Progressive Conservation Movement, 1890–1920.* Cambridge, Mass., 1959.

Healy, Laurin Hall, and Luis Kutner. *The Admiral.* New York, 1944.

Heindel, Richard H. *The American Impact on Great Britain, 1898–1914.* Philadelphia, 1940.

Hornbeck, Stanley K. *Contemporary Politics in the Far East.* New York, London, 1916.

Howe, Mark A. DeWolfe. *George von Lengerke Meyer: His Life and Public Services.* New York, 1920.

Ichihashi, Yamato. *Japanese in the United States: A Critical Study of the Problems of the Japanese Immigrants and Their Children.* Stanford, 1932.

Jenkins, Roy. *Asquith: Portrait of a Man and an Era.* New York, 1964.

Jessup, Philip C. *Elihu Root.* 2 vols. New York, 1938.

Johnson, Arthur M. "Theodore Roosevelt and the Navy," *United States Naval Institute Proceedings,* 84 (October, 1958), 76–82.

Kamikawa, Hikomatsu (ed.). *Japan-American Diplomatic Relations in the Meiji-Taisho Era.* Trans. by Kimura Michiko. Tokyo, 1958.

LaFeber, Walter. *The New Empire: An Interpretation of American Expansion, 1860–1898.* Ithaca, 1963.

Leech, Margaret. *In the Days of McKinley.* New York, 1959.

Leopold, Richard W. *Elihu Root and the Conservative Tradition.* Boston, 1954.

Leuchtenburg, William E. "Progressivism and Imperialism: The Progressive Movement and American Foreign Policy, 1898–1916," *Mississippi Valley Historical Review,* 39 (December, 1952), 483–504.

Levi, Werner, *Modern China's Foreign Policy.* Minneapolis, 1953.

Livermore, Seward W. "American Naval-Base Policy in the Far East, 1850–1914," *Pacific Historical Review,* 13 (June, 1944), 113–135.

———. "The American Navy as a Factor in World Politics, 1903–1913," *American Historical Review,* 42 (July, 1958), 863–879.

Livezey, William E. *Mahan on Sea Power.* Norman, Okla., 1947.

Mandel, Bernard. *Samuel Gompers: A Biography.* Yellow Springs, Ohio, 1963.

Marder, Arthur J. *From the Dreadnought to Scapa Flow: The Royal Navy in the Fisher Era, 1904–1919. Vol. I: The Road to War, 1904–1914.* London, 1961.

Matthews, Fred H. "White Community and 'Yellow Peril,' " *Mississippi Valley Historical Review*, 50 (March, 1964), 612–633.

May, Ernest R. *Imperial Democracy: The Emergence of America as a Great Power*. New York, 1961.

——. "The Development of Political-Military Consultation in the United States," *Political Science Quarterly*, 70 (June, 1955), 161–180.

Meadows, Martin. "Eugene Hale and the American Navy," *American Neptune*, 22 (July, 1962), 187–193.

Millis, H. A. *The Japanese Problem in the United States*. New York, 1915.

Minger, Ralph E. "Taft's Missions to Japan: A Study in Personal Diplomacy," *Pacific Historical Review*, 30 (August, 1961), 279–294.

Monger, George W. *The End of Isolation: British Foreign Policy, 1900–1907*. London, 1963.

Morgan, H. Wayne. *William McKinley and His America*. Syracuse, 1963.

Morison, Elting E. *Admiral Sims and the Modern American Navy*. Boston, 1942.

Morton, Louis. "Preparations for the Defense of the Philippines During the War Scare of 1907," *Military Affairs*, 13 (Summer 1949), 95–104.

——. "War Plan ORANGE: Evolution of a Strategy," *World Politics*, 11 (January, 1959), 221–250.

Mowry, George E. *The California Progressives*. Berkeley, 1951.

——. *The Era of Theodore Roosevelt, 1900–1912*. New York, 1958.

Murdoch, Walter. *Alfred Deakin: A Sketch*. London, 1923.

Neu, Charles E. "Theodore Roosevelt and American Involvement in the Far East, 1901–1909," *Pacific Historical Review*, 35 (November, 1966), 433–449.

Neumann, William L. *America Encounters Japan: From Perry to MacArthur*. Baltimore, 1963.

Nevins, Allan. *Henry White: Thirty Years of American Diplomacy*. New York, 1930.

Nish, Ian H. *The Anglo-Japanese Alliance: The Diplomacy of Two Island Empires, 1894–1907*. London, 1966.

O'Gara, Gordon C. *Theodore Roosevelt and the Rise of the Modern American Navy*. Princeton, 1943.

Pomeroy, Earl S. *Pacific Outpost: American Strategy in Guam and Micronesia*. Stanford, 1951.

Pressman, Harvey. "Hay, Rockhill, and China's Integrity: A Reappraisal," *Papers on China*. 13 (December, 1959), 61–79, Center for East Asian Studies, Harvard University.

Pringle, Henry F. *The Life and Times of William Howard Taft.* 2 vols. New York, 1939.

―――. *Theodore Roosevelt: A Biography.* New York, 1931.

Puleston, William D. *Mahan: The Life and Work of Alfred Thayer Mahan.* New Haven, 1939.

Rappaport, Armin. *The Navy League of the United States.* Detroit, 1962.

Reid, John G. *The Manchu Abdication and the Powers, 1908–1912.* Berkeley, 1935.

Scalapino, Robert A. *Democracy and the Party Movement in Prewar Japan: The Failure of the First Attempt.* Berkeley, 1953.

Schieber, Clara Eve. *The Transformation of American Sentiment Toward Germany, 1870–1914.* Boston, 1923.

Schull, Joseph. *Laurier, The First Canadian.* New York, 1965.

Skelton, Oscar D. *Life and Letters of Sir Wilfrid Laurier.* 2 vols. London, 1922.

Spender, John A., and Asquith, Cyril. *Life of Herbert Henry Asquith, Lord Oxford and Asquith.* 2 vols. London, 1932.

―――. *The Life of the Right Hon. Sir Henry Campbell-Bannerman.* 2 vols. London, 1923.

Sprout, Harold and Margaret. *The Rise of American Naval Power, 1776–1918.* Princeton, 1939.

Stephenson, Nathaniel W. *Nelson W. Aldrich: A Leader in American Politics.* New York, 1930.

Stillson, Albert C. "Military Policy Without Political Guidance: Theodore Roosevelt's Navy," *Military Affairs,* 25 (Spring 1961), 18–31.

Takeuchi, Tatsuji. *War and Diplomacy in the Japanese Empire.* Chicago, 1931.

Thorson, Winston B. "American Public Opinion and the Portsmouth Peace Conference," *American Historical Review,* 53 (April, 1948), 439–464.

Tompkins, Pauline. *American-Russian Relations in the Far East.* New York, 1949.

Treat, Payson J. *Japan and the United States, 1853–1928.* Stanford, 1928.

Trevelyan, George Macaulay. *Grey of Fallodon.* Boston, 1937.

Tupper, Eleanor, and McReynolds, George E. *Japan in American Public Opinion.* New York, 1937.

Varg, Paul A. *Missionaries, Chinese and Diplomats.* Princeton, 1958.

―――. *Open Door Diplomat: The Life of W. W. Rockhill.* Illinois Studies in the Social Sciences. Vol. 33, No. 4. Urbana, Ill., 1952.

Vevier, Charles. "The Open Door: An Idea in Action, 1906–1913," *Pacific Historical Review,* 24 (February, 1955), 49–62.

————. *The United States and China, 1906–1913: A Study of Finance and Diplomacy.* New Brunswick, 1955.

Ward, Robert E., and Dankwart A. Rustow (eds.). *Political Modernization in Japan and Turkey.* Princeton, 1964.

West, Richard S., Jr. *Admirals of American Empire: The Combined Story of George Dewey, Alfred Thayer Mahan, Winfield Scott Schley and William Thomas Sampson.* New York, 1948.

White, John Albert. *The Diplomacy of the Russo-Japanese War.* Princeton, 1964.

Woodsworth, Charles J. *Canada and the Orient.* Toronto, 1941.

Yanaga, Chitoshi. *Japan Since Perry.* New York, 1949.

Yarwood, A. T. *Asian Migration to Australia: The Background to Exclusion, 1896–1923.* New York, 1964.

Zabriskie, Edward H. *American-Russian Rivalry in the Far East: A Study in Diplomacy and Power Politics, 1895–1914.* Philadelphia, 1946.

2. UNPUBLISHED THESES (Ph.D. unless otherwise noted)

Bailey, Jackson H. "Prince Saionji: A Study in Modern Japanese Political Leadership," Harvard University, 1959.

Butzbach, Arthur G. "The Segregation of Orientals in the San Francisco Schools," M.A. thesis, Stanford University, 1928.

Esthus, Raymond A. "Diplomatic Relations Between the United States and Japan, 1905–1908," Duke University, 1956.

Hackett, Roger F. "Yamagata Aritomo: A Political Biography," Harvard University, 1955.

Kessler, James B. "The Political Factors in California's Anti-Alien Land Legislation, 1912–1913," Stanford University, 1958.

Lebra, Joyce C. "Japan's First Modern Popular Statesman, A Study of the Political Career of Okuma Shigenobu (1838–1922)," Radcliffe College, 1958.

Miller, Jessie Ashworth. "China in American Policy and Opinion, 1906–1909," Clark University, 1940.

Olson, Lawrence A., Jr. "Hara Kei: A Political Biography," Harvard University, 1954.

Pike, Albert H., Jr. "Jonathan Bourne, Jr., Progressive," University of Oregon, 1957.

Stillson, Albert C. "The Development and Maintenance of the American Naval Establishment, 1901–1909," Columbia University, 1959.

Thompson, Richard A. "The Yellow Peril, 1890–1924," University of Wisconsin, 1957.

Thomson, Ruth H. "Events Leading to the Order to Segregate Japanese Pupils in the San Francisco Public Schools," Stanford University, 1931.

# INDEX